HOSPITAL REIMBURSEMENT

Concepts and Principles

HOSPITAL REIMBURSEMENT

Concepts and Principles

Kyle Herbert

MBA, CPA, CMA, FACHE, FHFMA

CRC Press
Taylor & Francis Group
Boca Raton   London   New York

CRC Press is an imprint of the
Taylor & Francis Group, an **informa** business

A PRODUCTIVITY PRESS BOOK

CRC Press
Taylor & Francis Group
6000 Broken Sound Parkway NW, Suite 300
Boca Raton, FL 33487-2742

© 2012 by Taylor & Francis Group, LLC
CRC Press is an imprint of Taylor & Francis Group, an Informa business

No claim to original U.S. Government works

Printed in the United States of America on acid-free paper
Version Date: 20120516

International Standard Book Number: 978-1-4398-9894-9 (Hardback)

Library of Congress Cataloging-in-Publication Data

Herbert, Kyle.
    Hospital reimbursement : concepts and principles / Kyle Herbert.
        p. ; cm.
    Includes bibliographical references and index.
    ISBN 978-1-4398-9894-9 (hardcover: alk. paper)
    I. Title.
    [DNLM: 1. Hospitals--United States. 2. Reimbursement
    Mechanisms--United States. 3. Accounting--methods--United States. 4. Economics, Hospital--United
States. WX 157 AA1]

    363.11068'1--dc23   2012002217

Visit the Taylor & Francis Web site at
http://www.taylorandfrancis.com

and the CRC Press Web site at
http://www.crcpress.com

This book is dedicated to David Lee.

A great friend, an excellent teacher, a skilled motivator, a brilliant accountant, and an exceptional mentor.

I will be forever grateful for everything you have taught me.

Contents

Preface

Throughout my 12 years in the healthcare accounting field, I have read many books and articles that detail the numerous leadership strategies, physician integration methods, and healthcare reform issues that are applicable to being an effective hospital administrator. However, I found minimal literature on the fiscal concepts and reimbursement models that hospital leaders should understand. I have found few resources that explain how to complete a Medicare cost report or how to estimate a patient receivable. Indeed, there is a wealth of information that details billing requirements and coding guidelines, but there is little subject matter that details the revenue cycle as it specifically pertains to a hospital. The hospital reimbursement process is by far the most complex of any industry due to the numerous variables that affect revenue and cost. There are few businesses in which the bill is not paid by the client, and identical services may be paid at a lower or higher rate depending on insurance type. An additional factor is that hospital reimbursement is heavily affected by governmental regulation. I have attempted to formulate an easy-to-read text that any individual can use to better understand the various reimbursement methods that exist within a hospital setting. *It helps to have a working knowledge of the accounting field before you read this book, but it is not a requirement.* Several concepts and models in this book may seem overwhelming if the reader does not have at least an elementary financial background. I have included several boxed items, labeled "Critical Issue," to emphasize an important topic. I have also included several diagrams and flowcharts that I hope will make the process easier to understand. For your convenience, the forms in Chapter 8 are available at http://www.crcpress.com/product/isbn/9781439898949.

The actual process of reimbursement is defined as the repayment to a provider *after* services have been rendered. Healthcare is the only business that is compensated for services after the client has left the facility. In some cases, reimbursement for care is prospective in that the hospital knows what the payment will be regardless of the costs to treat the patient. The healthcare delivery system in the United States is complex not only because of the numerous reimbursement methods but also because of the link among health insurance, income, and the government. Numerous models are used to pay not only hospitals but also physicians, nursing homes, and other healthcare entities.

My goal is that, after reading this book, you will have a better technical understanding of the complex field known as hospital reimbursement. This dynamic industry is constantly evolving as the federal government continuously researches new methods to reduce health care costs while attempting to expand coverage for all citizens. Despite these modifications, the debits and credits of double-entry accounting have not changed, and assets will still equal liabilities plus equity. I hope that these chapters provide a better understanding of a field that few comprehend.

About the Author

Kyle Herbert has over 12 years of healthcare accounting experience, and he is licensed as both a CPA (certified public accountant) and a CMA (certified management accountant). Kyle received his undergraduate degree from the University of Richmond and his master's degree in business administration from The Citadel. In addition to these academic achievements, Kyle attained fellowships with both the Healthcare Financial Management Association and the American College of Healthcare Executives.

Kyle is a member of the American Institute of Certified Public Accountants, the Institute of Management Accountants, the South Carolina Society of Accountants, and the South Carolina Association of CPAs.

Chapter 1

Fundamentals of Accounting

Introduction

Before any discussion of hospital reimbursement can be given, a broad overview of the fiscal concepts that drive the accounting field needs to be addressed. The accounting profession has been in existence for hundreds of years, and there are numerous services an accountant can perform. These services range from those that are limited in scope to ones that are highly analytical. The rules and guidelines that accountants follow are formulated by regulatory bodies that have a responsibility to the public interest. Healthcare accountants are responsible not only for formulating the annual budget but also for creating financial statements. In addition, accountants who work within hospital systems are responsible for providing financial advice and direction when clinical initiatives are researched and developed.

Often referred to as the "language of business," the accounting field is a vast composition of subject matter that spans numerous industries. A majority of colleges and universities have some type of accounting program that prepares students to take either the certified management accountant (CMA) or certified public accountant (CPA) exam. The undergraduate curriculum begins with understanding the debit and credits that formulate the financial statements and advances into intermediate courses that detail the principles of taxation and auditing. The accounting field is historically separated into either financial or managerial accounting; financial accounting is the preparation of financial statements for external decision makers, while managerial accounting is designed to assist internal users within an organization. Historically, accountants have been categorized as either "tax" or "audit"; however, this classification has evolved due to the increased responsibilities of accountants and the expansion of the certification exams. An accounting professional need not obtain either a CMA or CPA to work in healthcare, but certification could increase compensation.

Many accountants find it difficult to describe their profession to those without financial experience because of the technical nature of the accounting field. It can be a challenge to describe the purpose of an audit or the significance of financial reporting. A broad definition is that *accounting is creating structure where there was once disorder so a decision can be made.* The disorder can be the various amounts of revenue and expense figures that need to be classified and analyzed. The structure is the numerous financial reports and statements that are formulated, while management represents the decision-making body.

History and Framework

The history of double-entry accounting can be traced to the 15th century; a Franciscan friar named Luca Pacioli published his theory of debit and credit rules in a mathematics text. Pacioli is often called the "father of accounting" because his research detailed the use of journals, ledgers, and a correlating trial balance. The theories and mathematical proofs that Pacioli created have been modified over the years, but the same accounting principles exist today. The basic accounting equation that "assets equal liabilities plus equity" is still in practice.

The Financial Accounting Standards Board (FASB) is the highest authority in establishing accounting standards and principles. It is a nongovernmental organization that develops and interprets accounting standards, and the SEC (Securities and Exchange Commission) has delegated this authority to the FASB. There are currently seven full-time FASB members, and they each serve five-year terms. Accountants adhere to generally accepted accounting principles (GAAP) developed and interpreted by the FASB. These GAAP regulations are used to prepare, present, and report financial statements for numerous entities, including not-for-profit organizations. In 2009, the FASB created a Not-for-Profit Advisory Committee (NAC) to obtain input from the various not-for-profit entities regarding how GAAP affects their job duties and financial reporting. This committee also assists the FASB in communicating these matters to the appropriate not-for-profit businesses. The NAC has developed three working groups whose purpose is to develop initiatives and recommendations that can improve the fiscal accountability of not-for-profit operations. The rules and regulations formulated by this committee will most likely have a significant impact on healthcare accounting. Table 1.1 lists the hierarchy of accounting standard setting (1).

Other countries do not have to adhere to either GAAP or FASB regulations because they have their own internally created standards. An increasing trend within the accounting profession is how to handle accounting issues with the increase of globalization.

The rules and regulations that are contained within GAAP are guided by specific assumptions, principles, and constraints. Unfortunately, it is not feasible to describe all the rules of double-entry accounting; however, an underlying conceptual framework can be discussed. The four primary assumptions of accounting are *economic entity, going concern, monetary unit,* and *periodicity.* The economic entity assumption states that the affairs of the officers and managers are separate from those of an entity such as a hospital. The going-concern assumption states that unless otherwise stated each business will continue operating indefinitely, which means that the liquidation values of assets is not important. The monetary unit assumption states that accounting records are best

Table 1.1   Hierarchy of Accounting Standard Setting

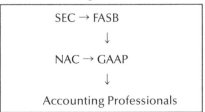

examined when they are reported in terms of money. The final assumption is periodicity, which states that financial information is best reviewed on a periodic basis, such as monthly or quarterly.

In addition to assumptions, there are several principles that are referenced when reporting financial information. The *revenue recognition principle* determines when sales or gains should be recorded in financial statements. Revenues are recorded when they are realized, realizable, or earned. *Realized* means that cash has been given, while *realizable* translates to a receivable being created. *Earned* occurs when the goods or services have been rendered, which is usually at the time of delivery or sale. The *matching principle* is a second principle that requires a company to match expenses with related revenues to report a company's profitability during a specified time interval (2). This principle is a critical aspect of accounting because it symbolizes the cause and effect of revenue and expenses. Basically, the expenses that are incurred in one time period must correlate with the revenue that is formulated within that same time period. In other words, the expenses recorded in March must be from the sales made in March. This principle is associated with the periodicity assumption.

Constraints are used within accounting to limit the process of recognition in financial statements. Two constraints that are used in all industries would be the *cost-benefit* and *materiality* constraints. The cost-benefit restraint of accounting basically states that the cost of any project or initiative should not exceed its benefits. Materiality is another constraint that is consistently used in accounting, and the basic premise is that something is material if its omission or misstatement could influence a decision maker. The concept of materiality is often used as a threshold within variance analysis and auditing.

Accounting Services

Accountants have historically performed four types of services or engagements, classified as compilations, reviews, agreed-upon procedures, or audits.

1. Compilation: Formulation and presentation of financial data without assurance
2. Review: A service that provides some assurance about the reliability of financial data
3. Agreed-upon procedure: An engagement to report on the procedures and findings relating to financial data
4. Audit: An examination of accounting records to formulate an opinion

Compilations and reviews are usually not completed within a hospital setting since most facilities employ their own accounting departments. Agreed-upon procedures are occasionally completed when compliance issues are in question; however, audit engagements are commonly used in the healthcare industry. A significant aspect of accounting services is understanding the difference between an attestation and an assurance service. An *attestation* engagement is a process in which an accountant reports on subject matter that is the responsibility of another party. The objective of attestation services is to create reliable information. In contrast, *assurance* services aim to improve the quality of information for decision makers. Auditing is a type of assurance service used by healthcare facilities to ascertain the validity and reliability of information. Assurance services are broader in scope than attestation services, and they focus on providing information rather than advice. Assurance engagements are also independent services that can be of a nonfinancial mature.

Auditing

Audits are used extensively throughout hospital reimbursement in that both Medicare and Medicaid will often employ the contract services of an audit firm to ensure that what a hospital is reporting is valid. Auditing is a type of accounting service that is performed to determine the credibility of data, whether financial or nonfinancial. The goal of an audit is to express an opinion on the subject matter in question. The audit *does not* guarantee that the information is free from mistakes but rather provides reasonable assurance that the statements are free from material error. Audit reports can be classified as qualified, unqualified, adverse, or a disclaimer of opinion (Table 1.2).

Some larger healthcare organizations employ both internal and external auditors to review both financial and nonfinancial subject matter. In comparison, the internal auditor's work is usually more detailed than the external auditor's work. The external auditor's primary purpose is to express an opinion on the fairness of the statements; the internal auditor attempts to improve the effectiveness and efficiency of the hospital's operations.

CRITICAL ISSUE

Audits do not guarantee that data are free from all errors. An audit is designed to provide reasonable assurance that the information is free from material error.

Another aspect of auditing is to provide an assessment of a hospital's internal control mechanisms. Internal control is the process designed to ensure reliable financial reporting and compliance with applicable laws and regulations. Safeguarding assets against theft and unauthorized use of equipment also falls within internal control. *A hospital can achieve effective internal control through the proper segregation of job duties.* The three principle job responsibilities that must be segregated are *authorization, recording,* and *custody.* These functions must be performed independently by separate hospital personnel, or an internal control weakness might exist. An example would be that only human resources should have access to changing pay rates, while the treasurer should only have access to signing checks. A weakness or deficiency is a control that adversely affects the ability to record financial data in accordance with GAAP. This weakness must also be *material* enough to affect the financial statements. It is the duty of the internal/external auditor to evaluate

Table 1.2 Types of Audit Reports

Unqualified: The financial statements are presented fairly in all material aspects in conformity with GAAP.
Qualified: The financial statements are presented fairly in all material aspects in conformity with GAAP except for effects of the matter to which the qualification states.
Adverse: The financial statements do not present fairly the financial position in conformity with GAAP.
Disclaimer: The auditor does not express an opinion on the financial statements.

Source: Henderson, K.J. 2011. What are the four types of audit reports? http://smallbusiness.chron.com/4-types-audit-reports-3794.html (accessed November 28, 2011).

the severity of each control deficiency to determine if any of these deficiencies are material. Audits are performed in accordance with GAAS (generally accepted auditing standards), while financial statements are formulated in accordance with GAAP. While GAAP rules may or may not be restrictive, it is the responsibility of hospital management to ensure that financial data are reliable. Despite the numerous types of internal control mechanisms, there are inherent limitations that could be the possible collusion of employees or faulty judgment of hospital personnel. There is also a risk of a competent auditor not finding the appropriate errors or misstatements when performing engagements. Audit risk is the risk that an auditor may unknowingly fail to modify the opinion of a materially misstated financial statement. The three components of audit risk are

1. Inherent risk: There are possible misstatements due to poor internal controls.
2. Control risk: Internal control is weak and will not prevent a misstatement.
3. Detection risk: An auditor will not find the mistakes that exist.

Of these three components, both inherent and control risk are dependent on the company or business being audited; however, detection risk can be minimized through the education and experience of the auditor. Whether for profit or not for profit, hospitals have some sort of annual audit performed on their financial statements. A majority of hospitals employ a clinical internal audit department that reviews medical records for proper coding and billing purposes; some larger facilities have internal audit teams that review financial data. It is not necessary for a hospital employee to know all the functions of auditing, but an accountant should be aware of the overall purpose and its effect on hospital operations.

CRITICAL ISSUE

It is the responsibility of hospital management to ensure that financial reporting is accurate and internal control is satisfactory.

Financial Concepts and Terminology

Much like other technical professions, the accounting vocation has specific terminology and jargon that is unique to the profession. Certain concepts and ratios guide the interpretation of the different reporting statements. Two concepts that are extremely common in financial analysis are *variable costs* and *fixed costs*. Variable costs move in direct proportion with volumes, whereas fixed costs are independent of volume. Salary and supply costs are examples of variable costs in that these items will increase or decrease as patient days or procedures increase or decrease. Fixed costs are incurred regardless of volumes, and they are relatively stable. Examples of fixed costs would be depreciation, interest expense, and the salaries of senior administration like the chief executive officer (CEO) and chief financial officer (CFO) (see Table 1.3).

Table 1.3 Variable and Fixed Costs

Variable cost	Fluctuates with volume	Example: medical supplies
Fixed cost	Does not fluctuate with volume	Example: depreciation

An additional type of expense unique to a hospital is termed a stepped-variable expense: The expense changes with volume but not in direct proportion. An example would be the nursing salary expense in a typical room-and-board department. If a unit had occupancy for 25 beds but only 12 patients were present, then assume no additional staffing is needed when 4 nurses are present (25 beds/12 patients/4 nurses). In this example, the assumption is that the appropriate staffing ratio is three patients for each nurse (3:1). If one or even two additional patients are admitted, then the staffing ratio would remain unchanged because the four nurses can handle the increased workload. However, assume that when the fifth patient (15 total) is admitted an additional nurse is needed (25 beds/15 patients/5 nurses). The addition of the extra employee is dependent on volume but not directly because the additional employee is "stepped" based on the staffing ratio for that nursing unit (15/5 = 3:1). Staffing ratios are predominantly dependent on the acuity of the service provided and the number of patients being treated. Clinical staff, not financial staff, is responsible for creating the appropriate staffing ratios. Senior management often benchmarks these staffing ratios against other hospitals to ensure that departments are operating efficiently.

The additional employee who was added to the mentioned staffing ratio represents an *FTE* or *full-time equivalent*. This term is consistently used in hospital accounting, especially for budgeting and monthly reporting. An FTE is an employee who works the full number of hours defined by the hospital. FTEs usually have the advantage of receiving fringe benefits such as health insurance and paid vacation. The standard definition of an FTE is an employee who works 8 hours a day, 5 days a week for the entire year (52 weeks in a year). Some FTE designations may be different due to different shifts and required number of work hours; however; the usual figure is 2,080 hours. The examination and maintenance of FTEs are critical to hospital budgeting because of the impact on salary expense.

One FTE = 2,080 hours (8 hours a day * 5 days week * 52 weeks in a year)

The addition of an FTE is significant because of not only the increased salary expense but also the correlating fringe benefits. The accurate budgeting of hospital FTEs is a job duty that each departmental manager must perform diligently. Typically, one employee might work in numerous departments in the hospital. For example, an imaging manager may be responsible for supervising five different imaging departments (magnetic resonance imaging [MRI], X-ray, computed tomographic [CT] scanning, ultrasound, and nuclear medicine), so instead of 1 FTE in a single department, there would be 0.20 FTEs in all five departments. The proper method of assigning this individual's salary expense would be to allocate one-fifth of the annual FTE expense to each of the five different departments. (Assume the imaging manager's salary is $100,000.) Table 1.4 lists the appropriate allocation.

The correlating 20% of the imaging manager's total FTE figure would also be classified in all five departments. The allocation becomes even more significant in a hospital setting since registered nurses (RNs) often work in more than one department. Due to the nationwide nursing shortage, some employees may be asked to work in the intensive care unit (ICU) for several days, then the following week may be asked to work in the obstetrics/gynecology (OB/GYN) department.

Another term that is commonly referred to in financial analysis is *margin*. There are several classifications of margin often used as performance measures. The primary components are contribution margin (CM), operating margin, gross margin, and profit margin. *Contribution margin* is defined as net revenue less variable costs, and it is one of the more significant financial measures in healthcare accounting. The CM represents the profit that would be incurred regardless if fixed costs were used. The use of the CM measure is significant when addressing and analyzing service

Table 1.4 Imaging Salary Expense Allocation

Department	Expense	FTE
MRI	$20,000	0.20
X-ray	$20,000	0.20
CT scan	$20,000	0.20
Ultrasound	$20,000	0.20
Nuclear medicine	$20,000	0.20
Total	$100,000	1.0

lines and departments. It is also beneficial when looking to purchase a new piece of equipment or offering a new clinical service. An example of an existing hospital service is given in Table 1.5.

In this example, the hospital service has produced net revenue of $1,000,000 with a correlating variable cost of $700,000, resulting in a CM of $300,000. The additional fixed costs of $500,000 have created a loss of ($200,000). By looking at this example, the service line might seem detrimental; however, the fixed-cost amount of $500,000 would be incurred regardless if this hospital employed the service or not. Without looking at other factors, the service line is actually beneficial to the hospital because it has produced a CM of $300,000. A hospital accountant should be aware of the financial significance of the CM to a healthcare facility.

Profit margin is a term used to measure how much of every dollar of revenue a healthcare organization keeps in earnings. Profit margin is often separated into either gross profit margin or net profit margin. Gross profit margin is basically gross margin divided by gross revenue. In this instance, gross margin is net revenue less the cost of goods sold (COGS). Net profit margin would be net income divided by gross revenue. The difference between the two is that the net profit margin takes into account all operating expenses, whereas the gross profit margin only entails the COGS figure. These two ratios are often used as benchmarked figures that measure a hospital's efficiency.

Another ratio that is commonly used is *operating margin,* which is defined as operating income divided by net revenue. This ratio is a measurement of how much net revenue remains after the payment of variable costs. The operating margin is useful in determining how much money remains for a hospital to pay its fixed costs, such as interest expense. The rule of thumb is that the higher the margin ratio percentages are, the better the performance will be for that facility.

Table 1.5 Net Income of a Sample Hospital Service

Net revenue	$1,000,000
Variable cost	$700,000
Contribution margin	$300,000
Fixed cost	$500,000
Net income	**($200,000)**

Additional Financial Terms

In accounting jargon, the terms *effectiveness* and *efficiency* are frequently used. Effectiveness is defined as completing the assigned task, while efficiency is maximizing output for a given input. Even though efficiency is vital to being successful, a healthcare professional should be more concerned with effectiveness. Since patient care is the primary goal of a healthcare system, efficiency should be sacrificed to achieve effectiveness. Two other significant terms referred to in healthcare are *liquidity* and *solvency*. Liquidity is essentially meeting short-term obligations, whereas solvency is the ability to meet long-term obligations. Liquidity measures a hospital's ability to convert assets into cash. Examples of liquid assets would be certain receivables and investments; examples of short-term obligations would be accounts payable or wages payable.

Both expenses and revenues can be further refined as either *incremental* or *differential*. These terms are often used interchangeably; however, they are quite different in nature. Incremental cost/revenue is incurred as a result of an additional activity, whereas differential cost/revenue is the result of two different alternatives. These cost variations become significant when comparing two alternatives. For example, assume a piece of lab equipment is not functioning appropriately and can no longer be repaired. Hospital staff has the choice of either replacing the lab equipment with an identical machine or upgrading to a new, more advanced piece of equipment. The cost between purchasing the new, more advanced machine and the identical previous lab equipment would be differential because the more advanced equipment has a higher cost. The cost between the two alternatives is the differential cost. Imagine if the lab equipment could be repaired; then, the choice would be to keep the old machine with the cost of repairs or purchase a new piece of equipment. The relevant costs would be the additional cost expense associated with purchasing the new lab equipment or the lesser expense by simply repairing the machine. The additional expense is incremental to the decision-making process.

Another type of cost that is significant to accounting is *opportunity cost,* which is the cost forgone by not utilizing another resource. Opportunity costs should be estimated when purchasing decisions are being researched. The calculation of an opportunity cost includes revenues that would not be received or the expenses that would not be incurred if another alternative was chosen. An example of an opportunity cost would be if a hospital decided to invest in a high-risk mutual fund that only yielded a 5% return. If the hospital decided to invest the same amount of funds in a less-risky U.S. Treasury bond, the return would have been 8%. That 3% loss represents the opportunity cost of not making the appropriate investment decision.

When determining the strategic direction of a hospital, a common technique that is employed by financial managers is *SWOT* (strengths, weaknesses, opportunity, and threats) *analysis*. By addressing these four aspects, hospital staff can determine what business venture or project needs to be pursued. SWOT analysis is performed using the mission and goals of the hospital. The facility identifies and examines the internal and external factors that are both beneficial and detrimental to hospital objectives. The strengths of a healthcare facility could be its geographic location or variety of services offered. The possible weaknesses could be anything that places the hospital at a disadvantage, such as the lack of a NICU (neonatal intensive care unit). Opportunities would be the external prospects that could increase profits for the hospital, such as increasing market share by advertising in a new district or county. Threats are the most significant aspect of SWOT analysis because they represent external issues that could hinder the hospital's ability to maintain operations. A threat could be a competing hospital filing a CON (certificate of need) to open more beds in their facility. Senior and middle management hospital personnel should be aware of the use of SWOT analysis and how it can benefit hospital operations.

Financial Statements

A primary function of any accounting department is formulating the financial statements that are reviewed and examined by management. Not only do internal users need financial information to assess hospital strengths and weaknesses, but also external users review the financial data for numerous purposes. Investors may need information to decide whether to increase or decrease their investments, while creditors desire financial statements to determine whether to extend additional credit. Employees of the healthcare facility may also need financial information to better negotiate wages and fringe benefits. In other words, *the users of financial information may or may not have a direct or indirect interest in the hospital.* The four basic financial statements that a majority of companies and for-profit hospitals utilize are the balance sheet, the income statement, the statement of cash flows, and the statement of changes in equity. In contrast, the four major financial statements that not-for-profit hospitals and other 501(c)(3) businesses use are the statement of financial position, statement of operations, statement of changes in net assets, and the statement of cash flows. The statement of financial position is similar to the balance sheet, while the statement of operations is somewhat similar to an income statement. The statement of operations is a significant document because of its prominence in budgeting and variance analysis. The statement of changes in net assets is a document specific to not-for-profit accounting, while the statement of cash flows is a fundamental report that separates the operating, investing, and financial cash components. *The primary reason why all financial statements are formulated is to support and assist the decision-making process.* There are also compliance and regulatory reasons, but the rationale for creating these documents is for those in management to make the appropriate decisions that will benefit the hospital.

Analyzing and reviewing financial information such as the income statement involve a working knowledge of financial principles. When formulating financial statements, accountants are under the assumption that those reading the documents already have an elementary, if not intermediate, comprehension of accounting. It is not the responsibility of the accounting staff to educate personnel on how to read financial statements but to create these documents in an efficient and effective manner. Certain for-profit hospitals may need to comply with SEC guidelines when preparing statements; not-for-profit facilities may create these statements for auditing purposes or for bond indenture agreements. Pro forma or projected financial statements are essentially estimated statements that may or may not reflect what the healthcare facility predicts will happen in the near future. Pro forma statements may be misleading because they may omit certain transactions that GAAP would require. As a rule of thumb, the validity of any financial statement labeled pro forma must be considered. An accountant may audit or review a pro forma statement; however, no investigation of internal control is required. When reviewing financial information, healthcare personnel often use what are termed *horizontal* or *vertical analysis* to analyze data. Horizontal or trend analysis compares data over a period of time, whereas vertical analysis compares figures over 1 year. An example of horizontal analysis would be comparing a hospital-specific ratio over a 5-year span to determine if the figure increased or decreased. An example of vertical analysis would be comparing a percentage of expenses to net revenue from 1 year to the next. This is completed by developing common-size financial statements, such as a balance sheet to determine what has increased or decreased over 1 year's time.

Budgeting

Regardless of the industry, almost every business employs some type of budget as a control mechanism to monitor revenues and expenses. The annual budget represents the strategic plan of the hospital, and it is formulated in accordance with the mission and long-term goals of the facility. Budgets are utilized to communicate objectives, evaluate performance, and motivate employees. Hospital budgets are typically segregated into the *operating budget, the capital budget,* and *the cash budget.* The operating budget is composed of the statistical budget, the revenue budget, and the expense budget. The statistical budget is created first, and it formulates the revenue figures for each department (Price * Quantity = Revenue). Examples of statistics would be the number of admissions, discharges, or emergency room (ER) visits. These figures are multiplied against the set prices for services listed in the hospital charge description master (CDM). The expense budget comprises the salary and nonsalary expenses used to achieve the revenue expectations. It is the duty of the departmental supervisor to estimate what these volumes and correlating expenses will be. An example of an operating budget issue would be that the highest hospital volumes are often incurred in the months of January through March, while the lowest statistics are usually in the summer months. The budget should reflect this decrease in both revenue and expense in the summertime. This seasonal variance in volumes is primarily due to the flu virus being active in the winter months.

CRITICAL ISSUE

The operating budget consists of the statistical budget, the revenue budget, and the expense budget.

The revenues and expenses that are budgeted in each department, such as the ICU or ER, are the responsibility of that department's supervisor. Accounting personnel assist and facilitate the process, but the actual managers are responsible for creating the departmental budgets. Termed *participative budgeting,* this process gives managers the ability to create the financial figures on which they will be measured. Obviously, a vice president or operations manager will review the figures to determine if they are accurate since some supervisors may "pad" or "sandbag" their annual budgets. Also referred to as *budgetary slack,* some managers may underestimate revenues and overestimate costs so that their actual budget monthly comparisons will be favorable in the upcoming year. The presence of budgetary slack is extremely detrimental to hospital operations, and senior hospital staff must review each department's budget to determine if it is accurate. The development of the hospital operating budget is a critical component of facility operations. All hospital staff must be aware of its significance in maintaining operations. If a department did not budget the correct amount of volumes or the appropriate expense figure, then the entire hospital could feel the ramifications.

Almost all hospitals use *incremental budgeting* as a method to plan the next year's operating budget. This method is based on the precedent that last year's revenue/expense figures will be a good indicator of what next year's figures will be. The current year's financials are used as a baseline to formulate what would be expected next year. This approach is simpler and less time consuming than the *zero-based budget* approach, which requires hospital staff basically to create each year's budget from nothing. The zero-based approach assumes that current-year operating revenues and expenses are not an appropriate barometer in what will occur next year.

CRITICAL ISSUE

Almost all hospitals use the incremental budget method in that current-year revenue and expenses are a sound predictor of what will occur next year.

A budget that is separate from the operating budget is the capital budget, which plans the financing of major expenses, such as fixed assets. These high-dollar items are excluded from departmental budgets because managers do not totally control the purchase of these items; therefore; the capital budget is excluded from the operating budget. Examples of capital budget items would be a CT scanner, an addition to a building, or a software upgrade. Some of these capital items may cost millions of dollars, and hospitals typically do not have the cash on hand to purchase these items. To finance these expenditures, hospitals can predominantly use three different techniques: *long-term debt, equity financing,* and *capital leases.* Long-term debt can be obtained from several sources; however, if the hospital is classified as not for profit, then tax-exempt financing can be used, which represents the lowest cost of debt. A restriction of using tax-exempt debt is that it must be used for tax-exempt purposes. An example of a purchase that would not be classified as tax exempt would be the purchase of a physicians' office building. The not-for-profit entity must use a third party to issue the tax-exempt debt, and the hospital must be classified as a 501(c)(3) organization. If the hospital does not qualify for tax-exempt financing, it can still qualify for numerous available long-term debt options.

A second source of debt financing is the use of equity, which can be either external or internal. Internal equity financing is less expensive, and it involves the use of retained earnings to purchase capital assets. External equity financing involves giving an ownership interest to those in exchange for funding. Both internal and external financing is used by for-profit hospitals. A majority of for-profit hospitals are part of larger organizations that are publicly traded, and these companies offer stock through public offerings. A disadvantage of a public stock offering is that control of the hospital system may be diluted or even lost if a third party purchases a majority of the shares.

A third source of debt financing is the use of capital leases, which gives the hospital the possession of an asset but not the ownership. In a capital lease arrangement, the benefits and risks of ownership are transferred to the hospital, but a third party retains the ownership of the equipment. The hospital pays a monthly fee to the third party for the use of the equipment. To be classified as a capital lease, one of four criteria must be met:

1. The lease contains a bargain purchase option.
2. The lease contains a transfer of ownership at the end of the lease.
3. The lease term is equal to 75% or more of the estimated economic life of the leased property.
4. The present value of the lease payments is greater than 90% of the fair market value of the asset leased (3).

If only one of these four criteria is met, then the hospital can capitalize the leased asset in the financial statements and depreciate it much like any other asset. An advantage of capital leasing is that the hospital gets to claim depreciation on the capital asset and deducts any interest expense in the lease payment. If the leased equipment does not meet any of the criteria, then it would be classified as an operating lease, and the item would not be capitalized in the hospital's general ledger. If an operating lease exists, the hospital does not have any ownership rights, and the payments to the third party are classified as expenses that flow in either the income statement or statement of operations. Operating leases comprise what is termed *off-balance-sheet financing* in that a risk exists from a liability that is not recognized on a financial statement. Other examples of off-balance-sheet financing involve unconditional purchase obligations or deferred compensation arrangements. Many of the new innovative financial instruments create some type of off-balance-sheet risk.

A significant difference between a capital budget and an operating budget is that capital budgeting involves ranking the numerous financial outlays to determine the best alternative. *Capital rationing* occurs when a hospital sets a limit on the amount of capital funds to be invested in a given time period, which is typically a year. In determining whether to purchase a capital item, financial personnel commonly rely on three methods: the *payback method, NPV (net present value),* and *IRR (internal rate of return).* The best way to rank such investments is to compare the estimated cash flow that each investment should produce. The payback method evaluates an investment based on the length of time to recapture the cost. For example, if a capital investment such as an X-ray machine costs $50,000 and the hospital expects the equipment to generate additional cash flows of $10,000, then the payback period would be 5 years. The advantage of the payback method is its simplicity; however, it ignores the time value of money. If the payback cash flows are not constant, then they can be calculated in cumulative form. The NPV method is a calculation that uses a discounted cash flow to calculate the present value of estimated future cash outflows of purchasing an item and comparing this figure with the present value of the estimated cash inflows. To calculate the NPV, a discount or hurdle rate must be estimated, which represents the minimum rate of return that a hospital will accept on a capital investment. The IRR calculation is similar to the NPV method; however, instead of producing an actual positive/negative figure, a percentage is formulated. The percentage is formulated through trial and error by selecting interest rates that make the NPV equal to zero. Therefore, the present value of the expected cash inflows equals the present value of the expected cash outflows. This percentage is compared against the internally created desired rate of return to determine if the capital investment should be made.

CRITICAL ISSUE

The three methods used to determine if a capital asset will be purchased are the payback method, NPV (net present value), and IRR (internal rate of return).

In addition to both the operating and capital budget, a healthcare facility must formulate a cash budget to deal with the necessary cash requirements that occur in a given time frame. A cash budget is usually prepared for each month of the year, and both a short-term cash budget (1 year or less) and a long-term cash budget (beyond a year) are created. The short-term cash budget is primarily used for daily operations, whereas the long-term cash budget is used for more strategic initiatives. The cash budget is the last component of the budget process, and it reveals if the other budgets are feasible. (If the cash budget is negative, then the operating and capital budgets must be reconfigured until the amount is positive.) Primarily, the cash budget is formulated using the cash receipts/disbursements method, which provides a picture of the increases and subtractions of cash transactions. The cash budget is an effective form of control that compares the net cash to a budgeted figure. The comparison of actual to budget is essential because cash is not only received from checks but also from electronic wire transfers. Healthcare financial personnel should always strive to maximize

Table 1.6   Example of a Lockbox to Decrease Check Float

A bank will charge an annual fee of $25,000 for the use of a lockbox, and a hospital estimates that this lockbox will reduce the float by 2 days. Assume that daily cash receipts are $500,000, and short-term interest rates are 4%.	
The healthcare accountant should first formulate the estimated increase in cash available, which would be $1,000,000 ($500,000 * 2 days), then estimate interest savings of $40,000 (0.04 * $1,000,000). The annual bank fee of $25,000 must be contrasted against the $40,000 in savings.	
Additional revenue by increasing cash by 2 days	$40,000
Expense of creating the lockbox	($25,000)
Net benefit of creating the lockbox	$15,000

the amount of cash available for investment while minimizing the expenses needed (bank fees) to maintain the appropriate cash balances. A significant step in collecting cash is to convert those funds into available bank balances. A problem that some hospitals have is that checks mailed from either patients or insurance companies may be from locations that are not in close proximity to the facility. When these checks are mailed, it might take several days before the post office can deliver the checks to the hospital. Also known as a *check float*, this is the time from when a check is mailed to when it is cashed by the receiving facility. Often, a check can take 3 to 5 days to reach a hospital before it can be deposited to a bank account. To decrease this float period, a lockbox system was created that decreases the float by instructing consumers to mail checks to a location closer to the check sender rather than mail the amount to the actual hospital. By doing so, the 3- to 5-day check float can possibly be reduced to 1 to 2 days, and a hospital can have quicker access to its cash. The use of a lockbox has its advantages, but its cost must be weighed against the benefits of its use. Table 1.6 is an example of a proposed lockbox submitted to a hospital to decrease its check float.

The end of the cash flow cycle is the disbursement of checks, which could be to a supplier or employees. Often, employees are paid through direct deposit, which is an agreement with a bank to electronically formulate an ACH (automated clearinghouse) entry, which wires the funds to the employee's bank account.

CRITICAL ISSUE

A goal of cash management is to minimize the check float of incoming checks and maximize the float of outgoing checks.

Cost Accounting

Even though healthcare is considered a service industry, the basic principles of cost accounting can be applied to improve decision making. *Breakeven analysis* is used to predict the relationships among cost and revenue at various statistical levels. It gives hospital management the ability to view the effects of volume changes as they apply to both variable and fixed costs. A significant

Table 1.7 Example of Breakeven Analysis in Units and Dollars

An endoscopy procedure is priced at $2,000 per procedure, and variable costs to perform this procedure are $1,000. The estimated fixed costs in this department are $50,000.
Breakeven Point = $50,000/($2,000 − $1,000) = 50 procedures
From this analysis, the department must perform 50 endoscopy procedures to break even.
Additional analysis could be completed to find the breakeven point in dollars, which is found by dividing fixed costs by the CM ratio. The CM ratio is the unit CM divided by the revenue per unit. Using this example,
Breakeven Point in Dollars = $50,000/($1,000/$2,000) = $100,000

component of any financial analysis is the formulation of the breakeven point, which is the level of volumes where total revenues equal total expenses. For hospital cost accounting purposes, the total revenue will be considered net revenue. The basic breakeven formula is defined as

$$\text{Fixed Costs/Unit Contribution Margin} = \text{Breakeven Point}$$

The unit CM is defined as sales less variable costs divided by units. It is the same definition as for CM except statistical volumes are divided into both net revenue and variable costs. The unit contribution is the amount needed from one sale to cover fixed costs. Table 1.7 lists an example of breakeven analysis.

Two assumptions used when performing breakeven analysis are that all costs are either fixed or variable and total variable costs change proportionately with volume. An extension of breakeven analysis is *cost volume profit analysis* (CVPA), which is a method used to predict volume trends in the healthcare organization. Much like breakeven analysis, both variable and fixed costs are needed to find a solution. An example of a typical cost volume dilemma is given in Table 1.8.

Table 1.8 Example of Cost Volume Profit Analysis

Assume a knee surgery is priced at $20,000; variable costs are $15,000. How would financial staff determine how many knee surgeries are needed to create a net operating income of 5% given that total fixed costs are $100,000?
An equation can be formulated to find the amount of volumes needed.
Revenue(x) = Fixed Costs + Variable Costs (x) + (.05)(Revenue(x)) $20,000x = $100,000 + $15,000x + (.05)($20,000)(x) $20,000x = $100,000 + $15,000x + $1,000x
The $1,000 is a result of multiplying 5% times the knee surgery charge of $20,000. The $15,000 and $1,000 are added together and subtracted from the $20,000.
$4,000x = $100,000 $x =$ 25,000
To achieve a net operating income of 5%, the hospital would need to perform 25,000 knee surgeries.

By using CVPA, the management of a hospital can be better informed of the company's profitability and cost utilization when implementing target goals. There are limitations of using this analysis because of the numerous assumptions needed; however, the overall analysis has a beneficial impact on decision making. Hospital accounting staff should be educated on the various cost accounting applications that can benefit operations.

Inventory Management

A hospital must maintain a substantial amount of inventory to treat the various patients who enter a facility. Supplies such as implants, sutures, and bandages are just a few items that need to be stockpiled. A purchasing or supply chain manager should be responsible for forecasting the correlation between inventory needed and patient volumes. The two primary goals of healthcare inventory management are to ensure that necessary medical supplies are available and to minimize the cost of holding these items. The supply chain is the flow of materials and services from their original sources to patients. This process involves more than one entity and several hospital departments. In theory, inventory is a cost that is not value adding since it has no benefit to a hospital as supplies are simply taking up space in a facility. Hospitals predominantly order material in a JIC (just-in-case) methodology rather than use JIT (just in time) because of the nature of patient care. A healthcare facility needs to have the appropriate inventory when a patient requires it. Stockout costs are those costs that occur when a hospital does not have inventory of a product. This cost may occur in other industries, but it can never occur in a hospital because this places the patient's health in jeopardy. Other costs associated with hospital inventory are ordering costs, receiving costs, and carrying costs. Carrying costs would be any cost associated with maintaining that inventory. Examples of carrying costs would be theft or product obsolescence. There are many expensive inventory items purchased by a hospital that could possibly be stolen and resold. Effective inventory controls must be implemented to safeguard assets against theft from employees, visitors, and patients. A hospital looking to improve performance or reduce costs must analyze and dissect all components of the supply chain.

CRITICAL ISSUE

The two primary goals of healthcare inventory management are to ensure that the necessary medical supplies are available and to minimize the cost of holding these items.

In addition, some inventory items, such as implants, have a limited shelf life, and they may expire if not used in a specific time frame. For example, certain implantable surgical devices such as cadaver bones cannot be used after several months. These expired items must be discarded, and they represent an immediate loss. To counteract this product obsolescence, hospital managers began purchasing certain items on *consignment*. When an item is purchased on consignment, the hospital does not own the product, and it does not record a financial transaction; however, the actual item is located in the hospital's inventory. The hospital only pays for the item if it is used. High-dollar items such as pacemakers and defibrillators are often purchased on consignment. The products are available for use by clinical staff, but they do not exist on the hospital financial statements. A close relationship with a vendor must be established and proper billing guidelines should be followed when implementing a consignment inventory system.

Sensitivity Analysis

A method used by accountants for both budgeting and other financial issues is sensitivity analysis. *Sensitivity analysis* is defined as a technique used to determine how different values of an independent variable will have an impact on a particular dependent variable under a given set of assumptions (4). This type of statistical analysis is used not only by accountants but also by engineers and actuaries in determining the possible increase/decrease in a figure if certain other variables were changed. Sensitivity or "what-if" analysis is used predominantly in budgeting to determine the increase or decrease in revenue/expense when additional statistics are added. An example of sensitivity analysis in an existing department is given in Table 1.9.

Currently, the revenue and volumes are $10,000,000 and 10,000, respectively, resulting in a revenue-per-statistic figure of $1,000. When formulating the possible increases in volumes, the manager has arbitrarily decided that the department may grow by either 10% or 20%; however; the payer mix of these new patients will not change. Assume for this example that the hospital has been collecting 40% of all revenue for this department (see Table 1.10).

After net revenue has been formulated the variable expenses must be formulated, which will increase as revenue increases. The fringe benefits for this example will be estimated at 20% of salary expense (see Table 1.11).

The variable cost per statistic includes salary and supply expense but does not include fringe benefit expense because that cost is a function of salaries rather than volumes. The current variable cost per unit would be $300 ($3,000,000/10,000). The 10% and 20% increase in volumes

Table 1.9 Volumes with 10% and 20% Increases

	Current	10% Increase	20% Increase
Gross revenue	$10,000,000	$11,000,000	$12,000,000
Volumes	10,000	11,000	12,000
Revenue per statistic	$1,000	$1,000	$1,000

Table 1.10 40% Collection Rate Assumption

	Current	10% Increase	20% Increase
Gross revenue	$10,000,000	$11,000,000	$12,000,000
Volumes	10,000	11,000	12,000
Gross revenue per statistic	$1,000	$1,000	$1,000
Net revenue (40%)	$4,000,000	$4,400,000	$4,800,000

Table 1.11   Correlating Variable Expenses

	Current	10% Increase	20% Increase
Salary expense	$2,000,000	$2,200,000	$2,400,000
Fringe benefits (20%)	$400,000	$440,000	$480,000
Supply and other expenses	$1,000,000	$1,100,000	$1,200,000
Total variable costs	$3,400,000	$3,740,000	$4,080,000
Variable cost per statistic	$300	$300	$300

Table 1.12   Total Costs

	Current	10% Increase	20% Increase
Salary expense	$2,000,000	$2,200,000	$2,400,000
Fringe benefits (20%)	$400,000	$440,000	$480,000
Supply and other expenses	$1,000,000	$1,100,000	$1,200,000
Total variable costs	$3,400,000	$3,740,000	$4,080,000
Variable cost per statistics	$300	$300	$300
Fixed costs	$750,000	$750,000	$750,000
Total costs	$4,150,000	$4,490,000	$4,830,000

would be a function of that $300 statistic; however, the fixed costs will remain constant despite the increase in volumes (Table 1.12).

After all variable costs and revenue figures have been calculated, the expected profit from the increase in volumes can be examined (see Table 1.13).

The sensitivity analysis of this sample department reveals that as volumes increase, the loss in the department decreases or profitability increases. The primary reason for the increase in net income is that fixed costs remained the same while other costs increased with volumes; however, this example also assumed that the payer mix of the department did not change with the increase in volumes. A more realistic sensitivity analysis would include several other internal and external factors that are unique to that department. The concept of sensitivity analysis may seem elementary, but it is consistently utilized throughout healthcare accounting in determining financial estimates. By adjusting the percentages, the hospital accountant can better determine the financial effect of increasing or decreasing volumes.

Relative Sales Value

Another accounting application that is used in healthcare is the relative sales value method. This technique is often used as a means of allocating a specific amount based on the total value of all

Table 1.13 Net Income

	Current	10% Increase	20% Increase
Gross revenue	$10,000,000	$11,000,000	$12,000,000
Net revenue	$4,000,000	$4,400,000	$4,800,000
Total variable costs	$3,400,000	$3,740,000	$4,080,000
Contribution margin	$600,000	$660,000	$720,000
Fixed costs	$750,000	$750,000	$750,000
Net income	($150,000)	($90,000)	($30,000)

variables. This method is often used when a variance occurs, and instead of omitting the variance, the amount is allocated to the remaining figures based on the percentage of total. For example, assume in Table 1.14 that several service lines had been formulated but they do not exactly tie to total hospital revenue.

In this example, the general ledger has recorded $135,000,000 in clinical hospital revenue, which is listed on the financial statements. This amount is referred to as the "source data" or the tie back into number. Service line reports and other ad hoc statements are occasionally created by IT (information technology) employees. Occasionally, these totals are formulated using estimates or allocations, and certain service line totals may be from numerous sources. In any case, there may be a small variance that needs to be allocated for presentation purposes. In this example, the variance is $1,579,231, which is approximately 1.17% of the total hospital revenue listed on the financial statements. This amount can be "pushed up" based on the percentage to equal the ledger figure because service line analysis is primarily used for trending/comparative purposes, and the variance is relatively immaterial. First, in Table 1.15 a percentage of total number is created for each service line. Second, each percentage of the total revenue amount is multiplied against the variance, and this summation is added to the service line total (see Table 1.16). These proportional variance figures can now be added back to each service line figure to tie back to the total revenue figure (Table 1.17).

Table 1.14 Sample Service Lines with Revenue

Service Line	Total Revenue
Cardiology	$54,926,825
Surgery	$35,458,756
Obstetrics	$24,556,236
Neurology	$18,478,952
Subtotal	$133,420,769
Total hospital revenue	$135,000,000
Variance	**$1,579,231**

Table 1.15 Revenue as a Percentage of Total

Service Line	Revenue as Percentage of Total
Cardiology	($54,926,825/$133,420,769) = 41.17%
Surgery	($35,458,756/$133,420,769) = 26.58%
Obstetrics	($24,556,236/$133,420,769) = 18.41%
Neurology	($18,478,952/$133,420,469) = 13.84%

Table 1.16 Percentage of Total * Variance

Service Line	Percentage of Total * Variance
Cardiology	41.17% * $1,579,231 = $650,161
Surgery	26.58% * $1,579,231 = $419,759
Obstetrics	18.41% * $1,579,231 = $290,739
Neurology	13.84% * $1,579,231 = $218,572
	Subtotal = $1,579,231

Table 1.17 Revised Total Revenue

Service Line	Total Revenue
Cardiology	$54,926,825 + $650,161 = $55,576,986
Surgery	$35,458,756 + $419,759 = $35,878,515
Obstetrics	$24,556,236 + $290,739 = $24,846,975
Neurology	$18,478,952 + $218,572 = $18,697,524
	Subtotal = $135,000,000

For presentation purposes, the total amount of the service lines now "ties back" or "foots" to the ledger figure listed in the financial statements. A significant theme of accounting is that *any report or financial analysis must tie back to the source data from which it came.* This preserves the integrity of the data and the reputation of the hospital accountant who produced the report.

Other Ratios

Hospitals predominantly formulate ratios using financial data for the purpose of performance evaluation; however, there are additional ratios that measure the financial health of the organization. *It is not feasible to memorize all the financial ratios that affect a hospital;* however, a general understanding of their purpose is needed. Currently, the economy is weathering what has been termed "the great recession," and many credit agencies have begun to downgrade the credit rating of certain healthcare organizations. A group of ratios that relates to the financial health of a hospital is termed the *profitability ratio,* and it generally examines financial data in the income statement or statement of operations. An example of a profitability ratio would be return on equity (net income/average equity), which indicates a hospital's ability to purchase new capital equipment without adding excessive debt. Another profitability ratio is return on total assets (net income/average total assets), which determines how effective and efficient a healthcare organization is in generating profits from its assets. A second group of ratios is called the *liquidity ratio,* which measures the ability of a hospital to meet short-term obligations. A liquidity or solvency ratio is significant to a credit agency because it reveals how quickly a hospital can pay current liabilities, such as payroll and accounts payable. An example of a liquidity ratio would be the days in accounts receivable (accounts receivable/net revenue per day) calculation, which measures the average length of time for a hospital to convert receivables into cash. An example is given in Table 1.18.

The formulation of the days in accounts receivable ratio may vary from hospital to hospital due to the fact that some facilities include/exclude other variables. Another example of a liquidity ratio would be the days cash on hand statistic, which indicates how much cash is available to meet operating expenses. Basically, if a hospital has operating expenses of $10,000,000 and cash available of $2,000,000, then it would have 73.00 days of cash on hand. ($2,000,000/($10,000,000/365)) A significant aspect of the days cash on hand ratio is that depreciation must be backed out of the operating expense amount before any calculations are made.

Another set of ratios that hospitals often use is called the *activity ratio,* which determines the relationship between revenues and assets. Also referred to as efficiency ratios, a common trait among these statistical measures is that all activity ratios have revenue as the numerator. An example of an activity ratio would be the total asset turnover ratio (net revenue/average total assets), which indicates how effective a hospital is in generating patient revenue from its assets. A second activity ratio would be the fixed-asset turnover ratio (net revenue/average fixed assets), which determines how much revenue is generated from the fixed assets of the healthcare organization. A final grouping of ratios is the *capital structure ratio,* and it reveals the level of debt a hospital is currently incurring. Capital structure ratios are extremely significant to healthcare organizations, and they are commonly formulated by lending agencies. A typical capital structure ratio would be the cash-to-debt ratio (cash/total debt), which measures the level of cash an organization has on hand compared to its short- and long-term debt obligations. Another example of a capital structure ratio would be the debt service coverage ratio, which determines the amount of earnings needed to meet interest and principal payments. An example is given in Table 1.19.

In this example, the debt service coverage ratio is 1.45, which is extremely good because if the ratio were below 1.0, it would represent a negative cash flow. For example, if the debt service coverage ratio were 0.85, it means that the hospital only had enough operating income to pay 85% of the annual debt payments. To appease loan officers and credit agencies, the debt service coverage ratio should ideally be over 1.0.

Table 1.18   Days in AR Calculation

A hospital has $25,000,000 in net accounts receivable and $109,500,000 in net revenue. The net revenue per day is ($109,500,000/365 = $300,000), which means the days in accounts receivable figure is 83.33 ($25,000,000/$300,000).

Table 1.19   Debt Service Coverage Ratio

A hospital has $1,500,000 in cash flow, interest expense of $100,000, and principal payments of $1,000,000. The debt service coverage ratio would be 1.45 (Cash Flow + Interest Expense)/ (Principal Payments + Interest Expense) or ($1,500,000 + $100,000)/($1,000,000 + $100,000).

Even though ratios have been extremely beneficial in dissecting financial information, they have limitations. Since many hospitals are different in size and services offered, the comparability of ratios may in some cases not be worthwhile. In addition, financial data that are formulated in statements are subject to numerous estimates. Ledger items such as depreciation and contractual expense are based on approximations and can be subject to change. Last, ratios are only financial measures, and they do not provide an encompassing view of hospital performance. The primary goal of a hospital system is to treat patients, while financial ratios only compare the fiscal performance of the facility.

Conclusion

The accounting profession is a broad and vast field that encompasses all businesses regardless of the industry. The terminology and concepts that exist in the accounting field can seem overwhelming, and the techniques used to analyze data may be confusing; however, these ratios and equations are vital to hospital decision making. The uniqueness of the healthcare industry makes applying the accounting principles and regulations even more difficult. A hospital accountant should be aware of the numerous tools and methods needed to analyze financial data properly.

References

1. Henderson, K.J. 2011. What are the four types of audit reports? http://smallbusiness.chron.com/4-types-audit-reports-3794.html (accessed November 28,2011).
2. Matching principle. http://www.accountingcoach.com/terms/M/matching-principle.html (accessed November 28,2011).
3. Capital lease. http://biztaxlaw.about.com/od/glossaryc/g/capitalleasdef.htm (accessed December 27, 2011).
4. Sensitivity analysis. http://www.investopedia.com/terms/s/sensitivityanalysis.asp (accessed November 29, 2011).

Chapter 2

Types of Hospitals/ Conceptual Framework

History and Introduction

In the 1940s, the citizens of the United States were faced with a world at war as the United States fought the axis powers in both Europe and the Pacific. To fight these battles, a draft was placed into effect that required all males in a certain age range to combat our enemies. While these soldiers were overseas, women were asked to perform jobs that were previously performed by men. Traditional manufacturing jobs producing textiles, clothing, weapons, and ammunition were needed since a majority of the male workforce was fighting on other continents. In response to this new population, the government enacted wage restrictions to ensure that one company could not offer higher wages to recruit female workers. Corporations responded to this governmental action by creating non-wage-related benefits such as health insurance. By offering this incentive, corporations could recruit and maintain the necessary workforce while male workers were not available. Hence, the need for job-related benefits began.

As the war ended, the returning soldiers qualified for Veterans Administration (VA) benefits, so the need for companies to offer benefits to these former soldiers was not essential; however, the seeds of offering employee health benefits had already been planted. In the 1960s, the government enacted Medicare and Medicaid, which protected the elderly and the poor; in the 1980s, EMTALA (Emergency Medical Treatment and Active Labor Act) was created, which stated that hospitals could not turn away patients who visit the emergency room. Currently, it is almost commonplace for a company to offer health insurance as a benefit of employment, and the federal government has attempted to reform the health care system by attempting to create universal coverage for all citizens. Despite these changes, the nation's population still has a substantial amount of uninsured citizens, and the costs of care are increasing at an alarming rate.

Throughout history, there has been a need to treat and care for those who are either sick or injured. Whether from treating casualties of war or tending for the elderly, the desire for a facility that specialized in medical care was needed. Hence, the *hospital* was created, which has been in existence for thousands of years and has been used for numerous purposes. The word *hospital* actually has a Latin derivation from the term *hospes,* which translates to "guest." Many ancient civilizations, from the Romans to the Egyptians, employed some type of hospital that treated patients. Over time, the hospital structure has evolved as medical technology has advanced and populations have become more civilized. In the present, virtually every country has some variation of healthcare delivery, and each state in the United States has numerous hospital systems.

Traditionally, hospitals have been classified as either investor owned, governmental, or not for profit. *Investor-owned* or *for-profit hospitals* are owned by a certain number of individuals with private equity interest. They provide the same quality of care as other hospitals except they are structured in a different manner. Healthcare systems like Tenet and Columbia HCA own several for-profit hospitals throughout the country that operate with the intent to maximize stock price and shareholder wealth. *Government-owned hospitals* are legally created public corporations that are controlled by a state or local government. An example of a government-owned hospital would be the VA hospital. A third hospital type and the kind primarily examined in this text is the *not-for-profit hospital*. The not-for-profit hospital structure was created after World War II as a result of the Hill Burton Act (Hospital Survey and Construction Act) in an attempt by President Harry Truman to improve the access and availability of medical care in the country. These facilities have no ownership interests, and they are exempt from federal income taxation. In addition, these hospitals receive contributions from third parties who do not expect anything in return. Not-for-profit hospitals depend on charitable contributions not only from various sources but also the state and federal governments to help pay for operating expenses. All three hospital classifications operate with the intent to treat patients, and they are staffed by nurses and physicians; however, the structure of each is different.

Not-for-Profit Hospitals

The predominant characteristic of a not-for-profit hospital is that the facility is classified as a tax-exempt business or has a 501(c)(3) status. A not-for-profit hospital seeks exemption from paying federal income tax by applying to the Internal Revenue Service, and the hospital must be organized and operated exclusively for charitable, educational, or social welfare purposes. Donors to the entity receive a deduction for charitable contributions made, and the business may be able to obtain debt financing at lower tax-exempt rates. A 501(c)(3) organization must be engaged in activities that further public purposes rather than private interests. The tax-exempt status of not-for-profit hospitals is a current topic of debate since these hospitals do not pay tax not only on clinical service revenue but also on non-patient-related revenue. Examples of non-patient-generated revenue would be sales from the gift shop, cafeteria transactions, or parking lot fees. There are several requirements to qualify for tax-exempt status; however, the primary conditions are that no earnings inure to any private individual, a governing board of directors composed of civic community leaders is present, and a full-time emergency room exists. The concept of *inurement* is paramount in that someone cannot use influence over a nonprofit for personal gains. Any private individual in this matter refers to anyone who has either a personal or a private interest in the not-for-profit hospital. To maintain the 501(c)(3) status, each year the facility must complete a 990 tax form, "Return of Organization Exempt from Income Tax," which asks for several financial aspects of the not-for-profit hospital. A significant aspect of Form 990 is Schedule A, which lists the compensation and benefits of the top five highest-paid employees as well as all employees paid in excess of $50,000. This listing of compensation also includes independent contractors. A recent addition to Form 990 is Schedule H, which details the estimated community benefit in dollars that the nonprofit provides to society. The Schedule H requests costs, not charges, of bad debt, Medicaid, and charity care services incurred. The recent inclusion of Schedule H in Form 990 reiterates the government's belief that healthcare organizations need to prove why they are not being taxed like other corporations. Some states have threatened to revoke the 501(c)(3) status unless a hospital can prove it is supporting its communities with uncompensated care and other social benefits. Common examples of community benefits would be the patient costs of payer classifications such as charity care, self-pay, and Medicaid. Not-for-profit hospitals typically incur annual losses of hundreds of thousands, and in some cases millions, of dollars treating indigent patients. Other examples of social benefits would be free-of-charge screenings for HIV or mammograms to detect breast cancer.

Another characteristic of a nonprofit hospital is that certain general ledger accounts, such as common stock or dividends declared, do not exist since the facility does not have a defined ownership interest that can be sold or transferred. Retained earnings is another ledger account that is common in other financial statements but does not exist in the financials of a 501(c)(3) company. Another noteworthy characteristic of a nonprofit hospital is that these institutions are more primarily concerned about the quality of services rendered and the ongoing ability to provide those services. Unlike other businesses that exist to make money, the not-for-profit hospital's primary purpose is to support the community. Therefore, the reporting needs of the decision makers in a tax-exempt hospital may be different from those who are operating in a different industry such as manufacturing.

Financially speaking, the nonprofit hospital adheres to the same accounting rules and regulations as other companies; however, there are certain differences. The primary difference is that fund accounting is used by not-for-profit hospitals not only for fiscal accountability purposes but also for compliance reasons. This model requires that nonprofit hospitals segregate all net assets into unrestricted, temporarily restricted, and permanently restricted figures at the end of each reporting period. These classifications are related to the existence of donor-imposed restrictions. The purpose of the net assets model is mainly for monitoring the balances of the various assets a nonprofit employs but also for internal and managerial control. The classification and balancing of these funds can be a cumbersome process, and each has its own self-balancing group of assets and liabilities.

Financial reporting in not-for-profit hospitals is different from other business because the main focus is to assist management in assessing the services the hospital provides and its ability to continue to provide these medical services. In addition, the financial statements evaluate the performance and financial stewardship of hospital managers. Not-for-profit hospitals typically utilize four different financial statements:

1. Statement of operations (income statement)
2. Statement of financial position (balance sheet)
3. Statement of cash flows
4. Statement of changes in net assets

The primary financial report is the statement of operations, which is comparable to an income statement used by other companies. The statement of financial position (similar to the balance sheet) states the proprietary theory that assets equal liabilities plus net assets, while the statement of cash flows segregates cash among operating, investing, and financing activities. The statement of changes in net assets is a report fundamental to not-for-profit businesses in that assets must be classified as unrestricted, temporarily restricted, and permanently restricted. A significant aspect of the change in net assets is that the financial document emphasizes aggregated information about the entity as a whole rather than the individual funds.

As part of its tax-exempt status, not-for-profit hospitals accept contributions from third parties, who in return can use the donation to reduce their taxable income. This act of contribution must be voluntary and nonreciprocal, and the contribution itself can include cash, securities, supplies, intangible assets, services, or an unconditional promise to give something in the future. The not-for-profit hospital records these contributions received at *fair market value*; however, an unconditional promise to give may be recognized at net realizable value. The term *unconditional* basically means that the likelihood is remote that the condition will not be met. Seldom do hospitals receive contributions for services, but they are recognized if they require special skills that would usually be purchased otherwise or if they create or improve an asset.

Not-for-profit hospitals sometimes have a separate entity that is apart from the facility but is responsible for raising money to help the hospital. Often called a *foundation*, this separate legal entity is usually chartered and contracted to raise funds to assist a specific hospital system. Even though the foundation's purpose is to provide funding to a hospital, it is typically not consolidated in that hospital's ownership structure. Foundations are usually a separate 501(c)(3) entity that has its own board of directors and employees. The duties of most charitable foundations are to meet with various businesses throughout the community in an attempt to raise cash to help support the hospital's mission. These charitable donations are given to the foundation rather than the hospital. It is at the discretion of that foundation how and when it gives these funds to the healthcare facility. Usually, there is some type of collaborative agreement between a charitable foundation and a hospital to determine when cash will be transferred to the hospital's bank account, and there are also various restrictions that are placed on these donations. For example, a donor may wish to give money to a hospital through a foundation, but the money can only be used to assist children who are affected with leukemia. Both the foundation and hospital must legally honor the request of the donor by using the cash donated for that purpose.

Unrelated Business Income

Unique to the not-for-profit hospital is the concept of unrelated business income (UBI), which would be any income that is not directly related to the mission of the organization. This income is taxed because it does not relate to the tax-exempt purpose of the hospital. UBI is generated in the hospital, but it is not directly related to patient care. The critical difference between classifying income as either "related" or "unrelated" is that related income is a business activity that helps sustain the primary mission of the hospital. Therefore, the related income is not taxable by the government. UBI is traditionally defined as meeting *all* of the three elements:

1. It is part of a trade or business.
2. It is regularly carried on.
3. It is not substantially related to the performance of tax-exempt functions.

Items that are generally *excluded* from UBI would be passive income such as interest income, any dividend income, or rental income. In addition, any income from property or equipment sales would be excluded from the computation of UBI. The income generated from selling items in the cafeteria and gift shop is also not considered UBI since it relates to the mission of the not-for-profit hospital. Items that would be taxed as UBI would be lab work performed for a physician's office. For example, if a family practice physician withdrew blood from a patient and submitted that fluid to be tested at a hospital, then the hospital is performing a service for someone who is not a patient at that facility. If the blood sample were from an existing patient, then the income would be business related; however, the patient is being treated at a physician office. The money paid by the family practice physician's office to the hospital would be considered UBI, and the not-for-profit hospital would be taxed on that income. If the UBI of a hospital comprises a significant amount of total revenue, then the facility may be at risk of losing 501(c)(3) status; however, the total UBI recorded for the year is usually minimal for most hospitals.

CRITICAL ISSUE

The defining characteristic of a not-for-profit hospital is that the entity is tax exempt and is organized for charitable purposes.

For-Profit Hospitals

Of all the hospitals in the United States, approximately two-thirds are not-for-profit, while for-profit and governmental facilities encompass the remaining balance. For-profit hospitals emerged in the 1980s, and companies such as HCA and HealthSouth represent the largest for-profit systems. Also known as investor-owned hospitals, the for-profit structure is similar to any other corporation. Their intent is to make a profit by providing inpatient and outpatient services to the public. Proponents of for-profit hospitals state that they provide better care at a lower cost because they operate in a very efficient manner. Critics believe that for-profit hospitals often place themselves in favorable geographic regions so they can better capture a more favorable payer mix. In addition, many believe that for-profit hospitals engage in profitable services such as cardiology and orthopedics, but they shy away from low-paying services such as psychiatric care. These stereotypes of for-profit facilities are for the most part inaccurate, and almost all for-profit hospitals have the same payer mix as not for profits. The distinction between for profit and not for profit does not refer to profitability but rather to the *limitations on the distribution of earnings and tax-exempt status.* For-profit hospitals predominantly perform the same procedures as other hospitals; however, they have chosen to be structured differently.

Most for-profit hospital systems consist of numerous facilities that treat patients in several different states. A large portion of these systems is publically traded and must adhere to certain regulations and laws. The Sarbanes-Oxley Act was enacted in 2002, and the legislation created the Public Company and Accounting Oversight Board (PCAOB) to oversee the audits of publically traded companies to protect the interests of investors. The act was a result of unscrupulous and illegal accounting practices performed by such companies as Enron, which forced the federal government to create new laws. The Sarbanes-Oxley Act also established the use of an independent audit committee and increased overall corporate responsibility. Violations of the Sarbanes-Oxley Act are deemed to be violations of the Securities Act of 1934.

CRITICAL ISSUE

The distinction between for profit and not for profit does not refer to profitability but rather to the limitations on the distribution of earnings and tax-exempt status.

Government-Owned Hospitals

Also known as public hospitals, the number of government-owned facilities has significantly decreased since the early 2000s. Government-owned hospitals can be funded at the local, state, or federal level, and they typically are located in poor, urban areas. Government hospitals almost always have some sort of graduate medical education (GME) or teaching program, and they typically treat a high number of indigent patients. Much like a not-for-profit hospital, governmental hospitals have the ability to issue debt that is exempt from federal taxation. Governmental hospitals may be a component of a medical school or university, and they present their financial statements using fund accounting. In addition, governmental hospitals must adhere to the financial reporting requirements created by the GASB (Governmental Accounting Standards Board). In contrast to for-profit and not-for-profit hospitals, governmental hospitals are only required to produce three basic financial statements:

1. Statement of net assets
2. Statement of revenues, expenses, and changes in net assets/equity
3. Statement of cash flows

Governmental hospitals are similar to not-for-profit hospitals in that they typically adhere to the fund accounting requirement of segregating net assets into unrestricted, temporarily restricted, or permanently restricted.

Board of Directors

The board of directors or governing board is the defining authority between the hospital and the numerous internal and external stakeholders. The board directors or trustees are appointed members who act on behalf of the community as a whole. Hospital board members are typically not compensated for their actions, and their duties should not create a conflict of interest. A board of directors is required in a not-for-profit hospital, and membership has five primary functions:

1. Select a CEO (chief executive officer)
2. Evaluate the performance of senior management
3. Establish the mission statement and vision of the hospital
4. Approve the hospital budget
5. Ensure quality of care through physician relationships

The governing board has numerous other job duties; however, these functions comprise the bulk of their actions. The board members have the responsibility of establishing and validating the hospital's mission, goals, and objectives. The mission statement of the hospital is a broad statement that is easily communicated throughout the organization and the community. It guides the hospital's planning and decision-making processes. Basically, the *board's performance is the overall hospital's performance*. A board duty that is specific to finance would be approving the hospital budget. The accounting department in every hospital spends numerous months working with both clinical and nonclinical departments in formulating the upcoming year's budget. Accounting personnel provide data, and they help facilitate the hospital budget, but they do not have final approval. It is the role of the board of directors to determine if the appropriate financial figures are congruent with the mission of the facility. For compliance reasons, an audit committee reports directly to the board of directors rather than the senior management. Members of the audit committee have the independence to comment to the board on any actions of senior management that are deemed unethical or contrary to the mission of the organization. Neither the chief financial officer (CFO) nor the CEO can serve on this audit committee.

Senior Management

In virtually every hospital, a senior management team exists whose purpose is effective implementation of the mission, strategies, and goals established by the board. The primary function of senior management is to create a culture of quality excellence and continuous improvement. This is accomplished by meeting the needs of all internal/external stakeholders and designing the organization to meet clinical and nonclinical needs. Senior management also has the duty of providing the board with the annual budget, which is defined as the hospital's mission transformed into reality. Senior management typically consists of the CEO, CFO, COO (chief operations officer), CNO (chief nursing officer), and the CMO (chief medical officer). Any additional members of senior management would be at the discretion of that individual hospital.

The CEO of the hospital is the highest-ranking member of senior management. The CEO is in charge of all management in the hospital, and he or she reports to the board of directors. The roles and responsibilities of the CEO range from figurehead to leader to facilitator. In healthcare, the CEO's job duties revolve around strategic growth and physician relationships. The COO is often considered the second-ranking individual in a hospital, and this position often carries the title of president. The job duties of the COO are defined in relationship with the CEO since the two positions have overlapping responsibilities. Many hospitals do not utilize the COO designation but instead have various vice presidents who preside over numerous departments in a healthcare environment. In contrast, some larger hospitals employ more than one COO if they have a complex organizational structure that offers numerous services. The COO position is often seen as a preliminary step in becoming the heir to the CEO, but that is not always the case. The CFO is almost always an accountant of some background who has numerous years of experience in the financial healthcare field. This officer reports to the CEO and is responsible for financial statement reporting, formulating the budget, and any other fiscal issues. The CFO is basically responsible for managing all financial functions in a healthcare organization. Often, this position is seen as an adviser to the CEO when clinical decisions are made. For example, if a hospital decided to add a new service such as bariatric surgery, then the CFO would be consulted to determine if this new procedure would make fiscal sense. Departments such as payroll, accounts payable, accounting, collections, decision support, and sometimes procurement fall in the CFO's managerial duties. Other industries may use titles such as treasurer or comptroller; however, these are seldom used in hospital accounting.

Specific to healthcare is the CNO, whose purpose is to lead and govern the various nursing departments that exist in a hospital. CNOs have numerous years of experience as a registered nurse (RN), and they usually have some type of graduate degree. The CNO reports to either the CEO or the COO and handles the day-to-day nursing issues that occur in a hospital. Often, nurses represent the largest population of hospital staff, and the CNO must coordinate nursing staffing levels as well as manage any clinical issues that arise. There are various nursing managers throughout a hospital who report to the CNO on the various clinical and nonclinical issues that occur. Another officer position in senior management that is healthcare specific is the CMO, who is a physician responsible for providing leadership and guidance to the medical staff. The CMO is responsible for patient care as well as safety. In addition, the CMO encourages the development of the physician staff and handles any issues that pertain to medicine.

There may be additional members of a hospital's senior management team, but that depends on the size of the facility and the services offered. Some smaller hospitals may not even have a CMO, whereas larger hospital systems might employ numerous COOs. Regardless of size and structure, the two primary senior management positions that all hospitals employ are the CEO and CFO. These two leadership positions are essential for a hospital to maintain effective and efficient operations.

CRITICAL ISSUE

Regardless of the size or structure, every hospital will have a CEO (chief executive officer) and a CFO (chief financial officer) to lead the facility.

Certificate of Need

Federal regulations prohibit any individual or company from building a hospital simply because the individual or company believes it would be a good business decision. The certificate-of-need (CON) program has been in existence since the early 1970s, and it is a legal document that is required in a majority of states before any medical facility can be constructed. The CON request is usually handled by the legal department in a hospital or outsourced to a law firm that has experience in the field. Usually, the Department of Health and Environmental Control (DHEC) in each state is responsible for approving CON requests, and there are numerous requirements in the document that need to be approved by the state. The primary reason for creating the CON is that legislators want to protect the community from oversaturating a market, which could possibly lead to overcharging or unnecessary hospitalization. The entity filing the CON must prove to the state that a definitive *need to the community* exists for this hospital to be constructed. A CON is needed not only to build a new hospital but also to expand any beds in an existing facility. For example, a CON would need to be approved by the state if a 100-bed hospital was at capacity and wanted to add 10 beds to treat additional patients. Arguments against the CON program are that it creates a monopoly for the existing hospitals, and new entrants are not allowed into the market.

Hospital Consolidation

As the future of health care reform remains uncertain, many healthcare providers are uniting or consolidating to protect themselves from financial risk. Whether classified as public or investor owned, hospital systems are currently researching the feasibility of merging. An integrated health-care delivery system can consist of both for-profit and not-for-profit hospitals. A parent corporation might exist, with the other hospitals classified as subsidiaries. The structure of these systems may be different, but the financial presentation is complex. The consolidation or merger of hospital systems is a complicated process that requires legal interaction, so only a broad overview of the topic is given for this text.

A significant issue that arises when hospital systems merge is how to account for the relationship between the new entities. Legal expertise is usually required because many options can be chosen that best reflect the needs of the new organization. A parent-subsidiary relationship might now exist, and financial institutions need to be aware of any additional disclosures that need to be presented and if the *equity method of accounting* needs to be used. Basically, the equity method is utilized when certain aspects of control or economic interest exist. In a consolidation, one hospital might have the direct ability to determine the direction and management of another hospital. Control exists when the rights and powers of the controlling entity are limited by the legal structure that was created (i.e., limited partnership, general partnership, etc.). Economic interest exists if one entity owns significant resources that must be used by the reporting entity to provide services (1).

Control and economic interest exist if the parent corporation has 20% or more ownership of the consolidated entities. The equity method would be used because the parent corporation has the ability to exercise significant influence over the other entities. Since not-for-profit hospitals do not have voting stock, it is usually difficult for hospital systems to determine what "significant influence" is. Regardless of the structure, a hospital system must disclose any transactions made using the equity method.

Unique to a not-for-profit hospital is the use of *equity transfers,* which are similar to ownership transactions for parent-subsidiary relationships. The equity transfer occurs when one hospital controls the other or both are under common control. The actual transfer involves no expectation of repayment or anything of value. The transfers are reported as changes in net assets and are excluded from income since no gain or loss has occurred. Often, what is termed an *eliminating entry* occurs, which removes the equity transfer on consolidation. The elimination needs to occur to ensure that a double count is not recorded when consolidating the hospitals. If an equity transfer occurs between not-for-profit entities but they are not consolidated, then the transfer should be reported at the discretion of the hospitals. The presentation of the equity transfer depends on the substance and nature of the transaction. However, if the equity transfer results in a change of ownership, then the transfer is accounted for as an investment. The financial reporting requirements for hospital consolidations are complex and beyond the scope of this text; however, a healthcare manager should have a basic understanding of how the process works.

When consolidating financial statements, an additional often-misunderstood ledger account is sometimes created. Termed *minority interest,* this account balance represents a share of the operating results or income of the hospital system if dissolution occurs. This account sits in the statement of financial position/balance sheet, and the amount does not often change. Within for-profit entities, the minority interest represents the portion of a subsidiary's stock that is not owned by the parent corporation.

Conclusion

The not-for-profit hospital predominantly maintains the same fiscal principles that other facilities employ with the exclusion/addition of a few financial concepts. The primary differences are the segregation of net assets, exclusion of certain ledger accounts such as retained earnings, and exclusion of any ownership interest, such as common or preferred stock. Even though nonprofit entities are primarily concerned with improving the community, *there is no law or regulation that states that non-for-profit hospitals cannot be profitable.* Through efficient protocols and effective management, a not-for-profit hospital can maintain a positive operating income. However, all profit is invested back into the facility at the discretion of senior management and the board of directors. For-profit hospitals are much like other businesses created to earn a positive margin. These hospital systems may provide dividends to shareholders depending on whether they are publicly traded. A governmental hospital is a state- or federally funded facility that shares many characteristics with a not-for-profit hospital. Regardless of the business structure, each hospital system has the same intent to treat sick or ill patients.

Reference

1. Woelfel, Charles J. 2011. Equity method of accounting. http://www.eagletraders.com/advice/securities/equity_method_of_accounting.htm (accessed November 28, 2011).

Chapter 3

Hospital Revenue Cycle

Introduction

Most businesses offer a product or service with the intent that either a cash or credit transaction will occur once a sale is completed. Revenue is recorded when realized or realizable, and a receivable is often created to reflect an obligation of payment. A majority of business operations are handled in this manner, and the traditional accountant has been educated on how to record and reconcile these transactions. The hospital accounting field, on the other hand, is not that simple. People who are in need of medical attention rarely expect to be in such a predicament, and the method of payment can be from various sources. Reimbursement for hospital care is often billed after treatment has been provided, and the amount of charges usually cannot be determined until the patient has been discharged. Patients may or may not even have the ability to pay for treatment, which places a tremendous financial burden on hospitals. All of these variables make the hospital revenue cycle an extremely complex and convoluted process.

Imagine owning a restaurant and offering a steak as a menu item; however, the amount paid is different, varying on the person who ordered it. The steak may be priced at $20, but some patrons may only pay $15, $10, or even $5, yet the quality of the steak must be the same for all customers. This scenario exemplifies the intricate nature of hospital accounting. The steak can be a cardiac procedure, and the money a hospital receives could be a certain amount from Blue Cross/Blue Shield, a different amount from Medicaid, and another amount from Medicare. Each amount the hospital receives may be different, yet the cost to provide this service is the same. A significant issue is how such a business can maintain operations when there is such a disparity between the price of services and the amount paid. This substantial gap between gross and net revenue is unique to the hospital revenue cycle. Even though hospital services are driven by patient care, it is the responsibility of financial personnel to transform patient revenue into cash and maintain fiscal responsibility. The primary business process that underlies a hospital system is its ability to be reimbursed for services rendered. In other words, the hospital revenue cycle begins with patient scheduling and ends with the collection of cash.

Patient Access

Preadmission

The first step in the hospital revenue cycle is patient access, which consists of four possible stages: *preadmission, inpatient admission, outpatient registration, and discharge.* The process of preadmitting a patient includes verification of insurance, obtaining authorization for services, estimating the patient portion of the bill, and collecting the point-of-service payment or deposit. The process of verifying insurance can be accomplished at any point in the medical stay; however, it benefits all parties if verification is completed before hospital services are completed. Many hospitals complete this process prior to scheduling, but some services, such as those in the emergency room (ER) require this information to be obtained at a later date. Many hospitals have automated the process of verifying eligibility/benefit data through a predetermined list of insurance providers. Authorization of services is a more time-consuming process since the hospital must coordinate with both the ordering physician and insurance carriers to determine the extent of medical treatment. The patient access department also has the critical function of calculating and communicating the amount of payment that is the patient's responsibility. Historically, the patient portion of the bill is formulated through three different steps:

1. Calculating the net amount from the gross figure
2. Calculating patient deductible and coinsurance payments
3. Considering any applicable annual/lifetime maximums or out-of-pocket limits

Even though a patient may have health insurance, most individuals are unaware of the extent and liability of their coverage. Through effective patient access protocols, the hospital can determine the potential risk of financial loss of treating each patient. *By no means can the patient access department restrict or deny treatment*; however, it does have the ability to educate and inform the patient of his or her rights and responsibilities.

CRITICAL ISSUE

The preadmission process does not decide who or who is not treated at a hospital. The main objective is to obtain and clarify information primarily before service so the hospital can gauge the financial burden of the services provided.

Since preadmission is utilized for nonurgent patients, the goal is to minimize the bottlenecks that occur in the "front end" of the hospital revenue cycle. A hospital can implement protocols that promote appropriate scheduling and financial planning before the patient even arrives at the facility. By collecting all relevant information, the hospital not only can lower the percentage of self-pay and bad-debt expense but also can reduce the amount of complaints from disgruntled patients. A hospital can also improve goodwill and overall customer service by preparing for a patient's visit to a facility. A benefit of an effective preadmission department is to create a "red flag" for each account that is most likely to be denied or have issues on the back end. These accounts are flagged based on previous experience of information being missing or excluded from the bill. These troublesome accounts can possibly be fixed on the front end before they become rework. Another growing trend in preadmission is to confirm the amount of payment prior to service. This verification of payment is completed because a hospital will bear a large portion of the expense if the medical procedure is not authorized. Not only can the estimated insurance payments be determined, but also a payment plan for the patient can be formulated before service. Recently, some hospitals have partnered with banks to provide loans for patients. Bad-debt expense can be minimized through the counseling of a financial representative as soon as the hospital schedules the patient's procedure.

Inpatient Admission

Even though a hospital has preadmitted a patient does not mean the process of collecting information has ended. The admission process has been quickened, but there is often additional demographic, insurance, and financial information that needs to be collected and verified. *The goal of the admission process is to be an extension of the preadmission department.* Whatever patient information is missing needs to be collected or authorized at the admission point. If this information has already been gathered, then the inpatient admission staff needs to confirm that these data are correct to ensure accuracy. Additional admission duties that can be completed at either preadmission or admission would be the administration of an Advanced Beneficiary Notice (ABN) and an MSP (Medicare secondary payer) questionnaire. The ABN is used to determine the patient's portion of a medical bill. Medicare and a majority of other payers require the use of an ABN, which informs the patient that Medicare will only pay for services that it determines are reasonable and necessary. If the patient's insurance does not cover the service, then the hospital representative must inform the patient that certain services will have to be paid out of his or her pocket. In addition, Medicare patients are required to complete an MSP, which is designed to identify patients who have insurance but also are Medicare eligible. *The MSP is significant because a hospital is not permitted to bill Medicare as primary for services if that patient has coverage through another insurance company.* A Medicare auditor will request all MSP questionnaires to ensure that fraudulent billing has not occurred. The hospital still has to send the primary bill to Medicare so it can track the encounter data but Medicare will not pay for services. The federal government's stance is that if a patient has insurance, then that company should pay first before Medicare does.

A significant aspect of hospital admission is the *coordination of benefits,* which is the process of coordinating the multiple insurance carriers that a patient might have. An individual may have various insurance plans that cover the same procedure at a different reimbursement rates. The patient access representative coordinates the insurance benefits of the patient to ensure that neither the hospital nor the patient receives more benefits then entitled. This process can be complex since some patients may be entitled or eligible for several different programs.

CRITICAL ISSUE

Medicare regulations require that all hospitals bill the primary insurance carrier if a patient has commercial insurance but is also eligible for Medicare benefits.

Outpatient Registration

For those patients who do not require an inpatient admission, the patient access department registers them as outpatients. Recently, the amount of outpatient visits increased due to various factors that have reduced the overall amount of hospital admissions. In addition, many low-income patients use the hospital ER as a family practice. Much like an inpatient admission, the registration of outpatients requires the collection and verification of patient information. Third-party insurance companies must be contacted to authorize coverage, and physician orders need to be verified before they can be administered. Typical outpatient visits would be imaging procedures such as a computed tomographic (CT) scan or magnetic resonance imaging (MRI). The amount of an average outpatient bill is much smaller than an average inpatient bill, yet the cost to collect either of the accounts is usually the same. For some hospitals, outpatient balances may even take longer to collect than inpatient accounts. In addition, a significant proportion of outpatient visits are classified as self-pay due to the use of the hospital's ER. The collection of patient information is vital during an ER visit because this may be the only time face-to-face interaction will occur. Patient access protocols should require that hospital personnel exhaust all methods to determine if the patient can qualify for either Medicaid or the hospital's internal charity care policy.

Discharge

If a patient is discharged appropriately, the process of billing and collecting is greatly facilitated. Most hospitals have a discharge checklist used as a reference point when patients exit from a facility. A *courtesy discharge* is when a patient directly leaves the hospital after discharge by their physician. The purpose of a courtesy discharge is not only to increase customer service but also to eliminate unnecessary traffic in the patient access department. The discharge point is usually the last face-to-face contact a hospital will have with the patient, so prompt collection of any copays or deductible amounts is stressed.

On discharge, the patient's medical chart is transferred to medical records or health information management (HIM) to be reviewed and coded. Even though the patient has physically left the facility does not mean that the collection and review of information have ended. Nurses and case managers review each patient's medical information in what is called a retrospective review to ensure that services rendered were medically appropriate. Usually, retrospective reviews are performed by registered nurses and occasionally by medical directors. *Each time a patient enters a hospital, it is the goal of the facility to ensure that appropriate care is given to that person not only while he or she is admitted to the hospital but also after discharge.* The retrospective review is a form of utilization management used to improve the outcome of hospital services. In addition to a retrospective review, hospitals may utilize concurrent or prospective reviews, which examine patient charts before discharge. A prospective review occurs before the patient is admitted, while a concurrent review is performed while the patient is still being treated at the facility. All three reviews can be used separately or in combination to ensure that the appropriate level of care is administered.

The patient access/registration department is a component of the revenue cycle that is occasionally overlooked; however, its function is vital to the capture of revenue in a healthcare facility. If a patient's insurance identification number is incorrect or the precertification of services is not verified, then billing could be delayed or even rejected. Unfortunately, the patient access department is also one of the lowest-paying departments in a hospital, thus perhaps attracting employees who may not be as knowledgeable as other hospital personnel. A patient access supervisor should create a defined and thorough training program to ensure consistency and reliability among departmental employees. In addition, the hospital should enact a well-defined plan to educate physicians and other clinicians on updated regulations and documentation requirements. Through effective management and training, a hospital can streamline the registration process to ensure that patient information is properly collected and verified.

CRITICAL ISSUE

Patient access is where billing issues are found, but it is not necessarily where they occur. Often, clinical departments are the culprit for billing issues.

Billing

The process of billing can be multifaceted due to all the numerous services a hospital offers and the various insurance carriers with hospital contracts. All orders and services completed are documented in the patient's chart, which acts as support for the correlating charges that are formulated after the chart has been coded. Once coded and examined, a finished bill is created that is sent to a third party. To simplify this procedure, the America Hospital Association (AHA) created a claim form, the UB-04 (Uniform Billing 04) or Form CMS-1450, which is used to submit hospital claims regardless of the insurance provider. The UB-04 is an attempt to standardize healthcare data collection, and it replaced the UB-92 claim form. Originally created by the National Uniform Billing Committee (NUBC), the formulation and usage of the UB-04 claim form prevents hospitals from having different forms to submit to the numerous providers that exist. The following is a sample list of some of the items required in the UB-04 claim form:

1. Demographic clinical and insurance information
2. Value codes: patient deductibles, copayments, and coinsurance
3. Occurrence codes: admission and discharge information
4. Condition codes: the basis of the patient's condition, such as whether the individual was hurt on the job
5. Other pertinent information, such as attending physician number

In addition to these items, there are numerous other financial and nonfinancial items that are keyed into the claim form, including the clinical revenue codes of which procedures were completed. A *present-on-admission* (POA) indicator states whether a patient had a medical issue prior to being admitted to a hospital. For example, the POA indicator would state if a patient already had a bedsore prior to admission. A form that is similar in use to the UB-04 is the CMS-1500 claim form. Much like a UB-04 form, the CMS-1500 form is a standardized claim form; however, it is predominantly used by physician practices and medical suppliers. A majority of the same information that is needed for the UB-04 is needed for the CMS-1500 except for the additional requirement of National Provider Identifier (NPI) figures. These NPI codes are unique identifiers used to indicate a health care provider in a transaction. In addition to formulating an invoice for services completed, the posting of revenue and the correlating receivable occur in the billing component of the hospital revenue cycle.

CRITICAL ISSUE

The UB-04 (Uniform Billing 04) is a standardized healthcare claim form used for all insurance providers.

A significant attribute of hospital billing that is specific to Medicare is the use of the *72-hour rule*. This billing rule states that all procedures and services conducted on an outpatient basis must be combined with inpatient charges if they are performed 72 hours prior to admission. Both inpatient and outpatient charges are lumped into one bill rather than two separate bills. If the inpatient services were performed after 72 hours, then a separate bill for inpatient and outpatient services are furnished to Medicare. This government-mandated billing mechanism is used for simplicity to reduce the number of total Medicare claims.

Revenue Sources (Payers)

Hospitals have historically relied on two primary sources of revenue: insurance companies and the government. Healthcare facilities also depend on charitable contributions from third parties and the patient's portion of the bill, but the majority of revenue typically comes from those with insurance and the federal or state government. Examples of insurance providers would be Blue Cross/Blue Shield, Cigna, and United Healthcare; government providers would be Medicare and Medicaid. Insurance carriers negotiate with clients and businesses to insure individuals and their families against health risks, and these companies pay the hospital a rate that is negotiated with that specific facility from the premiums collected from clients. Typically, if someone needs medical care in a hospital setting, Blue Cross/Blue Shield would pay a portion of the hospital bill, and the patient would be responsible for another portion. The percentage that a patient pays depends on the type of health insurance and acuity of service. This "allowable" or "adjusted" figure is the amount that remains after the gross figure is reduced to a net amount. In other words, a hospital may bill a third party for $50,000, but this figure may be reduced to $20,000 based on that particular service negotiated in that contract with that particular insurance carrier. Medicare and Medicaid reimbursement methodologies are quite complex; and they are addressed in further chapters.

Payer Mix

As previously stated, the patients or customers treated by a hospital may be insured by several different programs or providers. The total percentage of these patients is called the *payer mix*, and it is defined as the percentage proportion of patients treated at a facility classified by insurance carrier. A payer mix can be formulated for inpatients, outpatients, or both. A significant issue that each hospital faces is that the payer mix of a hospital primarily determines its ability to maintain operations. Basically, a hospital with a very high percentage of uninsured patients will be less able to function than a facility with a large percentage of insured patients. Since hospitals cannot theoretically influence who or who does not enter their facilities, the population of the payer mix is often the result of the geographic location of the hospital. A hypothetical payer mix for two separate hospitals is listed in Table 3.1.

Hospital A is more able to provide services than Hospital B since it has a more favorable payer mix. The reasoning is that the percentage of managed care (nongovernmental) insurance is 20% higher than Hospital B, and the proportion of of both Medicare and Medicaid populations is 10% less for Hospital A than Hospital B. Traditionally, the Medicaid and Medicare populations reimburse hospitals at a much lower rate than managed care providers.

Table 3.1 Payer Mix

	Hospital A	*Hospital B*
Medicare	30%	40%
Medicaid	20%	30%
Managed care	35%	15%
Charity	5%	5%
Self-pay	5%	5%
Other	5%	5%
Total	100%	100%

CRITICAL ISSUE

The payer mix of the hospital is a major factor in determining its ability to function.

Medical Records

Often called health information management (HIM), the medical records component of the revenue cycle is significant due to the increased complexity of hospital procedures and the federal government's mandate that patient records be digitized. The medical records department has the responsibility of *accurately and correctly translating what was medically performed to the patient into an existing numeric code.* The actual coding of the patient's medical chart is explained in a separate chapter; however, certain functions of the medical records department affect the length of the hospital revenue cycle. In every hospital, there are certain patient accounts that have not been submitted to a third-party payer because items in the bill are missing. Examples of such items could be an incomplete clinical code, an absent data item, or an inaccurate payer class. These accounts represent patients who have been discharged from the hospital but cannot be billed to insurance carriers (DNFB, discharge not final billed). The DNFB statistic is a detrimental, non-value-adding item that negatively affects the hospital revenue cycle. Since bills cannot be submitted, the amount of cash collected is delayed. The DNFB accounts represent bottlenecks in the revenue cycle that need to be minimized by staff.

CRITICAL ISSUE

DNFB is a statistic that represents those patients who have been discharged but not final billed by the hospital. This variable is detrimental to a hospital because it delays the inflow of cash.

Case Management/Utilization Review

In the hospital revenue cycle, patients often need additional care, advice, or referrals after they have been discharged from the facility. *Case management* is a term used to describe the process of hospital staff working with a patient to ensure a positive clinical outcome after hospital services have ended. The Case Management Society of America defines case management as a collaborative process of assessment, planning, facilitation, and advocacy for options and services to meet an individual's health needs through communication and available resources to promote quality cost-effective outcomes (1). Case management personnel basically work with the patient, the patient's family, and healthcare providers to ensure that all resources are being maximized. The healthcare delivery system in this country can be complex and overbearing for some patients, especially if this is their first time in a hospital environment. The typical job duties of a case manager are to coordinate referrals to specialists, arrange for additional care postdischarge, and review rates with providers who are not part of the network. Hospital case managers offer patients additional expertise and planning in an attempt to improve the outcome of the patient's health. Most case managers were previously employed as either registered nurses or social workers, so they understand the clinical and psychological issues that patients must endure. *The process of case management is not a billable action that a hospital can send to a third-party insurance provider.* The post-acute care process attempts to improve the ongoing health of the discharged patient through ensuring that medication is being taken, physical therapy is occurring, or appropriate lifestyle changes have occurred. Through these changes, a healthcare system can possibly decrease the number of patient readmissions, therefore reducing overall cost.

An extension of the admission process is the *utilization review* department, which has the ability to review the patient's medical record to determine if an admission clinically needs to occur. Utilization review can prevent the hospital from admitting patients who could be treated on an outpatient basis. Unnecessary medical admissions are detrimental to any quality improvement initiatives or goals in a healthcare facility. Medicare or recovery audit contractor (RAC) auditors will consistently review medical charts to determine if an inpatient admission was clinically necessary. The cost of providing services should never be considered when the patient's health is at risk; however, effective *clinical protocols* can be implemented that may possibly reduce waste and redundancy. A protocol determines the functional elements of how patient care is administered, and protocols are developed by clinical personnel. Clinical protocols are based on the belief that patients with similar symptoms or issues will have similar plans and can expect to have similar courses of action. These protocols have the ability to improve hospital efficiency and effectiveness by eliminating nonvalue activities, standardizing supplies, and regulating patient-provider relationships, such as nurse staffing ratios.

Cash Collections

Of all the general ledger accounts that exist in the financial statements, the debit balance in the cash account is by far the most critical. Without sufficient cash, employees cannot be paid and medical supplies would not be delivered. The importance of collecting cash is paramount not only in healthcare but also in all industries. The collection of both patient and insurance receivables usually has its own department that specializes in account maintenance. Collection of cash can be a tenuous process since most patients do not wish or may not feel they have an obligation to pay for medical care. Hospitals must design collection practices to be effective but not intrusive. Some patients may not have the necessary resources to pay for hospital bills. In other cases, patients may simply believe they do not need to pay even though they have the ability to do so. Due to the legal ramifications that exist, hospital staff needs to be aware of both the state and federal regulations regarding credit and collections. The five major laws that dictate cash collections are the Truth in Lending Act (TILA), Fair Credit Reporting Act (FCRA), Fair and Accurate Credit Transactions Act (FACTA), the Fair Credit Billing Act (FCBA), and the Fair Debt Collections Practices Act (FDCPA).

The TILA was created as part of the Consumer Protection Act, and its purpose is to protect consumers by having businesses disclose all relevant key terms of the financial arrangement. Regardless of whether the procedure was inpatient or outpatient, the individual usually does not have the necessary cash to pay for all of the hospital bills. Hospital staff is willing and able to create a payment plan for patients so the person will not incur a severe financial burden. Before any monthly payments are agreed on, the hospital must disclose all relevant financial information to the patient as part of the TILA. In essence, the patient is actually getting a loan from the hospital for medical services and is required to pay it back in monthly increments. The hospital must disclose the amount of payments, total price, and the finance charge or interest rate (if applicable). Hospitals must keep evidence that they have complied with the TILA for at least 2 years after the date of disclosure, and the penalty for not disclosing information can be severe. The components of the TILA are driven by whether the transaction was closed end or open end, and the legislation prevents creditors from baiting customers by advertising false credit terms.

The FCRA is a law that regulates the use and collection of consumer credit information. Credit agencies or consumer reporting agencies are entities that collect and report information about consumers used for credit evaluation and fiscal responsibility. The three big agencies (Equifax, TransUnion, and Experian) receive credit information from agencies that have some sort of fiscal relationship with an individual. Examples would be credit card companies, banks, or collection agencies. The FCRA is significant in that hospitals often use collection agencies as a mechanism to collect payment from delinquent accounts. These collection agencies have the ability to report negative information to credit agencies based on a discharged patient's inability to pay his or her portion of the medical bill. By law, the agency must give significant notice to the individual before submitting information to the credit bureau.

A third law that affects hospital collections is the FACTA, which is intended to protect consumers from identity theft. The FACTA requires that consumers can request a free credit report every 12 months, and that businesses must properly dispose of personal information such as Social Security numbers and dates of birth. A majority of this information is already explained in the HIPAA (Health Insurance Portability and Accountability Act) rules that every hospital must adhere to, but FACTA addresses some additional issues. For example, FACTA created the Red Flag Rules, which require certain institutions to develop identity theft prevention programs. Financial staff must be made aware that they have the ability to access patients' personal information, and hospital protocols must protect these data at all times.

The FCBA gives consumers the right to dispute errors listed by the reporting agencies. The dispute must be received within 60 days of the statement, and the credit bureau has 90 days to investigate the claim. An individual can actually sue the credit-issuing company for damages if there are errors in a credit report and they have not been amended. A significant aspect of the FCBA is that billing statements mailed to former patients must be sent at least 14 days before the payment is due. This gives the debtor ample time to make payment on the outstanding debt. Even though someone is entitled to view his or her credit history, they have no right to make an adjustment. The individual must request that the respective third party change the incorrect data.

A final law that is applicable to hospital collections is the FDCPA, which attempts to eliminate abusive practices in the collection of debt. This act is significant because *it predominantly applies to third-party collectors rather than hospitals; however, the collection agencies are "acting on behalf" of the hospital.* The actions of the collection agency reflect on the hospital, and their abusive collection efforts can result in negative goodwill. Collection agencies have to adhere not only to the FDCPA but also to any applicable HIPAA rules. A medical bill is considered debt because medical care is typically a service provided to a consumer. The FDCPA prohibits the use of deceptive or abusive practices of debt collection, such as contacting a debtor outside the hours of 8:00 AM and 9:00 PM, threatening the patient with arrest or legal action, using deception to collect debt, or using profane language to collect debt. Additional acts that are prohibited would be contacting the patient at work after being instructed that this is not acceptable and reporting false information about the individual's credit report. Hospital personnel should be cognizant of these issues to ensure that when patient balances are transferred to a collection agency they should be worked in an appropriate and professional manner.

Skip tracing or acquiring the location of a debtor is a method used by collection agencies to find debtors so the debtors may make payments on their debt. The FDCPA also addresses the numerous rules and regulations that exist when trying to locate someone. The location information that exists for a debtor would be the individual's residence, telephone number, and place of employment. It would not include the neighbor's address, work phone numbers, or names of work supervisors or relatives. The FDCPA is a strict liability law, which means that the patient need not prove actual damages if the debt collector violated the act. In addition, the Federal Trade Commission (FTC) has the authority to enforce violations according to the FDCPA. The FDCPA affects hospitals in that facilities must establish the appropriate protocols for outside collection agencies to act on their behalf. The debt collection companies are often not part of a hospital system, but they have a principal-agent relationship that can affect the hospital system in both negative and positive ways.

In addition to these five laws, some states have enacted legislation for a hospital to collect debt through a state income tax refund. Predominantly only not-for-profit hospitals can engage in such a program, and it varies from state to state. Another program used to recoup cash is the GEAR (Government Enterprise Accounts Receivable) program, which allows healthcare facilities to garnish wages and create bank levies. The minimum balance to qualify for the GEAR program is $300, and the cost to participate varies (2). Some states also have enacted what is termed a *doctrine of necessaries,* which means that both husbands and wives are responsible for their spouses and minor children. In other words, the medical bills of a wife can be the responsibility of the husband. This doctrine stems from common law, and medical services are generally considered to be a necessity for a spouse or minor child. This doctrine varies from state to state, and hospital personnel should be aware of its existence.

Table 3.2 represents a flowchart of the revenue cycle of a typical hospital.

Hospital Contracting

Any contract between an insurance carrier and a hospital that is not reimbursed at full charge creates some type of financial risk for the facility. The risk is dependent on the type of contract, the terms, and the type of services provided. A specific type of healthcare contract that is not as common as it used to be is referred to as a *capitated arrangement.* In this type of contract, the payment to the hospital is based on a fixed number of enrollees. The revenue that is recorded by the hospital

Table 3.2 Flowchart of the Hospital Revenue Cycle

Scheduling/Preadmission
↓
Inpatient Admission/Outpatient Registration
↓
Discharge/Case Management
↓
Coding/Medical Records
↓
Billing/General Ledger
↓
Cash Collection

is based on an agreement to provide care rather than the actual costs of treatment. For example, assume an insurance company has 2,000 covered members from whom it receives monthly or annual premiums. A hospital may negotiate a capitated contract with an insurance carrier that gives the facility a set amount per enrolled member. Assume the hospital negotiates a rate of $500 per covered member. In this scenario, the hospital would receive a cash payment of $1,000,000 (500 * 2,000) per month regardless of patient costs. Capitation payments are usually made at the beginning of the month, and a healthcare facility may or may not set up a receivable for this type of contract. The risk of such a contract is that some of those 2,000 enrolled members may not visit the hospital at all, resulting in pure profit, whereas some members may become extremely sick and absorb a substantial amount of expenses. It is at the discretion of hospital management to negotiate or accept these types of contracts because of the positive/negative contingency that might occur. Capitation payments are a fixed amount of cash given on a monthly basis regardless of how many patient visits. In addition, there are no outlier or complexity adjustments in capitated contracts. The PMPM (per-member, per-month) attribute of capitated arrangements makes the method a unique reimbursement structure.

A type of contract that is similar to a capitated agreement is a *global payment,* which is a fixed payment designated for all patient care during a given time period, such as month or a year. Global payments are similar but not identical to capitation payments in that a global payment is paid each time the patient is treated at the hospital. The purpose of global payments is to contain the cost utilized to treat patients and reduce unnecessary procedures. Hospitals have an incentive to decrease the length of stay and maintain efficiency so the cost of providing care will not exceed the global payment amount. Much like capitation, the hospital is placed at risk for outlier medical conditions that produce costs that exceed the global payment. An example of a global payment would be Medicare's reimbursement of home health's services (Home Health Resource Grouping, HHRG). Numerous types of home health services for physical or speech therapy are consolidated into a single payment. Critics of the global payment methodology believe that this increased risk will force hospital staff to reduce the quality of care given so the expected payment is not exceeded.

In an attempt to reduce losses, hospitals have negotiated certain clauses and mechanisms to hedge their risk. Certain contracts may contain a *stop-loss provision* that limits the amount of risk that a hospital incurs. Also known as the attachment point, the stop-loss provision limits the amount of outlier costs that can occur when a patient has an excessive length of stay or absorbs more costs than traditionally expected.

There have been some highly publicized lawsuits that have questioned the practice of hospitals charging self-pay patients the full price for hospital services while insurance carriers receive discounts of up to 60% or 70% of the full charge. From a socioeconomic perspective, those classified as self-pay are bearing the highest burden since they cannot negotiate rates with healthcare providers. The reason insurance providers receive these high discounts is *favored nation clauses*, which require hospitals to give discounts to payers equal to the discounts given to other third parties. Many hospitals choose not to use favored nation provisions in contracts because they state that the insurance provider must receive the lowest or most favorable rate of all insurance carriers that do business with the hospital. This is beneficial to the insurance company but not to the hospital. If an insurance company wishes to include a favored nation clause in a contract, then the hospital can counteract by reducing the membership of the network for that insurance provider. By reducing the membership, the hospital has reduced the cash flow (premiums paid) to the insurance company. This negotiation technique helps mitigate the use of favored nation clauses in insurance contracts.

Fraud/Abuse

Due to the complex billing procedures that exist in the healthcare revenue cycle, the opportunity for fraud or abuse has become a prevalent issue. To counteract the growth of healthcare fraud, the government created the HIPAA legislation in 1996, which authorizes the Office of the Inspector General (OIG) to conduct investigations relating to fraud and abuse. The purpose and mission of the OIG are to protect the integrity and welfare of the U.S. health system and its beneficiaries. The primary purpose of the HIPAA legislation is to protect the privacy and security of patient health information. The HIPAA laws were updated in 2009 with the passing of the Health Information Technology for Economic and Clinical Health Act (HITECH), which aims to improve the technological means by which patient information is accessed.

In addition to federal legislation, hospitals have formulated internally driven processes to protect themselves from unethical behavior. Virtually every healthcare facility has implemented an effective compliance program with which all employees should be familiar. A hospital's written policies and procedures should be able to lessen the risk associated with health care fraud and abuse. A healthcare facility should also create a code of conduct policy that should be tailored to the organization's goals and objectives. The internal code of conduct should take into account the regulatory exposure of each clinical and nonclinical function of the hospital.

Fraud occurs when a person *knowingly and willfully* makes a false statement or a misrepresentation of fact that results in a benefit. Fraudulent schemes can range from an individual acting alone to a highly sophisticated network of criminals. The most common forms of health care fraud are billing for services not rendered, misrepresentation of a diagnosis, or falsifying a patient claim. A component of legislation that applies to fraud is the Federal False Claims Act, which covers all federally funded programs with the exception of taxes. The False Claims Act was enacted during the Civil War to prevent fraud when military contractor's supplied items to the Union army. The act has been amended over the years, and the punishment for violating this act can range from civil to criminal charges. To be guilty of violating the False Claims Act, an entity must knowingly or willfully submit a fraudulent or false claim to the government. In addition to fraud, kickbacks are unlawful in that no finder fees or remuneration should be given for referrals. An example of a kickback would be a hospital leasing an office to a physician free of charge in exchange for the physician referring patients to that specific hospital. The illegal action is not the referral itself but the exchange of something monetary for the referral.

Legislation that specifically addresses referrals would be the Stark laws or physician self-referral laws, which were initially introduced in the early 1990s. The Stark laws address physician self-referral, which is the practice of a doctor referring a patient to a hospital in which that physician has a financial interest. This referral creates a conflict of interest because the physician can financially benefit from the referral. The Stark laws are separated into three correlating segments, with Stark 1 referring to lab services for Medicare patients, while the other components refer to other health services. Usually, the legal department of a hospital would handle any Stark law issues; however, a healthcare accountant should be aware of its purpose and how it affects the facility.

CRITICAL ISSUE

Fraud is a willful and intentional act; abuse only requires that a hospital engage in a practice that leads to unnecessary cost to a health care program.

Recovery Audit Contractors

A relatively recent addition to healthcare accounting is the federal government's implementation of the RAC program. The RAC began as a project in the Medicare Modernization Act of 2003, and its purpose is to identify potential over- or underpayments in Medicare inpatient admissions. Only a select group of states was initially chosen for the audit, and the results have been extremely successful for the federal government. The RAC program has the ability to request up to 10% of Medicare discharges but not more than 300 medical records every 45 days. The RAC auditors are attempting to review the medical record to determine if medically unnecessary services were billed or DRG (diagnosis-related group) miscoding occurred. The Medicare auditor would review the patient medical record to determine if the inpatient admission was legitimate or whether it should have been an observation day or even an outpatient visit. The use of the Medicare RAC has been so successful that individual states have begun plans to implement a Medicaid RAC program. Healthcare managers must be aware of the financial impact of the RAC audits due to the possibility of the government asking for its money back.

Form 990

The tax Form 990 is specific to tax-exempt organizations, and it details the financial items in a not-for-profit business. The Form 990 must be sent to the Internal Revenue Service (IRS) on an annual basis for all companies that are classified as 501(c)(3) with the exception of a few faith-based institutions and other state-funded agencies. There are numerous sections in this tax document, and beginning in 2010 a Form 990-EZ is used if the not-for-profit business had gross receipts of less than $500,000 and assets less than $2.5 million. If the company had less than $25,000 in gross receipts, then the 990 tax form need not be completed. Most not-for-profit hospitals have assets above $2.5 million, which means the accounting staff needs to complete Form 990 rather than the 990-EZ. Typically, the Form 990 must be submitted by the 15th day of the fifth month after its fiscal year ends. Examples of items requested in the tax form are the hospital revenues/expenses as well as the net asset fund balances. There are also accompanying schedules in the Form 990 that ask for ancillary information and community benefits. For-profit hospitals would not have to complete a Form 990; however, they would need to complete the necessary tax forms that any other business would complete. Most for-profit hospitals are part of a national organization that is incorporated and in some cases publically traded.

Conclusion

The revenue cycle of a hospital is a complex process that requires each step to be monitored closely to determine its effectiveness and efficiency. Health care personnel have what is termed *information asymmetry* in that the hospital has more knowledge about the patient's needs than the patient does. Patient access/registration is the front end of the hospital revenue cycle, and the collection and verification of patient information are vital to the billing process. The revenue cycle progresses to either an inpatient admission or outpatient registration and eventually leads to a discharge. The patient's medical chart is then transferred to medical records, where it is coded into an invoice. Accounting staff have the responsibility of not only billing the third party but also collecting payment for services provided. Hospital staff should also be aware of the numerous laws and regulations that affect the collection of these patient balances. The risk of loss that a hospital faces can also be mitigated through the appropriate negotiation of contracts with managed care insurance providers. In addition, senior management must enforce a code of compliance to ensure that fraud and abuse never occur in a healthcare setting.

References

1. Case Management Society of America. http://www.cmsa.org/Home/CMSA/WhatisaCaseManager/tabid/224/Default.aspx (accessed November 28, 2011).
2. Governmental enterprise accounts receivable collections. http://www.sctax.org/GEAR/default.htm (accessed November 28, 2011).

Chapter 4

Hospital Services

Introduction

The various types of services and procedures that a hospital offers to the public are the decision of that particular facility. Some hospitals may have the resources to perform advanced procedures, while others may not. Whether for profit or not for profit, the decision on what clinical services to offer is made by senior management and the board of directors. The types of services are reported in the bylaws or articles of incorporation. A majority of hospitals employ basic clinical services such as an emergency room (ER), birthing unit, pharmacy, imaging, and laboratory. Other teaching facilities may offer more high-acuity services involving cardiac or neurological care. That particular state's Department of Health or Department of Housing and Environmental Control agency would ensure that the hospital would adhere to specific federal and state regulations. Unfortunately, a practical description of each hospital service cannot be provided; however, the basic elements of the most prevalent services can be discussed.

Inpatient/Outpatient

The types of services and procedures that hospitals present to the public can range from routine to those that treat life-threatening conditions. A common type of hospital service is an inpatient admission, which is an acceptance by the hospital to provide medical care while the patient is lodged at the facility. In contrast, an outpatient visit is the acceptance by the hospital to provide medical care while the patient is *not* lodged in the facility. Traditionally, inpatient admissions have been classified as urgent, elective, or emergency. Urgent and elective admissions are scheduled before the patient arrives, whereas emergency admits require immediate attention. Elective admissions are those that can be scheduled anytime because the patient's health is not in danger; urgent admissions involve those patients who need hospital care so that their health will not be in further danger. Emergency admissions are those in which the patient's health is in serious jeopardy. In contrast, outpatient registrations are often classified as emergency, referred, clinic, or ambulatory. Of these four designations, typically only the emergency patients are treated at the hospital's ER. A referred outpatient is an individual referred by a physician to the hospital for treatment but will return to that physician after hospital care has ended. A clinic patient is treated by a hospital and remains a patient of the hospital after outpatient care has ended. An ambulatory patient commonly receives some sort of surgical service. By definition, *ambulatory* means outpatient, and this type of patient is receiving surgical care that does not warrant a hospital stay over 24 hours. In comparison to inpatient admissions, the rate of outpatient visits has increased since the year 2000 due to the growth of improved technology, such as advanced imaging equipment, and by the public's growing use of the ER as a primary medical care clinic.

Facility/Professional Fee

Hospitals often refer to the physician portion of the patient service as the *professional fee* in that a "professional" such as an ER physician is responsible for diagnosing the patient, ordering labs or imaging, and discharging the patient from the facility. Despite being performed at a hospital, these functions are billed separately from what is termed as the *facility fee* or technical fee, which is the hospital portion of the patient visit. In other words, a patient will receive a bill for both the professional fee and a facility fee. Usually, the particular physician's practice will be responsible for billing the patient's insurance provider and collecting payment for the professional fee. In contrast, the facility fee is billed and collected by the hospital. *The coding methodology for a physician's practice and a hospital are very different.* Physicians use the Resource-Based Relative Value Scale (RBRVS) method, whereas hospitals employ a CDM (charge description master, chargemaster) and are predominantly reimbursed using a Diagnosis-Related Group/Ambulatory Payment Classification (DRG/APC) model. If a patient is admitted to a hospital for a surgical procedure, then that individual will receive a bill not only from the hospital but also from the surgeon, the anesthesiologist, the radiologist, and any other physicians who treated the patient. These numerous invoices for the same patient are an issue that many lawmakers are currently attempting to reform or simplify.

CRITICAL ISSUE

Patients receive two bills from a hospital, which are termed the professional (physician) fee and facility (hospital) fee.

Emergency Room

Virtually everyone at one point has visited an ER, whether it is for an injury or illness to a family member, friend, or even oneself. Not-for-profit hospitals must employ ERs primarily to maintain tax-exempt status; however, for-profit facilities also employ them because of the significant benefit they provide to the community. For billing purposes, hospitals primarily use five different levels of ER visit charges. The type of level charge is determined from the acuity of the patient visit. Also known as a 450 revenue code, the purpose of the ER-level visit charge is to cover the *fixed costs* of providing the ER. In an ER visit, the charge nurse enters everything that was done to the patient, but he or she does not enter the level charge. The medical records (health information management, HIM) department is responsible for coding the level charge; however, this process is commonly automated due to the creation of decision support software programs. Medicare pays the same amounts for level 1 and 2 visits as well as a higher amount for level 3 and 4 visits. Due to the high acuity of services for levels 5 and 6, a much higher reimbursement figure is used because this patient most likely needed trauma-level care. The facility fee or ER-level visit charge for the ER is much like the room-and-board charge for other clinical departments.

CRITICAL ISSUE

The purpose of the ER-level charge is to cover the fixed costs for providing ER services to the community.

A problematic issue in the ER is the wait that occurs before a physician can be seen. If a patient enters the ER and sees the triage nurse but decides to leave, then the hospital can still bill for the triage charges. Most insurance providers compensate the hospital for the triage service even though the payment is minimal. Although the patient did not remain to be seen, the triage visit is considered a level 1 ER charge, and a 450 revenue code is attached to the bill. This additional billing mechanism is occasionally overlooked because some facilities will not bill a third party if an ER patient left without treatment (LWOT). The hospital may be able to recoup some minor expenses by billing for the triage visit; however, the LWOT statistic is detrimental to a facility because it means the wait for ER treatment is too long.

Unfortunately, a patient leaving the ER before treatment is a problem that cannot always be controlled because many people treat the local ER as a primary care provider, and due to federal Emergency Medical Treatment and Active Labor Act (EMTALA) laws, these patients cannot be turned away. EMTALA determines how and when a patient can be transferred or released from an ER. EMTALA was part of the Consolidated Omnibus Budget Reconciliation Act of 1986, and its purpose is to prevent hospitals from rejecting or refusing to treat patients who enter the ER. Prior to EMTALA, a hospital could transfer a patient to a charity or county hospital if the patient was not able to pay or did not have sufficient coverage. Hospitals must provide patients with an appropriate medical screening examination to determine if a life-threatening illness is occurring. If the patient is suffering from a serious condition, then the hospital must provide treatment until the patient is stable. For example, a pregnant woman who enters the ER and is in active labor must be admitted and treated until delivery is completed. All hospitals must post a sign in the ER that notifies patients of EMTALA, and this sign must be approved by the Department of Health and Human Services. If the patient is not suffering from an emergency medical condition, then the hospital has no further obligation to the patient. All hospitals that participate in the Medicare program must adhere to the EMTALA statutes. A 451 revenue code is used for ER screenings that meet the EMTALA guidelines. An ER bill must include either a 450 or a 451 revenue code but not both.

An interesting aspect of a hospital ER is that often facilities will not employ all the necessary ER physicians needed on a 24-hour basis. Hospitals often outsource the employment of ER physicians to a third party that specializes in staffing ERs. These companies are usually regional, and they handle all the appropriate liability and staffing issues that occur with the ER. The hospital will usually pay a monthly lump sum for the physician staffing services, and occasionally the hospital will bill the insurance companies for the ER professional fee of the medical bill. In the general ledger, there is often a separate receivable that consists of the ER physician accounts receivable. This receivable is billed and collected by the hospital as an added benefit for the physicians working at that particular hospital.

Surgery

A significant component of most hospitals is the surgery department, which is responsible for a majority of the profit and correlating expense in a healthcare facility. Surgeries can be classified as inpatient or outpatient, and they can range from simple to life saving. Hospitals either contract with surgical physician practices or employ full-time physicians to handle the surgical workload that a hospital must be prepared to handle. Often, facilities designate surgical floors or wings that only handle surgical cases; however, due to its complexity, a separate unit is designated for cardiac surgical cases. Once the surgery is completed, the patient is discharged, held in observation, or admitted. *A prominent difference with surgical billing is that hospitals often bill by the minute for time spent in these surgical wards.* In other words, the longer the surgery is, the higher the charge will be.

A by-product of surgery is the use of anesthesia services when performing surgical procedures. The administrators of anesthesia to patients are anesthesiologists or certified registered nurse anesthetists (CRNAs). Hospitals may choose to employ a combination of CRNAs and physicians or solely either one; however, the appropriate blend is a clinical issue that allows the surgical department to maximize volumes and costs. Unfortunately, providing anesthesia is expensive, and reimbursement for this service typically does not cover the cost. The CRNA charge is actually a component of the professional fee rather than the facility fee, and hospitals usually receive an add-on payment for CRNA services. To hedge the loss associated with this service, hospital staff often outsource anesthesia services to third parties. The outsourcing of this practice pays the anesthesia practice not only for the use of physicians and CRNAs but also for coverage in other surgical areas, such as obstetrics. These payments are formulated by examining the need for anesthesia services, the number of surgical rooms, and the payer mix of the hospital's surgical patients.

The use of CRNAs often results in inefficiency since most of these individuals are paid an hourly rate, which may result in overtime. Most hospitals pay at the minimum 8 hours a day for CRNA coverage regardless of the surgical workload that exists for that day. If a CRNA only services three patients during one 8-hour shift, then that CRNA is still paid for 8 hours. If the hospital incurs a significant workload and the CRNA works for 9 hours that day, then that CRNA may be paid 1 hour of overtime, which is usually paid at 150% of the hourly rate. The inefficiency of staffing CRNAs is a complex issue that clinical management should monitor to minimize cost.

Cardiology

In the early 1990s, there was a significant trend toward building hospitals that specialized in cardiac care. These facilities would service patients who needed open heart surgery, valve replacements, pacemakers, and other heart-related ailments. The financial justification for these cardiac hospitals was that the entity could "carve out" the higher-reimbursed procedures from the inpatient prospective payment system (IPPS) methodology. The cardiac hospital only serviced patients with heart conditions, meaning the hospital did not have to service other patients with lower-paying DRGs, such as psychiatric care. The federal government realized this disparity, and it has taken the appropriate steps to restructure the IPPS methodology. To level the playing field, the weights for the DRGs were reformulated so that hospitals that perform all procedures were rewarded, while those specialty cardiac hospitals were penalized. A large majority of both for-profit and not-for-profit hospitals offer cardiac services to the public; however, the acuity of procedures provided varies. Some hospitals only have a catheterization lab, while others have the ability to perform complex open heart surgery. Cardiologists are the physicians who diagnose and treat the patient, whereas cardiac or cardiothoracic surgeons actually perform the surgery. If a patient were treated at a hospital for a heart condition, then the individual would receive a bill not only from the facility but also from the cardiologist and the cardiac surgeon.

Even with the restructuring of the weights in the IPPS model, virtually all hospitals record a significant profit by providing cardiac care. Larger hospitals that offer cardiac services often construct not only separate wings for cardiac patients but also in some cases separate buildings. Hospital systems may erect a separate building and term the facility a heart hospital, but the entity is not freestanding. The heart hospital is a component or subsidiary of the hospital system, and the reimbursement model used for these cardiac services is driven by the hospital system, not the individual heart hospital.

Women's Services/Birthing Unit

Obstetrics and gynecology (OB/GYN) are the two medical/surgical specialties that deal with the female reproductive system in both the pregnant and nonpregnant state. Common services can range from normal childbirth to a hysterectomy. A majority of hospitals employ a women's unit or birthing center that offers rooms that are much more domesticated then a traditional hospital room. An example would be the use of a queen- or king-size bed instead of a single bed or the installation of polished hardwood instead of typical hospital floors. The décor of the birthing unit rooms is often designed to create a family-like atmosphere. The surgical cases that entail the female reproductive system are performed by an OB/GYN physician who specializes in that type of surgery.

In birthing cases, the mother and child are given two separate medical identification numbers, and they are billed separately. Often, the mother is treated in an independent OB/GYN department. Once the child is born, the baby enters the newborn department, where the child absorbs its own expenses and billable charges. The separation of charges/expenses for the mother and child is a unique billing structure that a hospital accountant should note.

Neonatal Intensive Care Unit

Few hospitals employ a neonatal intensive care unit (NICU) that specializes in the care of ill or premature newborn infants. The primary reason is that these units require a significant amount of resources to operate effectively. The NICU is staffed not only by nurses and technicians but also by a physician who specializes in neonatal care. The levels of care in a NICU can range from basic (level 1) to advanced specialty (level 3). A common sight in a typical NICU is an incubator, which is a fixed asset that is used to maintain conditions suitable for a newborn baby. These incubators provide protection from infection and cold temperatures in an attempt to heal the child. Due to the complexity of NICU procedures, most, if not all, insurance carriers reimburse hospitals with NICUs at very high rates. NICU services typically represent one of the few clinical services that state Medicaid agencies commonly reimburse on a per diem basis. Since only a small group of hospitals employs a NICU, the amount of transfer patients is quite high for this service. Other smaller hospitals will transfer the child to a hospital with a NICU once a neonatal issue has been diagnosed. Often, these children will remain a patient at the hospital for several weeks and even months.

Oncology

The field of oncology is the study of cancer, and it entails the diagnosis, surgery, treatment, therapy, and follow-up care that relates to a patient with cancer. Larger hospital systems have the ability to diagnose and treat those with oncology-related conditions; however, smaller healthcare facilities may not have the resources to provide appropriate care. The diagnostic methods used include advanced imaging technology or the biopsy of tissue. The biopsy or tissue diagnosis is considered the essential identification of cancer; empirical therapy is designated for those cases that are examined using only imaging equipment. Surgery is often the primary protocol when a cancerous tumor needs to be removed; however, chemotherapy and radiotherapy are often used in conjunction. The surgical component of an oncology case is billed just like any other surgical case. Both Medicare and Medicaid designate specific DRGs for the removal of tumors. The chemotherapy and radiotherapy aspect of cancer treatment is different because these services are completed on an outpatient basis over several months. Medicare Part B usually covers the outpatient prescription drugs required for oncology care. A significant aspect of Medicare billing is that the federal government pays physicians twice as much for administering chemotherapy drugs as it does nonchemotherapy drugs.

Radiology

Many believe that the future of healthcare lies in the advancement of imaging technology. Early detection of certain diseases or illnesses can prevent the progression to a more complex life-threatening diagnosis. Imaging equipment such as X-ray machines, MRI (magnetic resonance imaging) apparatus, and CT (computed tomographic) scanners have been extremely successful in assisting healthcare personnel combat a numerous array of medical issues. A majority of hospitals create departments specifically for the use of clinical imaging. A significant issue is how to absorb the cost of employing radiology physicians, who demand high salaries yet are vital to a hospital's operations. Radiologists are responsible for reviewing imaging results, which can lead to other clinical tests or procedures. Much like the ER and anesthesia, healthcare facilities often outsource the radiology services to a third-party physician group responsible for reading all imaging pictures. The hospital does not incur the radiologist's salary expense, but the facility incurs other variable and fixed costs associated with imaging procedures. An example of costs for a chest X-ray performed on a patient is given in Table 4.1.

In this hypothetical example, the hospital will receive an estimated $43 in profit per patient for performing this type of X-ray. (This example assumes that the patient had insurance that paid quite well for X-ray services.) The salary expense is low because the physician expense has been outsourced. The only remaining salary expense would be for those technicians and specialists who

Table 4.1 Sample Costs for a Chest-Ray

Charge per procedure	$350
Expected payment	$140
Salary expense per procedure	$25
Supply expense per procedure	$42 (outsourcing fee embedded in this cost)
Estimated fixed costs	$30
Net income per procedure	$43

operate the equipment. The supply expense is higher than the salary cost because the radiologist fee is embedded in this line item. A majority of hospitals will employ a vast array of imaging services because these services are relatively inexpensive to perform, and most insurance carriers will reimburse at high rates. The reason for high reimbursement is that many imaging services are used for preventive care, such as a mammogram. Despite the high margins, the profitability of imaging services must be balanced against the cost of purchasing the machinery. A majority of imaging equipment cost millions of dollars, and some items (e.g., MRI) require a CON (certificate of need) to be placed in service. The largest expenses in an imaging department are occasionally the fixed costs because of the high depreciation expense associated with the expensive imaging equipment. A healthcare accountant should be cognizant of the charge and correlating cost of the numerous imaging procedures a hospital offers to the public.

Pharmacy

Each hospital has a pharmacy that supplies the necessary drugs for maintaining clinical services. The pharmacy is an essential component of hospital operations since most patients in a hospital environment requires pharmaceutical care at some point. Historically, the pharmacy receives requests from other departments for drugs needed to treat patients. These drugs can range from life saving to pain relieving. A significant attribute of the pharmacy is what supply chain method is needed to ensure that each department receives the requested items in an efficient and effective manner. A majority of hospitals have some sort of electronic inventory system that monitors the requests of each clinical department. In addition, instead of consistently requesting the same drugs that are consumed repeatedly, a clinical department usually keeps a "par level" inventory system on that unit. This reduces the lead time of requesting drugs from the pharmacy since the medication is always accessible by clinical staff. The pharmacy will replenish these par level unit inventories on an as-needed basis. *Most hospital pharmacies bill based on drugs either dispensed to departments or those removed from the par level inventory.* These two methods should encompass the appropriate supply chain of drugs to a patient. A significant component of a hospital pharmacy is that most contain their own CDM or chargemaster that is independent of the hospital's CDM. The reason for this is that drug prices are updated on a continuous basis, and billing must reflect these changes. Some hospitals price their drugs using an average wholesale price (AWP); others use a specific markup percentage. Certain drugs may also be indexed differently based on their cost. The drug charges are entered into a patient's bill usually by interfacing from a pharmacy-specific inventory system to the hospital-wide billing system. Often, the pharmacy charges are specific to the product, not the dosage. The product has its individual procedure charge code listed in the pharmacy CDM, which is multiplied by the dosage administered. Even though most pharmacies employ their own chargemaster, the actual payment for pharmaceutical care will not be affected unless the payer's reimbursement model is based upon a percent of charges. If a patient is covered by Medicare, the payment would be fixed regardless of the charges.

CRITICAL ISSUE

A hospital's pharmacy has a separate charge description master (CDM) that is responsible for the pricing of the drugs administered to the patient. This pharmacy CDM is independent of the traditional hospital CDM.

Laboratory

Most hospitals employ a laboratory to analyze samples, such as blood and urine from patients. The types of lab procedures are sometimes separated by department, possibly classified as histology, cytology, or microbiology. These departments are utilized to test samples of tissue and to determine if certain diseases exist. The lab department, much like imaging, is critical to hospital operations due to its ability to diagnose medical conditions properly. Hospital protocols are often the result of what these lab tests reveal. The hospital lab predominantly bills for services like other departments with the exception of Medicare and Medicaid. The federal government has a fee schedule for all outpatient laboratory services, and these are paid outside the traditional APC methodology. If a Medicare patient is classified as inpatient, then all labs would be included within the DRG payment; however, if the procedure is classified as outpatient, then an additional payment is received for clinical lab work. Medicaid also reimburses hospitals at a fixed percentage of this fee schedule in a majority of states; however, it is traditionally lower than what Medicare pays. A common misconception about Medicare and Medicaid paying outside the APC realm is that a hospital will be getting reimbursed a higher amount; however, this theory is incorrect because the government reduced the traditional APC rates to correlate with the adjusted lab reimbursement.

If a patient is not classified as insured by Medicare or Medicaid, then the hospital-specific CDM master fee schedule applies. All lab charges for that specific hospital are embedded in the hospital CDM and are added to the patient's bill as services occur. The lab employee will perform the request generated by the physician and key the charges into an internal hospital system that interfaces to the billing system. If a patient comes to the hospital for several outpatient lab visits, then these charges are often compiled on a single claim called a *series account*.

CRITICAL ISSUE

Medicare reimburses hospitals using a separate fee schedule for outpatient clinical laboratory services, and this payment is outside the APC model. Most state Medicaid programs have mimicked this methodology.

Observation Days

Another service that hospitals offer is termed observation days, which are basically inpatient stays that do *not* warrant an admission. The most common departments that incur observation days are the ER, cardiology, and outpatient surgery. Other typical observation care patients include those with chest pain, asthma attacks, kidney stones, dehydration, and mild trauma. Observation days are for those who do not seem well enough to discharge but are not sick enough to be admitted. Once in the recovery room, the physician has the choice of discharging, admitting, or observing a patient. *The observation aspect is utilized because the patient does not warrant an inpatient admission, but the physician believes the patient requires temporary surveillance.* A hospital typically is paid less for an observation day than it would be for an inpatient admission regardless of the insurance provider. For most insurance carriers, the first hour of an observation day is usually billed at 50% of the inpatient room charge, and each additional hour is billed separately. Each additional hour is usually billed at 1/23 of the daily room-and-board charge. In theory, a patient could have an inpatient stay along with observation day charges. The observation day charges are classified as outpatient charges, and they are added to a patient's bill. If a patient was transferred from observation to inpatient status, then the hospital should classify the first inpatient day as the day when the patient was admitted, not when observation occurred. The observation day reimbursement methodology is driven by the theory that even though the patient observed occupies a bed, the reimbursement amount is less than the full room-and-board charge because the patient is not consuming the equal amount of expenses that a typical inpatient would absorb. Very rarely do observation cases exceed spans of 48 hours.

CRITICAL ISSUE

Observation days are a hybrid type of inpatient and outpatient services that are billed hourly. Often, the first hour is billed at 50% of the inpatient room-and-board charge, and each additional hour is billed at 1/23 of the daily room and board charge.

A significant issue occurs when a Medicare audit reveals that an inpatient stay should have been an observation day. In this situation, Medicare would take back the entire inpatient room payment and *not* pay the facility the respective observation day reimbursement. However, if a patient was allocated an observation day but Medicare discovered after an audit that it should have been an inpatient stay, then the hospital would receive the additional funds to compensate for inpatient charges not recorded. It would be conservative for a hospital to classify patients as receiving observation rather than inpatient care if the acuity of the patient were in question.

CRITICAL ISSUE

If a Medicare audit reveals that an inpatient admission should have been classified as an observation day, then Medicare will take back the entire inpatient room payment and not pay for the observation day charge.

Nursing Homes, Skilled Nursing Facility, Hospice Care

Nursing homes or intermediate care facilities do not perform the high-acuity services of a hospital, but they do care for patients who require constant nursing. A *skilled nursing facility* (SNF) is required when there is a need for more advanced nursing services, such as intravenous injections or physical therapy. A SNF could be a part of either a nursing home or a hospital, and patients are referred to a SNF because the physician believes their medical condition needs to be improved. Nursing homes and SNFs are reimbursed using a RUG (Resource Utilization Group) rate, which is also used for swing bed facilities. The RUG methodology used to be a set per diem rate that was either higher or lower based on the acuity of the stay. Recently, the federal government moved to a prospective payment system for skilled nursing care, but the RUG rate methodology is still used. Each RUG grouping is assigned a case mix weight that measures the acuity of the illness. A significant component of both a SNF and a nursing home is the use of custodial care. Custodial care is helping a patient out of bed, assisting with eating or bathing, and emptying colostomy/bladder containers, for example. *Medicare will not pay for custodial care if it is the only service given.* If a patient is discharged from a hospital to either a nursing home or SNF, then that patient will receive two separate bills (one from the nursing home/SNF and one from the hospital). A staffing difference between nursing homes and hospitals is that a majority of the caregivers at nursing homes are certified nursing assistants (CNAs) rather than registered nurses (RNs). Other employees, such as licensed practical nurses (LPNs), may also work in nursing home environments. The major difference between a RN and either a CNA or an LPN is the amount of education. RNs have more education, which allows them to perform more advanced services. An extension of an RN is a nurse practitioner (NP), who has additional expertise and training in areas such as family practice or pediatrics. Nurse practitioners usually have obtained a master's degree and completed some type of board certification.

A significant aspect of nursing home/SNF reimbursement is that if a Medicare patient stays more than 3 days in a hospital, then that patient can be discharged either to a nursing home or an SNF for up to 20 days and not pay any out-of-pocket fees. On the 21st day, the patient would be responsible for a daily nursing home coinsurance rate of approximately $120, while Medicare will pay for all other services. After 100 days of stay at the nursing home, Medicare will not pay for any services, and the patient will be responsible for all costs.

CRITICAL ISSUE

Both nursing homes and skilled nursing facilities (SNFs) are prospectively reimbursed using a Resource Utilization Group (RUG) rate methodology.

A *hospice* differs from a nursing home in that there are no prospective rates based on acuity. The hospice home engages in palliative care in that comfort and quality of remaining life replace the cure. The facility typically receives a flat per diem rate regardless of services performed. A prominent issue is that a hospital must negotiate a hospice rate for each hospice patient because most, if not all, hospitals do not have hospice beds, but they do have patients who may be extremely sick and eventually become terminally ill. *Respite care* is short-term care administered to a hospice patient so that a family member or friend can take time off from caring for the patient. The intent of respite care is to allow the individual who is caring for the hospice patient to have time away from administering care. The time away will decrease the stress involved in caring for the patient. Respite care is reimbursed in the same manner as hospice care.

An additional service that many believe is provided by a hospital is the use of an ambulance for transportation to a healthcare facility. Ambulance services are typically provided by the county rather than the hospital, and the ambulances are staffed with paramedics and emergency medical technicians (EMTs). If the patient is covered through Medicare, the ambulance service falls under Part B reimbursement only when other means of transportation could endanger the health of the individual. In addition, Medicare will only pay for the ambulance trip to the nearest medical facility. Typically, the patient will pay 20% of the Medicare-approved amount for ambulance care if the patient has met the annual deductible. Some commercial insurance carriers may or may not pay for ambulance services depending on the type of contract. If a patient is not covered by Medicare and has an ambulance trip to a hospital, then the patient usually receive a separate bill from the appropriate county for services rendered.

Home Health Care

Certain patients may be discharged from a hospital to their homes, but they may still need additional care. Home health care is a service in which a caregiver travels to a patient's house and administers some sort of clinical care. Typical home health services would be wound care, pain management, or physical therapy. Instead of using a DRG or APC model, Medicare implemented the Home Health Resource Group (HHRG) when reimbursing health care providers for home health care. Home health is billed using an episode of care, which is a 60-day period when an RN or home health aide will visit a patient at the patient's home and provide medical care. Often, hospitals will record a proportion of the home health patient revenue when that episode of care begins (usually 60–70%). The remaining revenue will be recorded or realized when the episode ends. During this time frame, the patient may heal before the 60 days allotted, and home treatment may no longer be needed. In these cases, revenue is adjusted using a low-utilization payment adjustment (LUPA) because the patient did not need receive the full episode of care. Before administering care, a home health agency is required to complete an Outcome and Assessment Information Set (OASIS) data set to measure patient outcomes. Some home health agencies may be a component of a hospital system, and others may be freestanding. If owned by a hospital, a separate billing module is usually implemented for home health care due to its complexity. Recording and reconciling an episode of care can be cumbersome, and the maintenance of home health care is usually isolated to a specific department. The revenue generated by home health care is classified as outpatient in an income statement or statement of operations.

CRITICAL ISSUE

Home health services are billed using the Medicare designated HHRG (Home Health Resource Group), which formulates a payment based on a 60-day episode of care.

Administrative Days/Swing Beds

Administrative days are those days restricted for patients who no longer need inpatient hospital care but are in need of nursing home care; however, a bed is not available. At discharge, the hospital cannot find a nursing home location that has an open bed for that patient. The reimbursement for administrative days begins when the patient is discharged from acute care. This coverage is terminated once a nursing home bed becomes available that is in a 50-mile radius from the hospital.

A *swing bed* is a bed that can be used for both acute care and nursing home services. The RUG methodology is used to reimburse healthcare facilities for swing beds. Some hospitals are classified as swing bed facilities; however, they must be located in a rural area and have less than 100 beds.

Osteopathic Medicine

An often misunderstood component of hospital care is osteopathy, which is basically the study of the musculoskeletal system to treat disease and disorder. Physicians who obtain the DO (doctor of osteopathy) have the same rights and privileges as medical doctors (MDs), and hospitals bill for their services using the same diagnosis codes. A majority of osteopathic services performed at a hospital would be classified as manipulative treatments, and they are nondiagnostic. A common misconception is that osteopaths are the same as chiropractors; however, there is a significant distinction. Osteopathic physicians differ from chiropractors in that the study of osteopathic medicine is based on the theory that disease is driven by a loss of structural integrity, whereas chiropractic medicine holds that disease is due to a lack of normal nerve function that originates in the spine. A significant difference between the two professions is that osteopaths can perform surgery and prescribe medicine, whereas chiropractors cannot. Osteopathic physicians can perform all the same functions in a hospital environment as a traditional doctor, and they do not require any unique billing mechanism. Basically, the DO credential is equal in stature to an MD.

Another term that is occasionally referenced in healthcare is the use of *allopathic* medicine. Allopathy is the use of pharmaceuticals or remedies in an attempt to treat or suppress medical conditions. An example of allopathic rationale would be the use of an antacid if a patient had an upset stomach or the use of a laxative if someone were constipated. The traditional medical degree (MD) requires training in allopathic medicine as part of the requirement to be a physician. Allopathy is a term that is often used to describe the education a traditional physician receives in comparison to osteopathy, which has a separate curriculum. An allopathic physician does not have a separate medical practice or specialty but rather this designation is a synonym for a conventional physician.

Conclusion

The services and procedures that are offered at a hospital can range across the clinical spectrum. Some teaching hospitals may offer complex procedures, whereas other rural facilities may only provide basic services. Regardless of size or services offered, the main objective of a hospital system is to treat and heal the patient. A traditional hospital may have numerous departments responsible for providing care, and some of these services may be outsourced to third parties. In addition to conventional inpatient and outpatient procedures, a hospital may offer other clinical services such as skilled nursing (in a SNF) or home health care. These programs allow a healthcare system not only to heal the patient but also to provide postacute care to improve recovery. It is not feasible for financial personnel to understand all the technical aspects of each hospital service; however, a working knowledge should be sufficient.

Chapter 5

Medicare

Introduction and History

The social insurance program known as Medicare is a federally administered plan that provides health insurance coverage to individuals who are age 65 and above or who meet other certain criteria. Medicare is the largest health insurance program in the United States, and it provides benefits to approximately 40 million people. The legislation was a result of the Social Security Act of 1965, and it was signed into law by President Lyndon Johnson. Medicare is administered by the Centers for Medicare and Medicaid Services (CMS), which is a component of the Department of Health and Human Services. The program was intended to provide coverage to the elderly; however, those with specific medical conditions, such as end-stage renal disease (ESRD) are also entitled to Medicare benefits. The components of Medicare coverage can be separated into four separate sections (A, B, C, and D). The first component is Part A, which covers hospital inpatient stays as well as other specific services, such as home health and hospice care. The funding to provide the cost of servicing the Part A population is imposed as a payroll tax; an employee pays 1.45% of his or her salary, and the employer pays a matching 1.45% (2.9% total). Part B generally pays for outpatient services such as imaging procedures, laboratory tests, ambulance services, and other treatments. Part B also covers certain durable medical equipment like wheelchairs, walkers, and prosthetic devices. In contrast to Part A coverage, funding for outpatient services is created through premiums paid by Medicare enrollees. Another significant aspect of Part B coverage is that these benefits are used to cover the broad range of preventive services, such as prostate screenings and mammograms. Part C of the Medicare program was established as part of the Balanced Budget Act of 1997, and it gives the beneficiary the option to have benefits administered by a third party. Also known as a Medicare Advantage Plan or a Medicare health maintenance organization (HMO), this arrangement substitutes the original Part A/Part B plans, and these programs are often administered by managed care companies like Blue Cross/Blue Shield. Their intent is possibly to create a profit by attempting to manage the Medicare population more efficiently. Those patients with ESRD are generally not allowed to enroll in Medicare Part C. Part D is a recently created addendum to Medicare that gives beneficiaries the ability to choose certain prescription drug plans that are administered by third parties. The federal government will assist the beneficiary pay for pharmaceuticals to a specified limit, which depends on which plan is chosen. Eligible Medicare beneficiaries can enroll 3 months before and after they turn 65. A significant aspect of Part D coverage is that most beneficiaries are capped at $2,400 in expenditures (referred to as the doughnut hole) until the beneficiary spends a certain amount of out-of-pocket expenses. This has become an issue since many Medicare recipients have chronic diseases that require expensive medications.

Even though Medicare is a federal government program, the administration of the plan is provided by third parties that have a contract with CMS. Previously, these contractors were called fiscal intermediaries for Part A services and carriers for Part B services. As a result of legislation in 2003, these fiscal intermediaries/carriers are now referred to as Medicare administrative contractors (MACs). The purpose of this was to simplify billing so that only one party rather than two would handle Part A and Part B claims. By law, Congress creates and signs the laws that affect the beneficiaries of Medicare, but CMS has the duty of interpreting how these laws will be implemented. CMS publishes numerous manuals, which are available on their Web site, that list the policies and procedures needed for billing. The CMS also creates transmittals, which are additions or changes to the manuals that hospitals should be cognizant of due to their financial effect. Besides the manuals and transmittals, there are other sources of authoritative information, such as rulings, but these rarely occur. Of all the major insurance providers that exist, Medicare represents approximately 30–40% of the payments for hospital care.

CRITICAL ISSUE

There is no cap or limit on salaries that are subject to the Medicare payroll tax. Regardless if someone makes $10,000 or $500,000 a year, the payroll tax will be 2.9%.

Cost Sharing

Despite the federal government's attempt to provide coverage for the elderly, there are numerous healthcare costs that Medicare beneficiaries must absorb themselves. Expenses like premiums, deductibles, and coinsurance are paid by the beneficiary. A substantial majority of Medicare patients do not pay Part A premiums; however, all Part B enrollees pay for coverage. In 2010, the inpatient deductible was approximately $1,100 for Part A services. In 2010, the premium was approximately $96 per month for Part B coverage, and this expense is usually deducted from the individual's monthly Social Security paycheck. In addition to the monthly premium, a deductible of approximately $162 applies for all Part B services. The reimbursement models for Medicare Part A and Part B services are very different, and by no means are Part B benefits to be used if Part A benefits are exhausted. There are additional Medicare supplemental policies (e.g., Medigap) that are administered and sold by insurance companies. Medigap policies do not cover prescription drugs, and they cannot be utilized if Part C is used. A significant issue with Medicare reimbursement is that a patient is not responsible for the payment of the deductible if the medical services are not "reasonable and necessary" to diagnose or treat an illness. This applies not only to Part A but also to Part B services. The healthcare facility must inform the beneficiary of such medically unnecessary services and refund any payments made if the facility failed to notify the patient. To protect the beneficiary, an Advanced Beneficiary Notice (ABN) of Noncoverage was created that alerts a patient of financial obligation when a medical service is performed. The ABN informs the patient that the procedure or service is not medically necessary, and it formulates an expected monetary figure that the patient will be responsible for paying. The patient must be presented with the ABN before any services are performed so that the individual can make an informed decision on whether to proceed. Previously, all hospitals had two types of ABNs that were for either general use or lab services. As of 2009, the federal government consolidated both forms into one form (CMS-R-131) for simplicity.

CRITICAL ISSUE

The purpose of a deductible is to delay insurance participation until a specific amount has been spent by the patient. The deductible attempts to rule out routine medical expenses. The purpose of a copayment is to deter unnecessary or inappropriate care.

As the population ages, many people are no longer retiring but continuing to work past the age of 65. Medicare could possibly be classified as a secondary payer depending if other insurance coverage is present. It is the responsibility of the hospital to determine if the patient has additional coverage besides Medicare and to verify that this coverage exists. It is also the responsibility of the facility to collect payments for the appropriate deductible/coinsurance payments, but *by no means can a facility restrict admission based on a patient's inability to make payment.* Often, a posting of this policy is placed somewhere in the admission department to inform patients that there is no undue pressure for prepayment.

Inpatient Prospective Payment System/Diagnosis-Related Group

Prior to 1983, hospitals were reimbursed for all costs provided to Medicare patients. Hospitals had no incentive to operate efficiently since all expenses were reimbursed by the federal government. Realizing a change was needed, the government initiated the inpatient prospective payment system (IPPS), which forced hospitals to operate in a more effective and efficient manner. The concept behind the IPPS methodology is that a hospital will receive a fixed amount regardless of the resources utilized to service the patient. All Medicare inpatients are classified into a *diagnosis-related group* (DRG) based on their principle diagnosis/procedure, and the hospital makes a profit or loss depending on the amount of expenses used on the patient. A hospital will receive the same predetermined payment each time the facility admits a Medicare patient with the same DRG. There are approximately 750 different DRGs, which were developed by Yale University in the 1960s, and they can vary from cardiac services to psychiatric care. The CMS reviews these DRGs each year to ensure that each grouping is concise and accurate. The DRG classification system expanded in 2008, and the revised system is now called *MS-DRG* (Medicare Severity-DRG). The change in 2008 was driven to better account for the severity of illness and resource consumption. A significant change in the MS-DRG classification was the addition of secondary diagnosis codes. An example of this change is given in Table 5.1 for what used to be classified as DRG 75, Major Chest Procedures.

The previous DRG 75 (Major Chest Procedures) was separated into three new DRGs based on severity. A hospital employee should be aware of the terminology changes in this revised inpatient coding model. The *MCC* means major complication/comorbidity, while *CC* stands for complication/comorbidity. In general, the higher the acuity of the patient's condition, the

Table 5.1 DRG to MS-DRG Example

Prior to 2008		
DRG	*Description*	*Weight*
75	Major Chest Procedures	3.0350
After 2008 (Medicare Severity)		
MS-DRG	*Description*	*Weight*
163	Major Chest Procedures W MCC	4.9549
164	Major Chest Procedures W CC	2.5164
165	Major Chest Procedures W/O CC MCC	1.7662

Note: W, with; W/O, without.

higher the assigned weight will be. In this specific case, the weight increases by 3.1887 (4.9549 – 1.7662) when the patient's DRG classification moves from 165 to 163 due to medical complications. The glossary of this text provides a list of all the current DRGs with the appropriate description and weight.

CRITICAL ISSUE

The DRG model is a form of provider risk sharing by which payment is based on the patient's condition rather than resources consumed. The federal government will pay a set amount regardless of the expenses incurred by the hospital.

Outpatient Prospective Payment System/APC Fee Schedule

In addition to the inpatient changes, CMS implemented a revised outpatient model, the OPPS (outpatient prospective payment system), in the year 2000 that introduced the *Ambulatory Payment Classification* (APC) system. Instead of a DRG methodology, Medicare uses a fee schedule to reimburse hospitals for all outpatient services. An APC is a grouping of clinical services that utilize similar resources. The relative weight of each APC is driven by both the operating and capital costs needed to perform that clinical service. The APC model is a prospectively set structure, so there is no contractual or reserve estimate needed. In addition, the APC system is not adjusted for any add-on payments like the Disproportionate Share Hospital (DSH) or indirect medical education (IME), and it is only used for hospitals. A national APC fee schedule exists that lists all the appropriate outpatient procedures that a hospital could incur. Some services are listed independently, and some are "bundled" into larger APC groupings. Numerous CPT (Current Procedural Terminology) and HCPCS (Healthcare Common Procedure Coding System) codes could create an APC, and often the payment to a hospital is based on a group of services instead of one individual service. Basically, the payment for each outpatient procedure is listed in the APC fee schedule, and this amount is multiplied against a geographic adjustment and a wage index figure. The basic APC payment/reimbursement for an outpatient (OP) Medicare procedure is listed as follows:

Medicare OP APC Payment = Fee Schedule Payment * Geographic Adjustment % * Wage Index %

Not only does Medicare use the APC methodology, but also numerous other payers like Blue Cross/Blue Shield and Medicaid use a rendition of this methodology when reimbursing hospitals. The wage index used in the APC methodology is the same calculation used in the DRG blend rate computation; however, the geographic adjustment is a percentage figure formulated by the government that cannot be influenced by the hospital. A hypothetical list of sample APCs from the national fee schedule is given in Table 5.2.

The following is an example of hospital reimbursement for a typical Medicare outpatient visit:

Sample: A Medicare patient is receiving an X-ray, magnetic resonance imaging (MRI) and lab work at a county hospital.
X-ray = Paid by APC fee schedule.
MRI = Paid by APC fee schedule.
Lab work = Paid to the hospital independent of the X-ray or the MRI. Lab work is paid outside the APC reimbursement methodology.

For an inpatient visit, a hospital will receive one payment based on the DRG assignment; however, several payments for one visit may occur in the outpatient setting. Certain outpatient procedures may be bundled into one payment; however, this grouping of payments depends on the services that the hospital provides. In addition, all clinical lab work paid to a hospital by Medicare is formulated using a separate fee schedule that is paid on top of any outpatient procedures. A patient may have several APCs but only one DRG.

As previously stated in the chapter on hospital services, the federal government currently pays for lab services outside the traditional OPPS realm and has implemented a fee schedule for outpatient lab services. To account for this separate payment to hospitals, Medicare has adjusted the APC reimbursement rates to consider the lab fee schedule payments. In theory, no hospital should benefit from the use of the lab fee schedule since Medicare has already lowered the rates in the OPPS methodology to account for this change.

Another aspect of Medicare reimbursement is the *72-hour rule,* which applies to outpatient services before an inpatient stay. In practice, all procedures and services conducted on an outpatient basis are combined with inpatient charges if they are performed 72 hours prior to admission.

Table 5.2 Sample APC Listing

APC Group Title	Relative Weight	Payment Rate	Copayment Amount
0019 Level 1 Excision/Biopsy	4.1677	$250.00	$45.00
0130 Level 1 Laparoscopy	31.6832	$1,700.00	$350.00
0275 Arthography	3.5084	$200.00	$40.00
0409 Red Blood Cell Test	0.1272	$8.00	$1.00
0662 CT Angiography	5.6204	$300.00	$64.00

All charges are lumped together into one bill, and the admitting department is responsible for ensuring that this process occurs. If the outpatient services are performed after 72 hours, then a separate bill for both inpatient and outpatient services will be formulated. The 72-hour rule applies not only to Medicare patients but also to all hospital patients regardless of payer.

An aspect of hospital reimbursement that used to be more prevalent before the change to the PPS would be the distinction between a *semiprivate* hospital room and a *private* hospital room. A semiprivate room is typically characterized by two patients sharing a room, with a curtain separating the patients. This model was cheaper for the hospital, but many patients were not happy due to the many privacy issues that may occur when two patients share a room. Most hospitals currently employ private rooms, which are created for one patient and have an adjoining bathroom. Prior to the IPPS, Medicare would only reimburse the hospital for the use of semiprivate rooms. The patient had to have a justifiable clinical reason to be placed in a private room, which was usually due to a communicable disease. The segregation between private and semiprivate rooms is no longer a concern since inpatient admissions are reimbursed prospectively on a DRG basis; however, some hospitals still employ semiprivate rooms because they do not have the resources to convert these to private rooms.

Physician practices, much like those of hospitals, used to be reimbursed on a fee-for-service methodology; however, the federal government reformed this system and created the *Resource-Based Relative Value Scale* (RBRVS), which established the Medicare reimbursement for physician services. The intent of this change was not only to decrease Medicare expenditures but also to decrease the disparity of payments between family practice doctors and physician specialists. Previously, those physicians in the cardiac or neurological field were reimbursed substantially higher for treating Medicare patients than those in family practice. The implementation of the RBRVS increased the weighted payment to family practice doctors by taking into account such variables such as history/physical exams and patient counseling.

In the RBRVS, the payments to physicians for Medicare patients are determined by cost, and a majority of other payers have mimicked this reimbursement model. Some managed care companies may pay at 120% of the RBRVS model, while Medicaid may pay less than 100%. The physician payments are formulated through three components: physician work component, practice expense component, and liability insurance component. Basically, the physician work aspect is the variable cost associated with the doctor; the practice expense represents the fixed cost. The liability insurance component is a minimal amount that comprises less than 5% of the RBRVS payment. In addition, payments are adjusted for geographical differences in resource costs.

Case Mix Index

The case mix index (CMI) is defined as the average DRG weight for all of a hospital's Medicare volume. The purpose of the CMI is to reflect the clinical complexity/diversity of hospital services, and a majority of hospitals have a CMI between 1 and 2, with 1 the lowest. The benefit of the CMI is that it balances out the numerous Medicare cases that are separated by acuity. A hospital can use the CMI as a comparative measure either month to month or year to year. Table 5.3 is an example of several different DRGs with the appropriate weight and volume.

To formulate the CMI, the Medicare inpatient cases must be multiplied against the appropriate DRG weight to form a preliminary figure. The sum of this figure needs to be divided by the total number of inpatient cases to calculate the CMI for that time period. In this example, the CMI decreased by 0.05 from year 1 to year 2. The decrease in CMI is significant for

Table 5.3 Case Mix Index

DRG	Description	Year 1			Year 2		
		Weight	*IP Cases*	*CMI*	*Weight*	*IP Cases*	*CMI*
37	Extra cranial Procedures W MCC	2.2630	8	18.10	2.9190	5	14.60
38	Extra cranial Procedures W CC	1.4686	3	4.41	1.4783	4	5.93
39	Extra cranial Procedures W/O CC/MCC	1.0909	5	5.45	1.0033	3	3.01
75	Viral Meningitis W CC/MCC	1.5369	7	10.76	1.6670	4	6.67
76	Viral Meningitis W/O CC/MCC	1.1439	4	4.58	0.8336	7	5.84
100	Seizures W MCC	1.2500	6	7.50	1.4778	6	8.87
101	Seizures W/O MCC	0.8258	2	1.65	0.7577	4	3.03
Subtotal			35	52.45		33	47.95
Total case mix index			52.45/35 =	1.50		47.95/33 =	1.45

Note: IP, inpatient.

reimbursement personnel because any decrease will negatively affect the operating income of the facility. The reduction in CMI acts as a barometer in that any changes in the figure reflect a change in the surgical and medical Medicare volumes in the hospital. The decrease in Table 5.3 may be due to the hospital not capturing the appropriate comorbidities and complications associated with higher-weighted DRGs. To improve the CMI, the hospital obviously cannot "up-code" any patients to a higher-weighted DRG, but hospital personnel can improve the process of physician documentation to ensure that all patient diagnosis citations are accurate. In theory, the higher the CMI, the higher the reimbursement will be because the facility is performing higher-acuity inpatient cases. Often, the CMI statistic cannot be influenced, but it definitely should be monitored.

CRITICAL ISSUE

The benefit and purpose of the CMI is that it balances out the acuity of Medicare volumes. A hospital can use the CMI as a comparative measure to monitor the types of Medicare cases serviced.

As technology increases and medical advances are discovered, the need for inpatient care is slowly being replaced by outpatient care. The effect of this migration is that the CMI will increase each year. Also known as *DRG creep*, traditional Medicare inpatients who are not as sick as other patients will move to an outpatient setting, while very sick Medicare patients will remain in the hospital. These sick patients not only will increase the overall hospital length of stay but also will absorb more costs. The CMI will increase to reflect the higher comorbidities and complications that occur with these sicker patients.

Medicare Blend Rate

The actual payment received for Medicare services is a complex computation that is shaped and adjusted by several factors. Each hospital has what is termed a "blend rate," which is specific to that facility, and this figure is multiplied against a specific DRG weight that is uniform for all hospitals. The formulation of this blend rate is extremely important due to the significant portion of a hospital's payer mix being populated by Medicare. An example of a Medicare payment for an inpatient heart procedure is given in Table 5.4.

A hospital's inpatient Medicare payment is formulated by multiplying the hospital-specific blend rate against a governmental formulated national DRG weight. In this example, the hospital will receive $23,106 in payment regardless of the services incurred in treating that patient (not including outlier payments). The payment includes all *fixed and variable* costs, including salaries, supplies, imaging, lab, depreciation, and any other patient-related expense. It is the responsibility of the hospital to determine *prospectively* what these expenses will be so that patient care will be administered in an effective and efficient manner. The MAC has 14 days to pay a hospital if a *clean claim* was electronically received. A clean Medicare claim is basically a submittal that does not require any further investigation or research. The government has 28 days to reimburse a hospital for claims submitted manually. All claims that are not classified as clean are termed other claims.

CRITICAL ISSUE

Medicare generally has 14 days to pay electronically submitted clean claims and 28 days for manually sent clean claims.

To influence the reimbursement of a hospital positively, a healthcare professional should be cognizant of how this blend rate is computed. Some of the variables in the formula can be altered; some cannot. A hospital employee can better understand the methodology of governmental

Table 5.4 Medicare Payment

DRG No.	Description	DRG Weight
DRG 234	Coronary Bypass w Cardiac Cath. W/O MCC	4.6212
County hospital blend rate = $5,000		
Medicare payment = $5,000 * 4.6212 = $23,106		

Table 5.5 Blend Rate Computation

A.	Standardized rate	$6,500
B.	Federal national standardized labor rate	$4,030
C.	Wage index	0.90
	Labor Rate * Wage Index	$3,627
D.	Federal national standardized nonlabor rate	$2,470
	Wage-adjusted base operating rate	$6,097

reimbursement by learning all the factors and issues that affect the blend rate. Table 5.5 is a sample blend rate computation for a hypothetical hospital with the appropriate description for each line item.

A. The standardized rate is supplied by the federal government, and this figure cannot be influenced by the hospital. The federal government adjusts this figure every year for market basket updates and other inflationary factors. A recent addendum to the standardized rate calculation is that if a hospital did not submit the necessary Medicare quality data, then the federal government would reduce the unadjusted standardized rate by 2%. In this example, a hypothetical amount of $6,500 is given, and if the hospital did not provide the appropriate quality data, then the labor rate would be $6,370 (98% of $6,500). This reduction is made before any wage index reductions. In this example we will assume all quality data was submitted.

B. The national labor rate is a product of multiplying the standardized rate against a given percentage. If the wage index of the hospital is above 1, then 68.8% of the standardized rate is used as the labor rate. If the wage index is below 1, then 62% of the standardized rate is used as the labor rate. In this sample, the wage index is 0.90, which means that the adjusted labor-related amount is $4,030 (0.62 * $6,500).

C. The purpose of the wage index is to account for the regional differences in the cost of labor and geographical areas. This amount is multiplied against the labor rate, and this can have either a positive or a negative effect. The wage index is designated by the federal government, and every hospital is classified as either urban or rural. Geographical areas with populations greater than 50,000 are considered urban, whereas all other areas are rural. The wage index is updated annually; the government formulates this percentage based on information from each hospital's cost report worksheets S-3 Parts 2 and 3. The geographical areas used in the wage index are derived from Core-Based Statistical Areas (CBSAs). *The purpose of the wage index is to level the playing field throughout the country to adjust for a community's cost of living.* For example, the cost of living in New York City will be different from that in Columbia, South Carolina. Recently, the federal government decided to look further at the wage index by requiring hospitals to complete a Medicare Occupational Mix Adjustment (MOMA), which asks for the salaries and correlating hours of nurses, technicians, and other clinical personnel. The purpose of the MOMA survey is to isolate the wage index to include only the price difference between a geographical area and a national average. The survey will attempt to complete this by removing the variation in skill mix across the labor markets. In theory, labor markets with an expensive occupational mix will have their wage index decreased, while markets with a cheaper occupational mix will have the wage index increased. A problematic issue with the wage index is that there is a 4-year lag in wage data. For example, a FYE (fiscal year end) 2011 wage index figure is based on cost report information in FYE 2007.

CRITICAL ISSUE

The wage index used in the blend rate computation adjusts the labor rate for each area's relative cost of living by comparing not only variances in the price of labor but also differences in the type of labor used.

D. The non-labor-related portion of the blend calculation is the difference between the standardized rate and the labor rate. In this example, the non-labor-related portion would be $2,470 ($6,500 standard rate – $4,030 labor rate). This nonlabor rate is combined with the adjusted labor rate to formulate a wage-adjusted base operating rate of $6,097. This amount is used as a baseline figure to formulate "add-on" payments in the blend rate computation.

Medicare Disproportionate Share Add-On

The federal government will give hospitals additional reimbursement for providing benefits to the community. The Medicare DSH payment is an add-on percentage to the base operating amount given to hospitals for treating a disproportionate share of low-income patients. These low-income patients are often less healthy than the general population, and they consume more resources. The basic formula for the Medicare disproportionate share payment is complex because one portion of the calculation is provided by the federal government, and the other is produced by the hospital.

$$\text{Medicare DSH Add-On \%} = \text{Medicare Fraction} + \text{Medicaid Fraction}$$

The Medicare fraction is a fixed amount provided by the federal government that the hospital cannot control. It is computed as:

$$\frac{\text{Days for Patients Entitled to Medicare Part A and Entitled to SSI Benefits}}{\text{Days for Patients Entitled to Medicare Part A}}$$

Supplemental Security Income (SSI) benefits are the benefits administered by the Social Security Administration for individuals with little income. These monthly benefits are for the basic necessities, such as food and shelter, and eligibility for these funds is driven by economic resources and other factors such as age or health status. The Medicare fraction is added to the Medicaid fraction component, which is formulated as:

$$\frac{\text{Days for Patients Eligible for Medicaid and Not Entitled to Medicare Part A}}{\text{Total Days for Patients in Acute Care Areas (Including Nursery)}}$$

A significant component of these fractions is the use of the terms *eligible* and *entitled*. Entitled generally means paid; eligible means should or could have been paid. A hospital can possibly influence the Medicaid fraction of the Medicare DSH add-on but cannot affect the Medicare fraction. Even though hospitals cannot add Medicare Part A beneficiaries to the numerator of the Medicaid fraction, they can still add Medicare Part C patients who are also Medicaid eligible (referred to as dual eligibility). A patient may be covered through the Medicare program yet still qualify for Medicaid benefits. In addition, hospitals can add all Medicaid patients to the numerator whether they were paid or not. The process of searching for these patients internally can be time consuming, so hospitals usually outsource this function to a third party with access to the national Medicaid database. The denominator of the Medicaid fraction is listed as the total days in the facility, not just Medicaid days. The total days consist of all patient days, including nursery days, regardless of the insurance provider. The total day statistic may be a fixed number that cannot be manipulated, but the reimbursement analyst should thoroughly review all patient day figures to ensure that the numbers are accurate. The theory is that the lower the total number of days, the lower the denominator of the Medicaid fraction, the higher the actual Medicaid fraction will be, resulting in a higher Medicare DSH add-on payment (see Table 5.6).

CRITICAL ISSUE

In terms of reimbursement, *entitled* basically means being paid, and *eligible* means could have or should have been paid. These terms are critical in formulating the Medicare DSH add-on payment.

Historically, all Medicaid days are found through two separate sources: the Medicaid billed days provided by the individual state (often called a MARS report or a state-issued PSR report) and all Medicaid secondary bills. A secondary bill is when a patient has primary insurance coverage but also could qualify for Medicaid. For hospital purposes, the insurance provider rather than Medicaid is billed simply because the expected payment will be higher. However, hospitals

Table 5.6 Effects of Influencing Medicare DSH

Lower Total Patient Days	Higher Total Patient Days
↓	↓
Lower Denominator	Higher Denominator
↓	↓
Higher Medicaid Fraction	Lower Medicaid Fraction
↓	↓
Higher Add-On Percentage	Lower Add-On Percentage

must track the encounter data, which are the Medicaid patient days even though the patient's commercial insurance was billed. *Although the hospital billed and received payment from the insurance provider, the facility can still put the patient's days in the numerator of the Medicaid fraction in the Medicare DSH computation if the patient is eligible for Medicaid benefits.* A significant issue is that these patients may be classified as commercially insured in the hospital financials rather than insured by Medicaid. Outsourcing this search function allows greater flexibility to find the Medicaid-eligible patients who have been placed in another patient population.

Once both the Medicare and Medicaid fractions are added together, a DSH adjustment factor calculation is used to formulate the actual percentage. Basically, if the combination of the Medicare/Medicaid fraction is less than 15%, then no operating portion of the Medicare DSH add-on is calculated. If the total of the Medicare/Medicaid fraction is above either 15% or 20.20%, then an additional computation is needed. (This will be addressed within the cost reporting chapter. The capital portion of the Medicare DSH is usually formulated by the cost reporting software; however, the formula is 2.71828 raised to the power of (.2025 * Medicare/Medicaid fraction total) less 1.

The Medicare DSH add-on percentage is also extremely important to a hospital not just because additional funds can be received for each Medicare patient. The 340B program was enacted as part of the Public Health Service Act of 1992, and it has the ability to save hospitals an estimated 20% to 50% of *outpatient drug expense* if their Medicare DSH add-on percentage is greater than 11.75%. This decrease in expense is absorbed by drug companies rather than the federal government. A significant requirement of the 340B program is that only nonprofit and government hospitals are eligible for the program. For-profit hospitals are not able to participate in the program.

CRITICAL ISSUE

To influence the Medicare DSH add-on payment positively, the number of Medicaid days must increase or the number of acute care days must decrease. A method to increase Medicaid days is to include all Medicaid secondary bills in the numerator of the fraction.

Indirect Medical Education Add-On

Much like the Medicare DSH add-on, the IME add-on calculation is an additional allowance that a hospital receives for providing social benefits to the community. A significant difference is that IME is only for teaching hospitals. The IME add-on payment is a ratio formulated by dividing the hospital's full-time equivalent (FTE) residents by the number of open beds multiplied by 1 to the 0.405 power. This formula is further multiplied by a geographic adjustment factor also provided by the federal government.

$$\text{IME Add-on} = (\text{FTE Residents/Number of Open Beds} * 1.405 \text{ power}) * \text{Geographic Adjustment Factor}$$

The IME calculation is trued up each year in the annual cost report, and hospitals can only report residents who service both inpatients and outpatients for clinical services. *The purpose of the IME add-on is to cover the tests (lab and imaging) ordered by resident physicians to enhance their learning.* Hospitals can also report residents who work at other facilities as long as they are *physically working and present* at the hospital claiming the IME. For example, if a resident employed at Hospital A works at Hospital B for several shifts a month, then Hospital B would be able to include that physician's shifts in the IME calculation, and Hospital A would not.

CRITICAL ISSUE

To influence the IME payment positively, either the number of FTE residents must increase or the number of open beds must decrease. A method to decrease beds is to subtract the beds that are not being used due to maintenance or clinical issues. Another method is to document the rotation of each resident to determine if he or she is servicing clinical patients.

The history of the IME add-on payment can be traced back to the early 1980s, when the federal government began looking at altering hospital reimbursement. While researching the feasibility of enacting the PPS, the government discovered that teaching hospitals predominantly incurred higher costs than nonteaching hospitals. The resident physicians employed at teaching hospitals not only work all hours of the day and night but also must be prepared to treat the traumatically injured or extremely sick. The existence of residents in hospitals intensifies the demand on other departments and increases overall staffing levels. The government realized that teaching hospitals require additional reimbursement for employing residents, and the IME add-on percentage was added to the DRG blend computation. The actual training of resident physicians is termed *graduate medical education* (GME). In the sample blend rate computation, the DSH and IME add-on percentages will be given as 20% and 10%, respectively. These percentages are multiplied against the base operating rate to formulate a monetary add-on amount to the blend rate (Table 5.7).

The total operating PPS payment is the sum of the wage-adjusted base operating rate, Medicare DSH add-on, and IME add-on amounts. This operating figure has not been adjusted for capital payments. Only a teaching hospital would adjust the operating PPS payment amount for the IME add-on figure.

Table 5.7   Blend Rate Computation

A.	Standardized rate	$6,500
B.	Federal national standardized labor rate	$4,030
C.	Wage index	0.90
	Labor Rate * Wage Index	$3,627
D.	Federal national standardized nonlabor rate	$2,470
	Wage-adjusted base operating rate	$6,097
E.	Medicare DSH add-on (disproportionate share) adjustment (20% of 6,097)	$1,219
F.	IME add-on (indirect medical education) adjustment (10% of 6,097)	$609
	Total operating PPS payment	**$7,925**

Capital Portion of the Blend Rate

Capital costs are defined as the fixed costs used to treat patients. Examples of capital costs would be computers, imaging equipment, and the building itself. The government provides capital payments in the blend rate because of the fixed costs needed to service Medicare patients. The federal government has created a standardized capital payment that is uniform to all hospitals, and this amount is adjusted by a geographical percentage that takes into account the capital cost differences in separate regions (lines G and H, Table 5.8). This geographical adjustment factor is derived from the wage index. The result of the geographical adjustment factor and the standardized rate is the *capital federal payment* (line I). In addition to the capital federal rate, the government will give extra capital add-on payments for Medicare DSH and IME. These amounts are formulated in the annual cost report, and these percentages are multiplied against the capital federal payment. A noteworthy aspect of the Medicare capital DSH add-on is that it is only paid to urban hospitals with more than 100 beds. Rural hospitals would not be eligible for the capital add-on payment. For the blend rate example, let us assume that the federal government capital rate is $400, and a hypothetical geographical adjustment factor is 95%. In addition, we assume that the capital DSH and IME amounts are 9% and 8%, respectively (Table 5.8).

The total capital PPS payment is the sum of the capital federal payment (line I), the capital DSH add-on (line J), and the capital IME add-on (line K). The total DRG blend rate computation is the sum of the operating and capital payments. This figure is multiplied against the DRG

Table 5.8 Blend Rate Computation

A.	Standardized rate	$6,500
B.	Federal national standardized labor rate	$4,030
C.	Wage index	0.90
	Labor Rate * Wage Index	$3,627
D.	Federal national standardized nonlabor rate	$2,470
	Wage-adjusted base operating rate	$6,097
E.	Medicare DSH add-on (disproportionate share) adjustment (20% of 6,097)	$1,219
F.	IME add-on (indirect medical education) adjustment (15% of 6,097)	$609
	Total operating PPS payment	$7,925
G.	Capital federal rate	$400
H.	GAF factor	95%
I.	Capital federal payment (0.95 * 400)	$380
J.	Capital DSH add-on (9% of $380)	$34
K.	Capital IME add-on (8% of $380)	$30
	Total capital PPS payment	$444
	Total payment for DRG weight 1.0	$8,369

weight to compute the reimbursement received from the federal government for each Medicare inpatient admission.

The computation of the blend rate is utilized not only by Medicare but also by other payers, such as TRICARE and the Veterans Affairs (VA) hospitals. Often, other insurance carriers may negotiate a higher figure, such as 120% of the hospital blend rate for inpatient services. Certain variables in this computation are fixed and cannot be influenced by hospital personnel; however, there are several figures that can be examined in detail possibly to increase the blend rate amount.

CRITICAL ISSUE

The Medicare capital disproportionate share add-on is only given to urban hospitals that have more than 100 licensed beds.

Outlier Payments

Occasionally, a hospital may treat a Medicare patient who generates an extraordinary amount of expenses. This patient may have had an excessive length of stay that required an unusual amount of supplies or pharmaceuticals. The federal government allows a cost outlier threshold for these rare cases so that the hospital will not incur such burdensome losses. Each hospital has a unique cost outlier threshold for each DRG that is based on the cost-to-charge ratios of that facility. Both the operating and capital cost-to-charge ratios are multiplied against the Medicare charges to create a cost assumption that is compared to actual costs to formulate a possible outlier variance. The theory for both inpatient and outpatient outlier payments is the same; however, few outpatient outlier payments are made. A majority of the outlier payments are derived from inpatient care. The following are four steps for calculating a Medicare outlier payment:

1. Determine the operating and capital DRG payment found in the blend rate computation.
2. Determine the operating and capital costs.
3. Calculate the operating and capital outlier thresholds.
4. Formulate the total outlier payment.

The federal government will reimburse hospitals at a higher rate because of outlier cases. A hypothetical patient's information is as follows:

Patient	DRG	Description	Weight	Charges	Variable Costs	Fixed Costs
John Doe	233	Coronary Bypass w Cardiac Cath W MCC	6.924	$225,000	$115,000	$25,000

Using the previously calculated DRG blend payment of $8,369, the hospital would have received $57,946 ($8,369 * 6.924) for services provided; however, assume this Medicare patient incurred complications and had to remain in the hospital for 30 days. The total expenses incurred to treat this 30-day length of stay amounted to $140,000 ($115,000 variable and $25,000 fixed).

Table 5.9   Step Two

Operating Costs = $225,000 * 35%	= $78,750
Capital Costs = $225,000 * 5%	= $11,250
Total expected costs for John Doe	= $90,000

Using step 1, the actual operating and capital payment for this Medicare case must be formulated from the $57,946 that was paid to the hospital. Usually, these figures can be computed by referring to the Medicare blend rate computation and multiplying the capital and operating figures by the appropriate DRG weight (Table 5.9).

Operating DRG Payment = (6.924 * $7,925) = $54,872
Capital DRG Payment   = (6.924 * $444) = $3,074
Total DRG Payment   = $57,946 ($54,872 + $3,074)

Using step 2, to determine if any additional reimbursement is allowed, the charges must be multiplied by the operating and capital cost-to-charge ratios from the blend rate to find the expected operating and capital costs. Assume for this example that the operating cost-to-charge ratio is 35%, while the capital cost to charge is 5% (see Table 5.9).

The operating and capital cost-to-charge ratios used in Table 5.9 are formulated in the previous year's cost report. According to these ratios, the total costs expected to treat John Doe should have been $90,000.

Using step 3, this $90,000 amount needs to be compared against the operating and capital thresholds dictated by Medicare. In 2011, the fixed loss threshold created by Medicare was $23,075. This amount is formulated by the government and cannot be influenced by a hospital. The methodology to formulate the operating and capital thresholds is detailed in Table 5.10.

Using step 4, determine the total outlier payment for the capital and operating portions of the individual case. Table 5.11 states that in addition to the $57,946 already received by the federal government, the hospital will receive an additional $14,555 to equal the total of the $72,501 outlier payment ($72,501 = $64,962 + $7,539). This additional money is due to the patient consuming an extraordinary amount of expenses because of unforeseen medical complications. The $72,501 in reimbursement does not equal the cost incurred of $140,000; however, it is an increase from the previous payment. Medicare auditors will examine the outlier payments made to hospitals to determine if the amount is accurate.

Medicare Pass-Through

In addition to the Medicare DSH and IME add-on payments, a hospital may receive additional governmental funding known as a *Medicare pass-through payment*. This payment is not part of the blend rate, and it is a combination of Medicare bad debt and direct medical education (DME). The government pays teaching hospitals a proportion of what is owed every 2 weeks, and hospitals usually set up a receivable specifically for this figure. The bad debt component of the Medicare pass-through payment is formulated in the annual cost report, which is addressed in a further chapter; however, the DME calculation can be derived from the number of resident physicians who are employed at that hospital. The DME equation is the

Table 5.10 Step Three

Operating Outlier Portion	
FYE 2011 fixed loss threshold (given by Medicare)	$23,075
Operating portion (Operating %/Total %) (0.35/0.40)	0.8750
Subtotal	$20,190
Labor-related share[a]	0.62
Subtotal	$12,517
Wage index from Medicare blend rate	0.90
Non-labor-related share	$11,265
Operating DRG payment (from step 1)	$54,872
Operating outlier threshold	$66,137
Capital Outlier Portion	
FYE 2011 fixed loss threshold (given by Medicare)	$23,075
Capital portion (Capital %/Total %) (0.05/0.40)	0.1250
Subtotal	$2,884
Geographic adjustment factor[b]	0.90
Subtotal	$2,595
Capital DRG payment (from step 1)	$3,074
Capital outlier threshold	$5,669

[a] Labor-related share of 62% is used if wage index is less than 1.0; a percentage of 68.8% would have been used if the wage index were above 1.0. See the computation of the Medicare wage-adjusted operating computation.

[b] Geographic adjustment factor is provided by Medicare.

number of residents either on contract or employed at the hospital multiplied by a government-produced rate, which is then multiplied by a Medicare utilization rate. The purpose of the DME payment is to cover both the *variable and fixed* costs of the teaching physicians who treat Medicare patients.

Medicare Pass-Through Payment = Medicare Bad Debt + DME

DME = Number of Residents * Government-Produced Rate * Medicare Utilization Rate

The Medicare utilization rate is defined as the number of Medicare days divided by total hospital days. Among the resident physicians, the primary care, emergency room (ER), and obstetrics/gynecology (OB/GYN) residents are reimbursed at a higher federal rate. To influence the

Table 5.11   Step Four

	Operating	Capital
Total costs for John Doe (see Table 5.9)	$78,750	$11,250
Less outlier threshold (see Table 5.10)	$66,137	$5,669
Subtotal	$12,613	$5,581
Marginal cost factor[a]	0.80	0.80
Outlier payment	$10,090	$4,465
Actual DRG payment (see step 1)	$54,872	$3,074
Total payment	$64,962	$7,539
Total Medicare payment for John Doe after outlier computation = $72,501 ($64,962 + $7,539)		

[a] Marginal cost factor is provided by Medicare.

Medicare pass-through payment, a hospital might possibly increase the amount of these primary care, ER, or OB/GYN teaching physicians. The purpose of the pass-through payments is that in the annual cost reports all medical education costs are backed out of the total cost to formulate a cost-to-charge ratio for Medicare patients (medical education is not backed out for Medicaid purposes). To compensate hospitals for eliminating these expenses, the federal government allows these costs to be paid back to teaching facilities every 2 weeks. Depending on the size of the facility and the number of residents, the DME payment used in the Medicare pass-through can range between $80,000 and $120,000 per year per resident. *If a facility is not a teaching hospital, then the Medicare pass-through payment would only consist of the allowable bad debt figure reported on Worksheet E of the cost report.*

CRITICAL ISSUE

To influence the Medicare pass-through payment positively, a hospital must employ or contract additional primary care, ER, or OB/GYN residents.

In addition to traditional resident physicians, resident fellow physicians are included in the Medicare pass-through payment. A resident fellow is a physician who has completed a residency (usually 3 years) and remains for additional years for educational purposes. An example would be a sports medicine fellow for an orthopedic physician. A hospital includes resident fellows but only at 50%. Previously, the government disallowed dental and psychiatric residents; however, these are now included in the Medicare pass-through computation.

Medicare Eligible Days

Simply because someone has turned 65 does not mean he or she can receive limitless medical care paid by the government. The federal government uses the term *spell of illness* to describe a time period when beneficiaries may receive Medicare Part A benefits. A beneficiary can be eligible for Medicare benefits on the first day of the month the individual reaches 65 years of age if that individual has been approved to receive Social Security benefits. However, each Medicare beneficiary has a certain amount of utilization days for time spent in a hospital, and this calculation of days is not determined by the calendar year. The maximum number of annual days for a traditional Medicare Part A patient would be 150 (60 days of regular Medicare, 30 coinsurance days, and 60 lifetime reserve days). The 60 days of regular Medicare and 30 coinsurance days are replenished after certain time periods have expired, whereas the lifetime reserve is never replenished; hospital staff must ask the patient before the lifetime reserve is used. The annual Medicare deductible that a patient is responsible for is approximately $1,100 for the 60 days, $275 per day for the coinsurance days, and $550 per day for the lifetime reserve days. The patient's benefit period begins on the first day of the hospital admission, and a tricky component of Medicare eligibility is how many remaining covered days a patient has after the patient has been admitted. For example, assume a Medicare patient is admitted on June 1 and stays for 30 days (discharged on June 30). If that same Medicare patient is readmitted on July 15, then that patient only has 30 days of regular Medicare and 30 coinsurance days remaining. However, if that Medicare patient is readmitted *61 days after the discharge date,* then the patient has 60 days of regular Medicare and 30 coinsurance days remaining (the 60 traditional Medicare days are replenished). The replenishment of Medicare days is an example of a *readmission window* in that eligibility is driven by the time between readmissions. The concept of patient eligibility can be confusing, which is why most hospitals employ a division of billing that solely concentrates on Medicare patient eligibility. Table 5.12 documents the complexity of remaining Medicare-eligible days postdischarge.

A crucial component of Medicare patient eligibility is understanding the financial ramifications of the patient's deductible and coinsurance/lifetime reserve payments. A patient is responsible for a $1,100 deductible for the first 60 days of hospital inpatient care. If the patient stays longer than 60 days, the individual will be responsible for a daily $275 coinsurance payment for up to 30 days. After the coinsurance days have expired, the patient is responsible for a daily $550 lifetime reserve payment for up to 60 days. If that Medicare patient stays longer than the total covered 150 days, then that individual will pay for all nondiagnostic services in the facility. These payments usually average about $1,500 per day (see Table 5.13).

Table 5.12   Medicare Eligible Days

Admitted	Discharged	Readmitted	Remaining Medicare Regular Days
June 1	June 30	July 15	30 days
June 1	June 30	September 1	60 days

Table 5.13   Maximum Medicare Patient Responsibility

60 traditional days:	Total deductible of approximately $1,100
30 Coinsurance days:	$275 per day (Maximum of 30 days = $8,250)
60 lifetime reserve days:	$550 per day (Maximum of 60 days = $33,000)
After 150 days:	Patient responsible for all nondiagnostic services

Another noteworthy issue is that most hospitals will bill Medicare for patients who stay for long periods and have not been discharged. Often called *interim billing*, hospitals will have a threshold, such as 30 days or even a monetary figure such as $200,000 in charges; hospitals will bill Medicare for services completed even though the patient is still receiving care. The problem with interim billing is that occasionally Medicare may overpay for services, and the hospital must pay back these funds when the patient is finally discharged. Another aspect of Medicare eligibility is that the federal government will not pay for more than 190 days of psychiatric inpatient care regardless of the number of utilization or reserve days. The 190 days is not for a specified time period but rather for the patient's entire lifetime; however, the psychiatric facility must be free-standing rather than a component of a hospital system.

Several years ago, the federal government gave the private sector an opportunity to manage the Medicare population, and these insurance providers became known as Medicare HMOs. These Medicare HMOs contract with the federal government to provide health insurance; in return, they receive a set amount from the government for each Medicare patient enrolled with them. Much like a capitated program, the Medicare HMO receives funds from the government regardless if the patient seeks medical attention. Examples of Medicare HMOs would be Medicare Advantage or Humana Gold Choice. The risk of being a Medicare HMO is that the stipend provided by the federal government will not cover the costs incurred by the Medicare patient. Hospitals cannot negotiate rates with Medicare HMOs, yet they can negotiate with Medicaid HMOs. The IPPS that is set by traditional Medicare patients is also utilized by Medicare HMO patients.

CRITICAL ISSUE

Hospitals can negotiate with Medicaid HMOs regarding reimbursement rates but cannot negotiate with Medicare HMOs. The same reimbursement from Medicare HMOs is received from traditional Medicare.

A reoccurring issue for a teaching hospital is when a Medicare HMO is billed and the IME add-on is excluded from the bill. Depending on the contract, some Medicare HMOs have left the IME portion of the bill with the federal government. The facility has to bill the MAC separately for the additional payment IME add-on payment that resides in the blend rate. This process is called *shadow billing*, and a hospital typically will not create a receivable for these funds. A significant issue in shadow billing is the general ledger presentation of these payments. The patient's account balance should not reflect the shadow bill since the Medicare HMO was not billed. When the cash is received from the federal government, the cash account should be debited, and a reserve account should be credited. The patient's balance should not reflect the IME cash received mainly because the account will have a credit or refund balance if the receivable is credited.

Medicare Hospital Designations

The federal government provides additional benefits to those hospitals that have certain limitations that restrict their ability to maintain operations. A *sole community hospital* (SCH) is a facility located at least 35 miles from a similar or like hospital and meets other criteria. The federal government will pay an additional 7.1% reimbursement above the standard outpatient Medicare payment rate and the higher of either the hospital's internal blend rate or an adjusted hospital-specific rate for inpatient Medicare services. The government gives extra money to an SCH because of its lack of proximity to other facilities and the fact the SCH is simply in a rural or remote location. In addition, SCH facilities are also not subject to the TRICARE inpatient DRG reimbursement methodology, which is a significant benefit to those facilities with high military patient populations. Each SCH hospital would have to negotiate a percentage of charge rate with TRICARE.

Another type of hospital that receives extra benefits is the *Medicare-dependent hospital* (MDH), which is basically a facility that has at least 60% of its payer mix populated by Medicare patients. If a hospital is an MDH, it cannot be an SCH; the MDH cannot have more than 100 beds, and it must be located in a rural area. A benefit of being an MDH is that Medicare inpatient services are paid the higher of the applicable blend rate or a combination of 75% of an adjusted specific rate and 25% of the blend rate. In addition, beginning in 2006 an MDH is not capped at 12% for Medicare DSH. This legislation was extremely significant because many SCHs switched to become an MDH to achieve the additional Medicare DSH add-on payment.

A third type of hospital that also receives added governmental benefits is the *rural referral center* (RRC), which is a facility that is located in a rural area and has more than 275 beds. A hospital must meet several requirements to become an RRC, and a significant necessity is that the facility must have at least 5,000 annual discharges. Much like an MDH, an RRC is not capped at 12% for Medicare DSH, and a RRC can qualify for 340B benefits with 8% instead of 11.75%.

A fourth and final type of rural hospital is the *critical access hospital* (CAH), which can have no more than 25 beds and an average length of stay of less than 4 days. This type of hospital must furnish 24-hour emergency services, and Medicare reimbursement is paid at 101%.

In addition to these benefits, an MDH, SCH, and RRC may also qualify for a low-volume hospital payment adjustment if certain criteria are met. The basic criteria to qualify as a low-volume hospital is that the facility be located more than 15 miles from the nearest hospital and have fewer than 1,600 Medicare discharges. Hospitals that qualify for the low-volume payment adjustment receive an add-on based on Medicare discharges; however, a CAH cannot qualify.

The federal government can access hospital statistical information in what is called the *MEDPAR file.* The MEDPAR (Medicare Provider Analysis and Review) file contains claims data regarding inpatient admission data for hospitals and skilled nursing facilities. The MEDPAR file allows the government to track and review the outcomes of patient care over a specified time period. A significant aspect of MEDPAR is that if a patient were admitted to a hospital then discharged to a skilled nursing home, it is classified as one stay. Additional data such as demographic information, diagnosis/surgery classifications, and resources consumed are included in the MEDPAR file. *MedPAC* (the Medicare Payment Advisory Commission) is an independent entity that advises the government on issues that affect the Medicare program. Established as part of the Balanced Budget Act of 1997, MedPAC researches and analyzes the payments to Medicare HMOs, hospitals, physicians, and any other recipient of Medicare funds. The goal of the commission is to improve the delivery of healthcare to those who are eligible for Medicare benefits.

Besides Medicare payments, a hospital may receive funds from the government that are not directly patient driven. Two examples of these funding sources are *appropriations* and *grants.* Appropriations are funds received by the hospital as a result of a legislative action; grants are awarded to a hospital based on a competitive bidding process. A hospital does not compete for an appropriation, and both of these revenue amounts are usually classified as "other revenue" in the financial statements. A hospital may receive numerous grants, especially if it is a teaching or not-for-profit hospital. In theory, a facility should not incur any profit for a grant since all expenses that are incurred by the hospital should equal the grant revenue received. In year-end financials, the net income of all grants received should be zero (not including timing differences).

Additional Issues

In 2008, the CMS began to penalize hospitals for treating hospital-acquired infections or conditions that were not present on admission. These hospital-acquired conditions can be urinary tract infections, pressure ulcers, and other infections that occurred while the inpatient was being treated at the facility. In theory, if the hospital was providing better care, these infections would not have occurred. The government basically will not pay for the additional cost to treat these infections because it believes these problems could have been prevented. The additional payment to a hospital would be the transition from a DRG with no complications to a DRG with complications. This increase in DRG weight can result in thousands of dollars of additional reimbursement. *The penalty that might be inflicted for an HAC (hospital-acquired condition) would only occur if the DRG changed. The federal government will not penalize a hospital if a patient incurred an infection but the DRG did not change.* The hospital has already incurred additional costs from treating the infection, which most likely resulted in a longer stay. This quality initiative highlights the government's belief that payments need to correlate to hospital performance rather than cost. Since this reimbursement change is relatively recent, there is not much information available to benchmark the financial effects of this modification. A coding indicator termed a POA (present on admission) allows hospital staff to track the occurrence of these infections. Even though financial personnel are not responsible for direct patient care, they should be aware of the federal government's reduction in reimbursement due to HACs that were not present on admission.

Occasionally, a Medicare patient will be admitted to a hospital and transferred to another facility. Such instances occur when a patient is transferred to either a skilled nursing unit or a rehabilitation facility. Medicare's methodology is that a hospital should not get a full DRG payment for treating that patient since he or she was transferred and not discharged accordingly. The Medicare transfer payment logic is given as

Medicare Transfer DRG Payment = Full MS-DRG Payment/Average Length of Stay for that DRG * (Number of Days Treated at the Hospital + 1)

Medicare auditors will examine and review traditional patient discharges to determine if the patient was truly discharged or transferred to a rehabilitation or skilled nursing facility.

A Medicare program that has recently grown is the *PACE* (Programs of All-Inclusive Care for the Elderly) program, which provides care and service to those above the age of 55. The purpose of the program is that the beneficiary has the benefit of staying at home and receiving care from numerous providers while the federal government hopes to reduce overall Medicare costs by keeping the patient out of a hospital or nursing home. Most states have adopted this program to include Medicaid patients as well as Medicare enrollees. Typical PACE services would be primary care, hospital care, prescription drugs, physical therapy, and adult day care. A significant benefit to the program is that the individual can leave PACE and not be penalized. In addition, the program offers transportation to and from activities and clinical appointments. The actual PACE program is often a component of a hospital system, and the facility is paid identical Medicare rates for PACE enrollees. In theory, Medicare created the PACE program in an attempt to minimize the admission of senior citizens to a nursing home. These clinical programs are often staffed and administered by a geriatrician, who specializes in caring for the elderly.

Conclusion

The Medicare reimbursement methodology implemented by the federal government is a complex model that is not easily understood. The inpatient reimbursement is driven by a DRG, while an outpatient payment is formulated by an APC. The blend rate is the cornerstone of Medicare reimbursement, and a healthcare professional should be aware of how it is computed and influenced. There are numerous add-on payments and adjustments that affect Medicare reimbursement depending on the type of hospital. The most significant condition would be if a facility is a teaching hospital. As a social benefit, the federal government gives additional funds to those hospitals that teach and educate resident physicians. In addition, Medicare allows outlier payments to hospitals for treating patients with excessive lengths of stay. Calculating the amount of covered Medicare days can be complex since the figure is replenished based on certain readmission criteria. The formulation and computation of Medicare reimbursement is an evolving process with many variables that may possibly change in the near future.

Chapter 6

Medicaid

Introduction

Medicaid is a program funded at both state and federal levels that is intended to provide health coverage to those families with low incomes. Created as a part of the Social Security Act of 1965, the Medicaid program is administered by each state, but the Centers for Medicare and Medicaid Services (CMS) has established the requirements for eligibility and funding. A significant difference between Medicare and Medicaid is that Medicare is solely funded at the federal level, whereas individual states are responsible for a substantial portion of Medicaid funding. Medicaid is basically a social welfare program in which eligibility is largely based on income. States are often required to cover certain mandatory groups and are given the option to cover other populations. In contrast, Medicare eligibility is based on national guidelines; Medicaid rules vary from state to state. California employs a system known as Medi-Cal, while Tennessee has a program called TennCare. Even though states administer these programs, they must conform to federal guidelines to receive matching funds from the federal government. Some states receive matching federal government payments at levels as high as 3:1 or even 4:1; this ratio is primarily driven by the income of the residents in that particular state.

The rates of coverage and reimbursement for Medicaid services do vary from state to state, but overall *the goal of Medicaid reimbursement is to pay hospitals at cost*. Hospitals are not supposed to earn a profit from treating indigent patients, so in addition to paying on a claim-by-claim basis ,a cost report settlement is often formulated in arrears to ensure that hospitals are compensated only for the expenses used to treat Medicaid patients. Discussing the process of Medicaid reimbursement is difficult since each state employs a different methodology. For this text, an overview of the most prevalent models used in the 50 states is given.

Much like a Medicare health maintenance organization (HMO), states have used private companies to manage the care of their patient populations. Termed a *Medicaid HMO* or a Medicaid managed care program, these companies contract with each state and receive a fixed rate per Medicaid enrollee. As stated in the Medicare chapter, a hospital may negotiate rates with a Medicaid HMO but not with a Medicare HMO. The goals and purpose of a Medicaid HMO is to improve the health of its members, lower the costs of treatment, and increase access to healthcare services. Similar to a Medicaid HMO is a *medical home network* (MHN), in which a state Medicaid agency contracts with a primary care provider to care for and treat a Medicaid-eligible patient. The MHN is a voluntary program reimbursed for services on a fee-for-service methodology accompanied by an additional monthly management stipend. If a MHN-insured patient were serviced at a hospital, then the facility would bill traditional Medicaid in that state rather than the MHN. The hospital would receive the same rates of reimbursement for the MHN patient as a regular Medicaid patient.

Reimbursement

States typically reimburse hospitals for treating Medicaid inpatients on either a diagnosis-related group (DRG) or per diem basis. The DRG methodology often represents approximately 75% of the total structure, whereas per diem payments represent about 25%. Nonfrequent services for trauma and neonatal intensive care are often paid on a per diem (daily) basis. Traditionally, Medicaid agencies administered by each state do not use the federally mandated Medicare blend rate but a similar computation. These amounts are eventually cost settled in future years, but the particular state has to pay hospitals something on an interim basis for the current year. Listed in Table 6.1 is a sample Medicaid DRG blend rate computation used for inpatients.

The discharge base rate and capital add-on are fixed amounts provided by each state for each individual hospital. Commonly, the Department of Health and Environmental Control (DHEC) of each state will formulate these amounts based on historical data for each hospital. The direct medical education (DME) and indirect medical education (IME) add-on amounts are formulated in that hospital's previous year's cost report, and they are only applicable for teaching hospitals. The DME and IME components of the blend rate can be influenced by the hospital, whereas the other components cannot. The actual Medicaid blend rate computation may be different for each state; however, a majority of states employ some sort of DRG reimbursement methodology to compensate hospitals for treating patients. Much like Medicare, each state has a weighted listing of all possible Medicaid DRG-reimbursed medical procedures; however, some states separate which procedures are reimbursed on a DRG basis and which services are reimbursed on a per diem basis. Table 6.2 is an example for a Medicaid patient for whom the hospital is reimbursed through a state-driven DRG grouper listing.

In this example for a sample Medicaid admission, the hospital will be paid $8,834 regardless of the expenses and length of stay at that facility. This listing of DRG weights may be different from state to state; however, the overall methodology is usually the same. Eventually, the hospital will be paid at cost for the service provided, but in 2010 the payment was $8,834. In addition to DRG reimbursement, most states pay hospitals per diem rates for inpatient and outpatient services. Table 6.3 provides a sample Medicaid per diem blend rate computation.

Table 6.1 Medicaid DRG Blend Rate

	2010	*2009*
Per discharge base rate	$5,100	$5,000
Capital add-on	$310	$300
Direct medical education add-on	$520	$500
Indirect medical education add-on	$715	$700
Total	**$6,645**	**$6,500**

Table 6.2   Medicaid DRG Reimbursement

DRG No.	Description	DRG Weight
DRG 085	Pleural Effusion W CC	1.3295
2010 county hospital blend rate = $6,645		
Medicaid payment = $6,645 * 1.3295 = $8,834		

Table 6.3   Medicaid Per Diem Rates

	2010	2009
Inpatient multiplier	0.82	0.80
Outpatient multiplier	1.25	1.20

Usually, states employ a uniform established rate for per diem services, and these amounts would be adjusted by either the inpatient or the outpatient multiplier amounts. The following is an inpatient example that details a Medicaid-qualifying neonatal intensive care unit patient who stayed in the hospital for 20 days.

2010 Statewide Inpatient Medicaid per Diem rate: $3,000

Hospital A Reimbursement for Services = $3,000 * 0.82 = $2,460 * 20 days = $49,200

The per diem model exhibits the state-established uniform rate, which is adjusted by hospital-specific inpatient and outpatient per diem rate percentages. The hospital-specific per diem rates are created by that particular state, and hospital reimbursement staff usually cannot influence this figure. Some states may or may not even employ a per diem reimbursement model. Most Medicaid agencies reimburse hospitals for outpatient procedures using a fee schedule. Usually, only one category of service based on the highest classification is paid per claim. The fee schedule consists of all services that are either surgical or nonsurgical. The following is an outpatient example that details a Medicaid patient who had a cyst surgically removed:

2010 Statewide Outpatient Medicaid Fee Schedule Rate for Removal of Cyst: $500

Hospital A Reimbursement for Services = $500

The hospital knows the Medicaid reimbursement for the outpatient surgical procedure in advance. This $500 in payment is made for all the laboratory, radiology, anesthesia, blood, and supplies used to treat the patient. The outpatient fee schedule reimbursement model is much simpler than the inpatient model, and it includes all nonsurgical services, such as any imaging or lab procedures.

Often, a patient is *dual eligible* in that the individual qualifies for both Medicare and Medicaid benefits. In these instances, the hospital will always classify Medicare as the primary payer and Medicaid as the secondary payer. Most states that administer Medicaid will pay the allowed amount less the reimbursement paid by Medicare or the coinsurance/deductible figures (whichever is less). Most state Medicaid programs cover hospital services that are medically necessary to the patient. These services can range from surgical, dental, or even those that are substance abuse related. These covered services must be directed toward the maintenance, improvement, or protection of the patient's health. A typical service that would not be covered by most Medicaid programs would be any cosmetic procedure.

Medicaid Add-On Payments

As a benefit for being a teaching hospital, Medicaid has traditionally given add-on payments just as Medicare does. Typically, the state pays each teaching hospital a DME add-on payment; the purpose of this payment is to compensate hospitals for the fixed and variable costs of the teaching physicians, who provide an additional benefit to the community. This amount is paid on a claim basis (part of the blend rate), and the add-on amount is formulated from the previous year's cost report. The DME add-on is typically computed as follows:

DME = (Total Hospitalwide Medical Education Costs * Medicaid Utilization Rate) divided by the Number of Medicaid claims

Some states may add additional variables to this computation, but overall the methodology is similar. A significant issue to the DME add-on payment is that to qualify for the money the teaching physicians must have "teaching or faculty privileges" in that facility. Another issue is that some states have kept the DME billing portion in-house rather than give Medicaid HMOs the ability to administer this service. If the particular state has decided not to outsource the DME add-on portion to Medicaid HMOs, then a hospital receivable needs to be created for all the Medicaid HMO DME add-on payments since these previously billed claims do not reflect this amount. This variation of billing depends on the Medicaid program being administered in that particular state; however, South Carolina would be an example of a state where DME add-on payments are not included in Medicaid HMO billing. Teaching hospitals must bill the state of South Carolina directly for the additional add-on payment for Medicaid HMO patients who were treated. This amount can be significant, depending on the number of patients covered in a Medicaid HMO program.

In contrast, the IME add-on in the Medicaid blend rate is usually based on the same computation used in the Medicare blend rate; however, the number of Medicare inpatient claims rate is substituted with the number of Medicaid inpatient claims.

IME Add-on = (FTE Residents/Number of Open Beds * 1.405 power) * Geographic Adjustment Factor divided by the Number of Medicaid Inpatient Claims

The method to influence this equation positively is to either increase the number of residents or possibly decrease the number of open beds. As stated in the Medicare chapter, the IME calculation is trued up each year in the cost report, and hospitals can only report residents who service both inpatient and outpatient patients for clinical services. Hospitals can also report residents who work at other facilities, such as a nursing home, as long as they are physically working and present at the hospital claiming the IME. A method to decrease beds is to subtract the beds that are not being used due to maintenance or clinical issues.

Medicaid Teaching Supplement and Trauma

In addition to the medical education payments, some states have created add-on payments for the teaching of physicians who treat Medicaid patients. One such add-on is called the Medicaid teaching supplement, which is paid on a claim-by-claim basis. An additional percentage of charges is received for treating both qualified traditional Medicaid and Medicaid HMO patients. Much like the Medicaid DME computation, a payment is received only if the hospital employed or contracted a physician who has "teaching or faculty privileges." For each inpatient and outpatient visit, the hospital will receive an additional percentage regardless if the patient is enrolled in traditional Medicaid or a Medicaid HMO. The additional percentage can range from 15% to 35% of hospital charges. Hospitals may or may not decide to create a receivable for this money depending on the amount of Medicaid patients. This additional teaching reimbursement paid to hospitals is not given in every state. Some states may believe hospitals deserve more cash for treating Medicaid patients; others may not.

In addition to the DME, IME, and teaching supplement, some states give extra funds to hospitals for employing trauma services; however, the amount of funding varies. Typically, a state will budget a certain portion of money for all hospitals in the state that employ trauma services. Instead of only Medicaid patients, a facility will receive more funds if it has a larger indigent patient population. Historically, all indigent patients are classified as Medicaid, charity care, and self-pay. Much like the Medicaid teaching supplement, the trauma service payments vary from state to state.

Hierarchy of Indigent Patients

Even though federal and state governments have budgeted funds to cover the medical costs of low-income patients, most indigent people do not realize they are eligible for Medicaid benefits. *It is the responsibility of the hospital to ensure that billing representatives attempt to transfer uninsured patients to Medicaid based on that particular hospital's established criteria.* Medicaid eligibility is based on family size, income, and assets, and to qualify for coverage a patient must usually bring in tax forms for verification. Hospitals typically classify families who are eligible for Medicaid at 200% of the poverty level, which was approximately $21,660 in income for the head of household in 2010. Depending on the particular state, the percentage of the poverty level may vary, but the annual limit of income increases as the number of children or family size increases. Generally, a single male is not eligible for Medicaid because a majority of state programs are intended for women and children. The following is an example of the guidelines for 200% of the poverty level in a state (information is available on the CMS Web site, www.CMS.gov):

Family Size	Annual Limit
1	$21,660
2	$29,140
3	$36,620
4	$44,100
5	$51,580
6	$59,060
7	$66,540
8	$74,020
Note: The 2010 national poverty guideline was $10,830.	

Using this example, if a woman had less than $21,600 in income (200% of the poverty level), then she would be eligible for Medicaid and not be responsible for any payment of her bill. If a mother with a child had less than $29,140 in income, then she would also be eligible for Medicaid and not be responsible for any bills she or her child incurred.

CRITICAL ISSUE

A single male is generally not eligible for Medicaid coverage. The Medicaid program is intended to cover the cost of medical services provided to women and children.

The billing department will adjust a Medicaid case to zero once any payment from the government is received. The justification is that Medicaid-qualifying patients should not have to pay any portion of their bill. *There is no patient portion of the bill if a patient qualifies for either Medicaid or charity care.* If a Medicaid patient incurs $100 in charges and only $25 is received from the state, then the remaining $75 is adjusted to zero. In accounting terms, the $75 adjustment credits the receivable balance of that particular Medicaid patient, and the correlating debit is a $75 increase in the contractual figure, which is an operating expense that reduces net income.

A significant issue of Medicaid eligibility is that those who represent the *working poor* will not qualify for Medicaid because their income is commonly above the threshold. These individuals will possibly qualify for charity care, which is reserved for those who do not qualify for Medicaid yet they still represent an indigent portion of the population. If a patient does not qualify for Medicaid or charity care, then the individual would be classified as self-pay (see Table 6.4).

To be eligible for charity care, a patient must meet the hospital-specific unique criteria for those who can be classified as charity care patients. Much like Medicaid, these patients do not pay any portion of their bills; however, unlike Medicaid, the hospital does not expect any payment for these services. Treating patients who are classified as charity care results in an immediate loss since there is no expected payment for these services.

Self-pay patients represent the patient population with excess income or assets that place them above the threshold to qualify for either Medicaid or charity care. Unlike charity care, the hospital expects payment from these patients for services provided. The self-pay population represents those who have no insurance but are either not eligible for Medicare or Medicaid or too wealthy for charity care. The treatment of this patient population is a significant burden for hospitals because these individuals often will not pay for their treatment, whether for inpatient or outpatient services. Hospital collection personnel will concentrate their efforts to collect self-pay patient balances; however, this population is predominantly responsible for driving the bad debt expense in the facility.

Table 6.4 Hierarchy of Indigent Care

Medicaid (Poorest)
↓
Charity Care (Does Not Qualify for Medicaid)
↓
Self-Pay (Does Not Qualify for Charity Care or Medicaid)

Medicaid Cost Settlement

A hospital bills traditional Medicaid and Medicaid HMOs just like any other insurance carrier; however, there is a cost settlement that occurs in arrears. Most states will typically use some type of source data (sometimes called a MARS report or state-issued PSR report) as a source document to determine what it under- or overpaid hospitals. This state-formulated document typically contains all charges, payments, and volumes that were submitted and paid by that particular state for all traditional Medicaid patients at that particular hospital. Medicaid HMO payments are usually not listed on these state reports; however, occasionally Medicare and other third-party payments are listed. These "other-than-Medicaid" patients listed in these government reports represent those who had insurance but had Medicaid as a secondary payer.

CRITICAL ISSUE

The annual cost report settlement is usually only for traditional Medicaid patients. Most states do not include Medicaid HMO patients in this computation.

Medicaid's reimbursement model is largely based on the cost-to-charge ratios provided by hospitals; however, there is a timing lag when formulating this information. As previously stated, Medicaid pays each claim on either a DRG or per diem basis, but that is only a best-guess estimate to what the cost of Medicaid services will be. The actual or final payment to hospitals for servicing Medicaid patients is often settled years after the patients are discharged. Traditionally, the 12-month FYE (fiscal year end) for state agency billing runs from October through September rather than the typical 12-month CYE (calendar year end) time period of January through December; however; the following example uses a calendar year. The following information provides a 2-year timeline for a typical Medicaid cost report settlement. Understand that some states may employ different timelines and regulations, but this hypothetical example exemplifies the overall methodology. The financial information of a sample Medicaid patient is given in Table 6.5.

Since the individual was discharged on June 15, 2010, the patient is classified in CYE 2010. The hospital billed the state based on the DRG weight and blend rate that was classified to that hospital. This resulted in a payment of $8,834. To treat this Medicaid patient, assume the facility

Table 6.5 Information for Sample Medicaid Patient

DRG 085	Pleural Effusion W CC	1.3295
2010 county hospital blend rate = $6,645		
Patient discharged June 15, 2010		
Total hospital charges = $40,000		
Medicaid payment = $6,645 * 1.3295 = $8,834		
Total costs = $15,000		
Loss on Medicaid patient = $6,166 ($15,000 – $8,834)		

incurred $15,000 in costs, resulting in a loss of $6,166. The DRG payment by the state was an estimate of what the costs should have been for treating a patient for that type of procedure.

> The CYE 2010 (January 2010 to December 2010) claim-by-claim payments were based on the state-supplied DRG/per diem reimbursement rates for CYE 2010.

As previously discussed, most states reimburse hospitals at 100% of cost, yet some states reimburse at 80% or even 75% of cost. The cost report that is submitted to the government attempts to find a cost-to-charge ratio for each line item and apply that ratio against the Medicaid charges to formulate an estimated cost. This amount is contrasted against the payments already received by the hospital for treating Medicaid patients. *A significant attribute of cost report settlements is that cost-to-charge ratios used to find cost are formulated in arrears.* In other words, the cost information may be from several years ago. In this hypothetical example, the state government is using cost report data from 2 years previous and will pay hospitals 100% of this cost for treating Medicaid patients.

> The CYE 2010 Medicare cost report is filed 5 months after the end of the year. Actual reimbursement rates are based on FYE 2008 cost-to-charge ratios multiplied by a 90% state overpayment contingency.

The 10% that is held back is to account for possible overpayment to hospitals. States typically implement a 5% or 10% reduction against total cost as a buffer to protect their cash flows. To account for this underpayment to hospitals, some states often add an inflationary adjustment to the ratio. Prior to any cost report settlement, the sample hospital currently has a loss of $6,166 for treating this example Medicaid patient. This loss was created using not only variable costs but also any fixed costs. Assume for this example that after completing the FYE 2008 cost report it was revealed that the cost-to-charge ratio in the respiratory grouping was 32.25%. (This clinical grouping applies to DRG 085 pleural effusion WCC.) After applying this ratio to the total charges, the expected cost of treating that Medicaid patient is $12,900 instead of the actual costs incurred of $15,000.

> Cost Report Respiratory Cost to Charge Ratio = 32.25%
> Expected Cost for Treating Respiratory Patients = (0.3225 * 40,000 = $12,900)

By cost settling this Medicaid claim, the state believes that the hospital should have incurred $12,900 in costs to treat this particular patient. This $12,900 in expected costs is different from the actual $15,000 incurred by the facility. Since this example assumes that Medicaid pays at 100% of cost, the newly formulated cost report amount must be compared against the previous payment received of $8,834 to determine if the state government owes the hospital additional funds. Since we are assuming this state reimburses at cost, the net revenue/payment for this patient will increase from $8,834 to $12,900. This payment increase of $4,066 reflects the cost report adjustment that is settled in arrears. This hospital will still incur a loss in this example; however, the amount will not be as severe.

> Loss on Medicaid Patient prior to Cost Report Settlement $15,000 – $8,834 = ($6,166)
> Loss on Medicaid Patient after Cost Report Settlement $15,000 – $12,900 = ($2,100)

Using the same example, assume that the FYE 2008 cost report formulated a cost-to-charge ratio of 21.25% in the respiratory cost center. After applying this ratio to the total charges ($40,000), the new expected cost of treating that Medicaid patient is $8,500 instead of the actual costs incurred of $15,000.

Cost Report Respiratory Cost-to-Charge Ratio = 21.25%
Expected Cost for Treating Respiratory Patients = (0.2125 * 40,000 = $8,500)

By cost settling this Medicaid claim, the hospital has formulated that it incurred $6,500 more in cost than expected in treating this patient ($6,500 = $15,000 – $8,500). The adjusted cost figure is compared to the previous payment received of $8,843, which results in a Medicaid overpayment to the hospital in 2010. The overpayment of $343 ($8,500 – $8,843) must be paid back to state government for the overpayment of Medicaid services.

Loss on Medicaid Patient prior to Cost Report Settlement $15,000 – $8,834 = $6,166
Loss on Medicaid Patient after Cost Report Settlement $15,000 – $8,500 = $6,500

These two examples represent only one Medicaid patient, while the entire cost report entails an entire year's population for all Medicaid patients. The annual cost report settlement is a way of ensuring that the state reimburses hospitals at cost; however, an issue is that the definition of cost varies from year to year for providing services. Some states may or may not reimburse at 100% of cost depending on the Medicaid population in that state.

CRITICAL ISSUE

A significant attribute of cost report settlements is that the cost-to-charge ratios used to formulate current year cost are from a previous year's cost report. In other words, the payment for Medicaid services in 1 year may be from data compiled from 2 or even 3 years previous.

After the cost report is filed, an initial settlement is created using the updated cost-to-charge ratio information. The costs reported to treat Medicaid patients for services in FYE 2008 are now used as a basis for reimbursement rather than the previously mentioned DRG/per diem methodology. *The DRG and per diem payments are a temporary method to pay hospitals for Medicaid services. The cost settlement in arrears is the final method to find the net payment for medical care.* A significant issue is when hospitals actually are reimbursed by the respective state government for the discrepancy between cost and payment. It depends on the state, but most Medicaid programs formulate an initial settlement 18 months after the cost report is filed. This initial settlement could result either in a hospital owing money to that state's Medicaid program or in that particular state owing additional funds to the hospital. A permanent settlement usually occurs 4 years after the cost report is filed. A permanent settlement means that an independent auditor hired by Medicaid audits the cost report to determine if the figures reported were accurate. Basically, the auditor is performing due diligence to determine if the cost report was completed accordingly.

A significant aspect of the cost report settlement is how the asset/liability is reported on the hospital financial statements. Reimbursement analysts can estimate the Medicaid cost report

Table 6.6   FYE 2010 Medicaid Cost Report Settlement Asset/Liability

FYE 2008 Cost to Charge Ratios * FYE 2010 Medicaid Charges = FYE 2010 Cost-Settled Payments
FYE 2010 Cost-Settled Payments Compared to Medicaid FYE 2010 Actual Payments = Settlement Asset/Liability

liability/asset settlement figure once the cost report is filed. The cost-to-charge ratio found in the current cost report can be multiplied against the Medicaid charges supplied by the state government to find the expected Medicaid payments. This amount is contrasted against the payments received from the state-administered Medicaid program.

In Table 6.6, the sample state uses 2008 as the previous year for the cost-to-charge ratios. Some states may use ratios from 1 or even 3 years previous; however, for this text we assume that a 2-year lag is used. The 2008 ratios are multiplied against actual 2010 charges to formulate an expected payment amount. This expected payment amount is contrasted against actual payments received. If the expected payments are higher than the actual payments, then an asset is created since Medicaid owes the hospital additional funds. If the expected payments are less than actual payments, then a liability is created since the hospital owes money to the state.

Medicaid Disproportionate Share Calculation

A majority of states that administer Medicaid have two separate programs that are matched by the federal government. The first is the traditional fee-for-service or UPL (upper payment limit) program in which hospitals are paid on a claim-by-claim basis for patients treated. The second is the *Medicaid DSH (Disproportionate Share Hospital) payment,* which is paid to hospitals not only for Medicaid patients but also for all indigent patients. The federal government typically matches the budgeted Medicaid funds appropriated by a particular state on a pro-rated basis such as 4:1 or 3:1, and how these funds are collected is a multistep process. Most not-for-profit hospitals in a state pay a quarterly "DSH tax invoice" or intergovernmental transfer (IGT) to the state-administered Medicaid program to fund both the traditional fee-for-service (UPL) and DSH programs initially. The amount of tax a hospital will pay is derived proportionally from the operating expenses of all the hospitals in that state. *The purpose of the DSH tax is that the appropriate state can use these received funds as evidence to be reimbursed by the federal government for treating low-income patients.* The Medicaid DSH portion of the Medicaid funds is matched and in some cases doubled or tripled by the federal government to treat patients; however, this figure is capped at a certain amount per state. The remaining DSH tax funds from each hospital are lumped into the traditional Medicaid bucket that is used to reimburse hospitals using either a DRG or per diem methodology. Table 6.7 is a hypothetical example of a state-administered Medicaid DSH

Table 6.7   Sample Medicaid DSH Formulation

A.	DSH tax collected from state hospitals	$200,000,000
B.	Amount allocated to DSH payment (60%)	$120,000,000
C.	Amount allocated to fee-for-service (40%)	$80,000,000

Table 6.8 Segregation of Medicaid DSH

A.	DSH tax collected from state hospitals	$200,000,000
B.	Amount allocated to DSH payment (60%)	$120,000,000
C.	Amount allocated to fee for service (40%)	$80,000,000
D.	DSH funds that are matched by the federal government for all indigent patients (3:1 basis)	$360,000,000 ($120 million * 3)
E.	DSH funds that are matched by the federal government for traditional Medicaid (3:1 basis)	$240,000,000 ($80 million * 3)
F.	Total Medicaid funds	$600,000,000 ($360 + $240)

formulation assuming that the federal government will match funds on a 3:1 basis and a 60/40 split of DSH tax collected.

A. $200 million was raised by the state-administered Medicaid program through DSH tax payments from state hospitals. All hospitals pay the DSH tax, usually on a monthly or quarterly basis. The amount that each hospital pays is often driven by their operating expenses.

B. and C. The $200 million is separated into the traditional Medicaid and DSH components. The proportion of this segregation is at the discretion of the individual state (Table 6.8).

D. and E. The federal government usually matches the DSH payments accumulated by each state on some type of pro rata basis. For this example, we are assuming the federal government will match the DSH tax payments at 3 to 1. This matching figure is usually driven by the income of the population in the state.

F. After the federal match, the total amount of statewide funds for Medicaid spending is $600,000,000. This amount represents the total money that a state can pay its hospitals for traditional Medicaid and DSH payments.

The next step for the state-administered Medicaid program is to disburse the Medicaid DSH payments to all hospitals in the state for their treatment of low-income patients. Each state will create its own unique model of paying hospitals; however, for this example we assume that each hospital in the state is paid DSH money using a cost report cost-to-charge ratio that was reported in arrears. Items G through K in Table 6.9 display the methodology for how a sample facility (Hospital A) will be reimbursed for Medicaid DSH funds.

G. A hospital will report all the charges associated with both charity care and self-pay patients. These charges will be multiplied against a cost-to-charge ratio to formulate an estimated cost figure. *The Medicaid DSH component is often used to reimburse hospitals for treating charity care and self-pay patients in addition to Medicaid patients.*

H. The hospitalwide cost-to-charge ratio was formulated in the Medicare/Medicaid cost report from 2008. We are assuming in this example that the state is using a cost report from 2 years ago. Some states may use the cost-to-charge ratios from 3 years ago or even 4 years; however, the purpose of this is to use a valid percentage in which an initial settlement has been formulated. Medicaid usually adjusts this cost-to-charge ratio for

Table 6.9   Medicaid DSH Payment

A.	DSH tax collected from state hospitals	$200,000,000
B.	Amount allocated to DSH payment (60%)	$120,000,000
C.	Amount allocated to fee for service (40%)	$80,000,000
D.	DSH funds that are matched by the federal government for charity care and self-pay patients	$360,000,000 ($120 million * 3)
E.	DSH funds that are matched by the federal government for traditional Medicaid	$240,000,000 ($80 million * 3)
F.	Total Medicaid funds	$600,000,000 ($360 + $240)
G.	Self-pay and charity care patient charges reported by Hospital A	$50,000,000
H.	FYE 2008 cost to charge ratio for Hospital A	30%
I.	FYE 2010 estimated DSH costs	$15,000,000 (0.30 * 50,000,000)
J.	Payment's already received on self-pay and charity care patients by Hospital A	($500,000)
K.	Total Medicaid DSH payment to Hospital A	$14,500,000

annual inflationary adjustments. This percentage represents an average cost of all services performed at Hospital A.

I. The estimated cost to treat indigent patients is the average cost-to-charge ratio multiplied against the total self-pay and charity charges (15,000,000 = 30% * 50,000,000).

J. This amount represents the payments already made to that hospital for self-pay and charity care patients. This figure is often internally derived in the hospital's patient accounting system. This amount should be minimal because of these patients' low income.

K. The subtotal is the estimated DSH cost less the payments already received from treating indigent patients. This amount will be paid to a hospital in that appropriate state for treating indigent patients other than Medicaid.

In some states, the amount of DSH money available cannot cover the total cost of care given to indigent patients. Often, states must pro rate the total DSH money to hospitals based on the proportion of indigent patients in that state. Table 6.10 lists all charity care and self-pay charges reported in a fiscal year for all state hospitals ($400,000) and Hospital A ($50,000).

In this hypothetical instance, Hospital A is treating 12.50% of the total charity care/self-pay patients in the state. If there were *not enough funds* to cover all the costs of indigent care, then Hospital

Table 6.10   Indigent Patient Allocation

Hospital A Indigent Patients	*Entire State Indigent Patients*	*Percentage of Total*
$50,000	$400,000	12.50%

A would receive 12.50% of the pro rata share of Medicaid DSH money that is available. This pro rata adjustment is common among many states due to the poor status of the nation's economy.

A significant issue that healthcare accountants face is how to present the DSH tax and DSH payment in the financial statements. Some hospitals may present the tax payment as an operating expense, whereas others may record it as a receivable. Using T-accounts, a brief explanation of recording the Medicaid DSH tax in both manners is given.

Record DSH Tax as Receivable

Cash

(B) $30,000,000	(A) $10,000,000
$20,000,000	

DSH Receivable

(A) $10,000,000	(B) $30,000,000
	$20,000,000
(C) $2,000,000	
	$18,000,000

Other Revenue

	(C) $2,000,000
	$2,000,000

A. A hospital pays the quarterly DSH tax invoice of 10,000,000 to the state with the intent that the federal government will match these funds. Cash is reduced (credited), and an "upside down" receivable is created (debited).

B. The federal government matches the DSH tax amount provided by the appropriate state on a pro rata basis (3:1). This money is allocated back to all hospitals in the state on an equitable basis. This $30,000,000 is paid to the hospital on a quarterly basis; cash is debited, and the receivable is credited.

C. *Since the money received from the government is more than the DSH receivable, a credit balance will occur.* To reduce this credit balance, a portion of the DSH payment is allocated from the receivable to an other revenue ledger account. This figure may be based on months in the year or other factors. For this example, we assume that $2,000,000 is reclassed to other revenue on a monthly basis.

An issue with recording the DSH tax as a receivable is that a credit balance will consistently exist in the balance sheet/statement of financial position due to the timing of receiving the respective DSH payments. The entire credit balance cannot be reclassed to other revenue because the money has not been earned yet. This monthly adjusting entry adheres to the accounting principle that revenue is realized when it is recorded or earned.

Another method of presenting the DSH payment is to record the tax as an expense and not create a receivable.

Record DSH Tax as Expense, Not Receivable

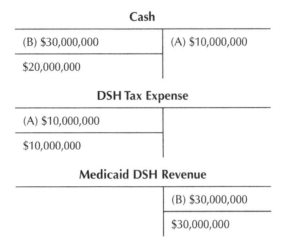

Cash

(B) $30,000,000	(A) $10,000,000
$20,000,000	

DSH Tax Expense

(A) $10,000,000	
$10,000,000	

Medicaid DSH Revenue

	(B) $30,000,000
	$30,000,000

A. A hospital pays the quarterly DSH tax invoice of 10,000,000 to the state with the intent that the federal government will match these funds. Cash is credited, and the tax expense ledger account is debited.
B. The federal government matches the DSH tax amount provided by the appropriate state on a pro rata basis (3:1). This money is allocated back to all hospitals in the state on an equitable basis. This hypothetical $30,000,000 is paid to the hospital on a quarterly basis; cash is debited, and a unique revenue ledger account is credited.

The benefit of recording the Medicaid DSH payment as an expense is the simplicity of debiting an expense and crediting revenue for the cash received. There is no additional monthly adjusting entry to move the money from one account to another. The correlating issue of recording the Medicaid DSH tax as a receivable is that, due to the timing issues of receiving payment, the receivable will almost always have a credit balance. It is at the discretion of the accounting manager to determine which method is a best fit for that hospital.

State Children's Hospital Insurance Program

A problematic issue in Medicaid reimbursement is how to insure or cover services provided to a child if the parents did not qualify for a government program. Many states have enacted a *State Children's Hospital Insurance Program* (SCHIP) that covers children under the age of 18 for hospital services. The rates a hospital receives for treating SCHIP-qualifying patients is the same for Medicaid, which is usually defined as cost. If a child is covered under Medicaid, then that child cannot be classified as covered by SCHIP. A child is in either one program or the other. The same reimbursement methodology used for SCHIP patients is used for traditional Medicaid patients.

Conclusion

The Medicaid program is both state and federally funded and is designed to cover those with little to no income. Most states employ a Medicaid program that reimburses hospitals using both a state-driven DRG methodology and a per diem rate. Much like Medicare, the Medicaid system offers add-on payments like IME and DME for those hospitals that have teaching programs. In addition, *Medicaid is cost settled using the same cost report that Medicare uses.* A majority, if not all, of states employ some type of Medicaid system that depends on matching federal dollars, and most state programs attempt to reimburse hospitals at some portion of cost. The two federally matched programs are usually separated into the traditional claim by claim Medicaid UPL and the Medicaid DSH program. These two methodologies are responsible for hundreds of millions of dollars that each state budgets to cover the medical costs of its indigent citizens. By understanding the formulation and manipulations of these figures, a healthcare professional can better comprehend the healthcare budgeting issues that affect both the state and federal government.

Chapter 7

Other Insurance Providers

Introduction

Medicare and Medicaid typically account for almost one-half to two-thirds of the patient populations at most hospitals throughout the United States. The remaining insurance carriers represent what is often termed nongovernmental payers. Examples of these payers would be insurance carriers such as Blue Cross/Blue Shield (BCBS), Cigna, or Kaiser Permanente. Due to the vast amount of insurance providers that currently sell health coverage, it would not be feasible to list the reimbursement method of each company; however, certain models can be addressed. Insurance carriers reimburse hospitals using a variety of methods that depend on the contract negotiated. Typical forms of payment could be a per diem rate, a percentage of charges, or the traditional Medicare Diagnosis-Related Group/Ambulatory Payment Classification (DRG/APC) model. The reimbursement methodology usually depends on what is negotiated between that particular hospital and the insurance carrier.

Managed Care (Health Maintenance Organization versus Preferred Provider Organization)

In 1973, the Health Maintenance Organization Act was passed and created organizations that attempted to reduce the cost of providing care while improving quality. These managed healthcare providers developed relationships with doctors and hospitals by negotiating lower rates in return for referrals of patients. These companies also managed the cost of care through a select group of healthcare providers, and they absorbed the risk of insuring patients. A majority of the growth and success of managed care is due to the minimization of costs while maintaining expected quality outcomes. The two most popular components of managed care are the health maintenance organization (HMO) and the preferred provider organization (PPO). An *HMO* is a managed care company that contracts with physicians and hospitals to provide health care for those who are insured in that plan. The HMO earns revenue from the individuals who pay premiums for health coverage. Those who are covered must see a primary care physician in the network that negotiated with that HMO or they will pay for expenses out of their own pocket. Typically, the HMO has some sort of capitated contract with a physician's office, which pays a monthly fee based on the number of enrollees. In theory, HMOs work best when there are young and healthy people enrolled in the program.

HMOs can exist in various forms, but most are usually classified as either a staff or a group model. In a staff model, the physicians are direct employees of the HMO; the group model does not employ physicians but contracts with several physician practices. Kaiser Permanente is a managed care organization that exhibits the group model. A detriment to being in a HMO is when a family practice physician refers a patient to a specialist who is outside the network. The patient may have to pay out of pocket expenses to see this specialist. To offset this negative referral, the HMO may decrease the monthly payment to the doctor's office. Health maintenance organizations are regulated at both the federal and state levels, and they have been criticized for some of the restrictions they have placed on those patients they service.

In comparison, a *PPO* is a managed care plan in which a covered individual does not need to select a primary care physician, and a referral is not needed to see a specialist. A distinguishing feature of most PPOs is the use of an annual deductible and copayment when visiting a physician. Like a HMO, the individual must see a physician in the PPO network, or the amount of out-of-pocket costs will significantly increase. PPOs earn revenue by charging an access fee for the use of their network of physicians, and a majority require the use of precertification when a hospital admission is needed. The use of the PPO model has grown over the years since they have higher premiums than HMOs, and they offer their clients more flexibility.

The argument about which model is more effective is currently under debate. Some believe that the HMO has increased efficiency, while others believe that there is no direct correlation between the cost of care and quality. The PPO has given the patient more rights, but it has also created a bottleneck of patients for physician specialists. A healthcare accountant need not know all the intricacies that exist in the managed care realm, but a working knowledge is needed.

Regardless if a managed care organization is structured as a PPO or HMO, the entity utilizes two basic indemnity concepts: *assignment of benefits* and *balance billing*. The assignment of benefits refers to a managed care company paying a hospital rather than a patient for services provided. For this to occur, some type of contract must exist between the insurance provider and the hospital. Most hospitals have some department or senior administrator that specializes in the negotiation of these managed care contracts. Balance billing is the practice of the hospital billing a patient for the portion of the services not paid by the insurance carrier. Almost all managed care contracts prevent balance billing from occurring, with the exception of copayments and deductibles. The variations in billing and payment for hospital services in HMOs and PPOs can be vastly different. Some companies use a fee-for-service arrangement that may be discounted to a more manageable rate, whereas other businesses may pay a hospital on a percentage of gross charges. Occasionally, a hospital may negotiate a *letter of agreement* with a managed care company, which is basically a shorter form of a contract. A letter of agreement is a document that both parties submit to, while a formal contract is being further negotiated. A letter of agreement may be 2 to 3 pages, while a contract may be 18–20 pages. Both a contract and a letter of agreement are binding for all parties.

Blue Cross/Blue Shield

The Blue Cross/Blue Shield Association is one of the most recognizable health insurance organizations in the country. The company provides insurance to over 100 million Americans, and it is headquartered in Chicago, Illinois (1). The history of the company goes back to the beginning of the 20th century when separate companies existed. Blue Cross was originally created for teachers in Texas while Blue Shield was intended to provide coverage to lumberjacks in the Pacific Northwest. The original difference between the two was that Blue Cross was intended for hospital coverage, and Blue Shield was created for physician services. In the early 1980s, the two companies merged to form one of the largest health insurance companies in the nation.

BCBS offers some type of health insurance coverage in every state and provides coverage to both federal and state employees. In the BCBS umbrella, there are both public and private companies that offer a range of services and products. WellPoint and Anthem are the largest members in BCBS, and they are publicly traded; CareFirst and Premera are smaller components. In addition, each state typically has its own unique BCBS independent licensee, like BCBS of Nebraska, BCBS of Ohio, or BCBS of South Carolina. The company also acts as third-party administrator (TPA) of other health insurance programs, such as Medicare. A *third-party administrator* is an entity that processes insurance claims or other employee benefit plans for another entity. The use of a TPA is common when companies decide to self-insure their employees; therefore, the risk lies with the employer rather than the TPA. Since the employer has chosen to finance the cost of employee health care, a majority of the duties of a TPA are to manage membership status, process claims, and monitor provider networks. The basic reason why companies employ other companies like BCBS to become TPAs is that it is more cost efficient for them. Health insurance companies already have the economies of scale to handle claims processing, whereas other business do not have the resources to do so.

A significant issue for a hospital is that a patient may have BCBS coverage but the plan is administered in another state. A typical national health insurance chain such as BCBS has clients throughout the country that may need medical care for a variety of reasons. A BCBS-insured patient who lives in Georgia and receives care at a hospital in South Carolina may have a different reimbursement rate than a BCBS patient from Ohio. To compensate for this discrepancy, the hospital in South Carolina will price the inpatient or outpatient services at BCBS South Carolina-negotiated rates rather than the Ohio or Georgia BCBS rates. In other words, it does not matter what state the patient is from if a patient has a national healthcare provider. The incorporated state in which the hospital resides will receive the same payment from the national provider regardless (see Table 7.1).

TRICARE

TRICARE is a managed health care program created by the Department of Defense that provides coverage to both active duty and retired members of the military. Covered organizations

Table 7.1 National Health Care Insurance Provider Example

	Patient A	*Patient B*
Patient residence	Georgia	Ohio
State where hospital services were provided	South Carolina	South Carolina
Reimbursement amount	South Carolina hospitals are paid at South Carolina rates for both patients	

would be the Army, Navy, Air Force, Marines, Coast Guard, U.S. Public Health Service, and the National Oceanic and Atmospheric Administration (2). Formerly known as CHAMPUS (Civilian Health and Medical Program of the Uniformed Services), TRICARE is available worldwide and managed domestically and internationally in six different regions. The United States is separated into three different regions, and they are managed by independent administrators (Triwest in the west, Health Net Federal in the north, and Humana Military in the south). Not only are active duty and retired members of the military eligible for TRICARE benefits but also the dependents of these individuals. These additional dependents may be spouses, children up to age 21, and children up to age 23 if they are full-time students. Patient access is the hospital department that verifies TRICARE coverage, and this usually is completed when the patient provides a Uniformed Services ID card. Another type of military identification is the Common Access Card (CAC); however, this ID does not prove TRICARE eligibility. In addition to reviewing the hospital military ID card, the patient access representative can verify through an online Web site that the patient is covered by TRICARE. A significant issue occurs when a patient is eligible for both Medicare and TRICARE benefits (dual eligible). A patient may be older than 65 and have accrued benefits through both insurance programs. Hospitals will classify Medicare as the primary payer and TRICARE as secondary; however, the patient must have purchased Part B benefits.

CRITICAL ISSUE

TRICARE is the secondary payer when beneficiaries are entitled to Medicare Part A and they purchase Medicare Part B benefits.

In other cases, a patient may be eligible for both TRICARE and Veterans Affairs benefits. In these cases, the patient has the option to use either program, but no duplicate payments will be made. In the TRICARE plan, there are three options for a patient to choose if the patient is less than 65 years of age:

1. TRICARE Prime
2. TRICARE Extra
3. TRICARE Standard

TRICARE Prime is very similar to a HMO in that beneficiaries select a primary care physician. TRICARE Extra is comparable to a PPO, while TRICARE Standard is much like a fee-for-service contract. In addition to these three options, the TRICARE for Life plan is available for all beneficiaries provided that they are entitled to Medicare Part A and they purchase Medicare Part B.

Unfortunately, hospitals do not have the ability to negotiate with the Department of Defense for reimbursement of services. A hospital that services TRICARE patients is classified as either participating or nonparticipating in that the facility either does or does not have a contractual relationship to administer treatment. A participating hospital agrees to the allowable reimbursement for services or what is termed the TRICARE allowable charge. By agreeing to the rates, a hospital "accepts assignment," and the facility is reimbursed on a claim-by-claim basis much like other providers. A nonparticipating hospital is a facility that has not agreed to the TRICARE rates and can possibly bill 15% above the allowable charge; however, this rarely occurs. For the most part, hospitals typically accept assignment and agree to the TRICARE allowable charges.

Much like an Advanced Beneficiary Notice for Medicare patients, TRICARE beneficiaries must be informed of the services that are not covered by their insurance and are subject to patient payment. Also known as a *hold harmless policy*, the hospital must obtain a signed legal waiver from the patient or all costs of care are absorbed by the facility. This waiver must be signed before care is provided. TRICARE predominantly pays for inpatient admissions using the DRG/APC methodology used by Medicare; however, there are some minor differences. TRICARE utilizes Value Options as a subcontractor that administers behavioral and psychological services for service-men and -women. The use of behavioral care for military personnel is extremely critical with soldiers returning from military operations and experiencing PTSD (post-traumatic stress disorder). Examples of behavioral care would be psychotherapy visits, medication management, and partial hospitalization for mental health/substance abuse.

TRICARE reimburses for outpatient services similar to the APC model by Medicare. This methodology is a change from the previous technique used prior to 2009. TRICARE also utilizes the RUG (Resource Utilization Group) rate for skilled nursing home admissions. The TRICARE outpatient system differs from Medicare in that certain deductible and coinsurance fees are eliminated, and other services such as oncology-related procedures are reimbursed on a fee-for-service basis. Hospitals are required to submit all claims electronically, and claims must be submitted within 1 year from the date of service. A significant issue is that TRICARE is a secondary payer to all health benefits plans with the exception of Medicaid.

CRITICAL ISSUE

TRICARE is a secondary payer to all health benefits plans with the exception of Medicaid.

Much like the Medicare pass-through payment, an additional receivable is set up for TRICARE patients and is based on total TRICARE days divided by total hospital days. This percentage is multiplied by both the capital and GME (graduate medical education) costs for an additional annual payment to the hospital. The educational costs are derived from residents, whereas capital costs are basically depreciation expenses. Any hospital (for profit or not for profit) can file for the additional TRICARE funds, but the teaching facility must have TRICARE days to receive the money.

Workers' Compensation

The workers' compensation laws that exist are designed to relieve employers from liability involving negligence in exchange for becoming responsible for medical costs. As a federally enforced law, companies must have a workers' compensation plan that insures employees from injury. The purpose behind the workers' compensation laws is to minimize interaction with lawyers and court trials by providing a single remedy and income/benefits to work-related injury victims. The methodology to how worker's compensation is administered can vary depending on the circumstances. If an employee is injured while working, then he or she can file a workers' compensation claim regardless of how the injury occurred. The employee is entitled to all hospitalization services, but sometimes a patient must see the doctor that is chosen by the employer or the insurance representative. Rules vary state to state, but usually employees are notified about the status of their claim within 7 days of the reported injury. A significant issue regarding workers' compensation is that the employee is not entitled to benefits unless the employer has been notified of the injury as soon as possible after it occurs. An employee cannot notify a supervisor of a work-related injury several weeks after it occurred. Dependents of employees who die as a result of a work-related injury may also be eligible for benefits.

In a hospital environment, the billing methodology for a workers' compensation patient is different from that for other insurance carriers. When a patient is seen for any work-related injury, the hospital will first bill the patient's insurance (if any) for reimbursement. The insurance company will perform due diligence and realize that if it is work related, then the hospital needs to bill that employee's workers' compensation provider rather than the insurance provider. *Workers' compensation is a form of strict liability in that no fault needs to be shown.* The cost of workers' compensation flows through as an operating expense through the company in which the victim/worker is employed. In terms of reimbursement, the workers' compensation insurance provider is seen as another insurance carrier. Historically, the reimbursement from a workers' compensation provider is the Medicare rate plus a certain percentage, such as 30% or 40%. This additional percentage varies by state, but typically it is an add-on to the Medicare rate for both inpatient and outpatient services.

CRITICAL ISSUE

An insurance carrier will transfer a claim to an employer's workers' compensation insurance carrier if it is work related. Workers' compensation is a form of strict liability in which no fault needs to be shown.

Veterans Affairs

Otherwise known as CHAMPVA (Civilian Health and Medical Program of the Department of Veterans Affairs), this program is responsible for providing coverage to qualified veterans who are not eligible for TRICARE. This patient population can consist of a veteran or the spouse or child of a veteran who either has died or become disabled. A majority of hospitals classify CHAMPVA as secondary to Medicare if the patient is Medicare eligible. *Hospitals that participate in the Medicare program are required by law to accept CHAMPVA patients for inpatient hospital services.* Patients rarely have any out-of-pocket expenses in the CHAMPVA program; however, they are responsible for an annual deductible, which is approximately $50 per year or a maximum of $100 per year per family.

To accommodate the number of military families, the government has created a specific healthcare facility that handles those who have or had an affiliation with the military. Termed a VA (Veterans Affairs) hospital, the presence of these hospitals has become increasingly significant with soldiers returning from the wars in Iraq and Afghanistan. Even though these facilities perform extensive medical procedures, the VA hospital is often considered more of a skilled nursing home than a hospital because high-acuity procedures are usually performed elsewhere. A VA hospital usually performs some surgical procedures and has multiple behavioral health services, but complex procedures are often completed at nearby hospitals. Typically, the VA pays other hospitals a variation of DRG/per diem reimbursement for such high-end services. A significant component of VA hospital reimbursement is the use of POS (point-of-stabilization) model. *The POS model pays hospitals to a certain point or time period in the patient's treatment.* For example, if a VA hospital-qualifying patient enters a hospital emergency room and is admitted, then the VA may only pay a per diem amount until the point of stabilization, which is based on the acuity of care. The POS can vary from 1 day to several days based on the cause of the patient's admission. The justification for the POS reimbursement model is that the VA theoretically can handle the care needed for the patient after the individual has been stabilized by the hospital. Usually, hospitals are not reimbursed for any services or procedures after the point of stabilization.

Conclusion

Throughout the country, there are various insurance carriers that negotiate with hospitals to provide services for their clients. Unfortunately, it is not feasible to discuss each insurance plan, but a majority of companies reimburse healthcare facilities by mimicking existing methodologies, such as Medicare's DRG/APC system. Other carriers have introduced a percentage-of-charge structure or strictly adhere to a per diem model. Regardless of the reimbursement structure, the hospital must be able to sustain operations despite the numerous carriers that pay hospitals varying amounts. Managed care contracts must be carefully negotiated and examined by hospital staff to ensure that the contract is manageable and equitable.

References

1. About the Blue Cross Blue Shield Association. http://www.bcbs.com/about-the-association/ (accessed November 26, 2011).
2. What is TRICARE? http://tricare.mil/mybenefit/ProfileFilter.do?puri=%2Fhome%2Foverview%2FWhatIsTRICARE (accessed November 26, 2011).

Chapter 8

Governmental Cost Reporting

Introduction

One of the more significant yet less-understood aspects of hospital reimbursement is the formulation of the **Medicare cost report**. The cost report is similar in concept to a tax return, and its completion is mandatory if a hospital participates in the Medicare program. *Of all the chapters in this text, the cost-reporting component is the most important because there is little information currently available that addresses this topic.* Regardless of how a hospital is incorporated, a facility must submit the Medicare cost report 5 months after the fiscal year ends. Many hospitals do not have the necessary resources or personnel to complete the cost report, so they outsource its completion to healthcare consulting firms that specialize in cost reporting. The benefits of outsourcing the cost report is that external consultants are aware of recent changes in Medicare regulations; since many firms solely work in hospital reimbursement, they have more expertise on how to complete the report. The downside to outsourcing is that the hospital has a loss of control, and management may not be cognizant of all the factors that affect hospital reimbursement.

The annual cost report is formulated using a step-down methodology that attempts to find the costs of performing hospital services. These costs are allocated into groupings to find a cost-to-charge ratio for each specific clinical grouping. The cost-to-charge ratio statistic is arguably the most significant component of the cost report and hospital reimbursement. The annual cost report reflects the activity of the hospital in that time period; however, certain expenses are excluded. The source data for all costs reported are derived from the general ledger, and the cost report classifies expenses as either allowable or nonallowable. The cost-to-charge ratios are created by formulating data from treating all patients, not just Medicare or Medicaid patients. *The cost report has numerous purposes; however, the primary objective is to formulate the cost of providing care to both Medicare and Medicaid patients.* This cost information is vital to the federal government because the Department of Health and Human Services can compare what was actually paid to the expected cost of providing treatment. In other words, the information compiled in the annual cost report is used as a measure to determine the gap between payment and cost. Other managed care insurance companies use the information provided in the cost report as a negotiation tool when dealing with hospital systems. In addition, most state-administered Medicaid agencies reimburse at either cost or a percentage of cost, which makes the cost report a critical document in formulating hospital payments for Medicaid patients. Other reimbursement concepts such as Disproportionate Share Hospital (DSH) and indirect medical education (IME) reported in the Medicare blend rate are also formulated in the cost report.

CRITICAL ISSUE

The cost-to-charge ratios formulated in the cost report are derived from expenses used to treat all patients in the hospital, not just Medicare and Medicaid patients.

Prior to 2011, all hospitals were required to submit the report via governmental Form 2552-96. This form was recently revised; starting in 2011, all hospitals are required to submit a form 2552-10. The changes from the 96 to the 10 form are not extensive, and the overall methodology remains the same; however, additional worksheets and groupings were added to the report to improve simplicity and comparability. Electronic filing of the cost report is mandatory, and both the chief executive officer (CEO) and chief financial officer (CFO) of the hospital must sign the document to ensure its authenticity. Several vendors offer software that can be purchased, like HFS (Healthcare Financial Services), but the vendor software must be approved by the federal government.

For most facilities, the annual cost report is due 5 months after their fiscal year end, and it is electronically submitted to the hospital's MAC (Medicare administrative contractor). Extensions for filing a cost report are allowed; however, if the document is not filed on time and no extension is requested, then the government will severely penalize a hospital. In 2011, the government penalized a hospital with a 100% reduction in payment if an extension was not appropriately requested. The MAC is responsible for auditing and settling the Medicare cost report, and a tentative settlement is usually given to facilities 60 days after the filing date if the hospital is owed funds. However, if a hospital actually owes money to the federal government, then the MAC will request that a check be mailed immediately.

In this text, a sample cost report is formulated using the appropriate worksheets. Not every worksheet in the cost report is referenced; however, the usual and customary worksheets are addressed. Other worksheets could be used, but that depends on the size of the facility and services offered. The cost report worksheets primarily addressed (and displayed) in this chapter are:

Worksheet A, A-6, A-8, A-8-2
Worksheet B-1, B Part 1
Worksheet C Part 1
Worksheet D-3, D-5
Worksheet E Part A

The initial documents in the cost report ask numerous yes/no questions about the hospital; they are labeled *S worksheets*. These questions pertain to whether the facility is a teaching hospital or if specific subproviders are being included. Basically, the more questions that are answered "yes" will require more worksheets in the cost report. Additional components in Worksheet S ask for statistical data, such as patient days and FTEs (full-time equivalents). The primary components of Worksheet S are S-1 through S-4; however, some facilities may use Worksheets S-5 through S-10. The data entered in all the S worksheets are pertinent to the completion of the cost report, but for this text an examination of Worksheet S is omitted to concentrate on Worksheets A through E.

It is very difficult to explain and formulate an entire Medicare cost report within one chapter. After reading this chapter, one should have an <u>improved but not complete</u> understanding of the annual hospital cost report.

Worksheet A

The initial worksheet in the cost report is Worksheet A, which classifies expenses from the trial balance into both clinical and nonclinical groupings. The expense groupings in Worksheet A are segregated into subgroupings such as General Service Costs, Inpatient Service Costs, and Ancillary Service Costs. Lines 1 and 2 in the General Service Costs are listed as "Capital-Related Costs." These lines replace the "new and old capital" expense listings from Form 2552-96, and they encompass all the depreciation expense and possibly interest expense in the facility. A major change in classification groupings from 2552-96 to 2552-10 is that new specific groupings for implantable devices charged to patients, magnetic resonance imaging (MRI), and computed tomography (CT) scan are available. Previously, the MRI and CT scanner costs were lumped into the radiology diagnostic line, and implants were classified in medical supplies. *Even though Medicare has listed several account groupings, it is the responsibility of the hospital to determine what is classified in each line item.* Some lines may have to be added to Worksheet A, while some may not be used at all. The additional line items that need to be added are referred to as subscripts. The classification of expenses is often driven by the size and acuity of services provided at the facility. A significant attribute of Worksheet A is that it separates costs into "salary" and "other" components. A hospital should always retain the source data for how Worksheet A was formulated for each fiscal year. Medicare auditors will request a *crosswalk* that acts as a justification for how trial balance accounts were grouped into the appropriate cost report line items. Generally, the hospital trial balance should tie back into Worksheet A less bad debt and contractual expense. The classification of expenses in Worksheet A should be consistent from year to year, and the crosswalk figure should be used as a reference tool when any new general ledger expense codes are added.

CRITICAL ISSUE

The expenses listed in the hospital trial balance should tie back to the expenses listed in Worksheet A of the cost report less the bad debt and contractual expense.

A sample listing of a hypothetical hospital's trial balance is listed in Table 8.1. Most hospitals will have a much larger listing of departments, but for this sample cost report, the following amounts are given: Revenues are listed as negative; expenses are listed as positives. Reference to the appropriate cost report worksheet is given next to the expenses.

The trial balance represents all the hospital ledger accounts for that fiscal year. The expense figures listed in the trial balance need to be classified in Worksheet A of the cost report (less the contractual amount and bad debt expense). From this trial balance, a loss of $265,000 is formulated; total salary and non-salary-related expenses are $33,265,000. The $33,265,000 in total hospital expense ties to the total amount listed in Table 8.2 (Worksheet A), line 29, column 3. (All cost report worksheets are at the end of this chapter.)

Table 8.1   Trial Balance for County Hospital: Fiscal Year 1

Adult and Pediatrics–Inpatient Revenue	($15,000,000), WKST C
Adult and Pediatrics–Salary Expense	$2,000,000, WKST A, Line A
Adult and Pediatrics–Employee Benefits	$400,000, WKST A, Line B
Adult and Pediatrics–Supply Expense	$800,000, WKST A, Line C
Adult and Pediatrics–Drugs	$50,000, WKST A, Line T
Adults and Pediatrics–Professional Fees	$50,000, WKST A, Line C, and WKST A-8-2
Nursery–Inpatient Revenue	($8,000,000), WKST C
Nursery–Salary Expense	$1,000,000, WKST A, Line D
Nursery–Employee Benefits	$200,000, WKST A, Line B
Nursery–Supply Expense	$400,000, WKST A, Line E
Nursery–Drugs	$25,000, WKST A, Line T
Nursery–Professional Fees	$20,000, WKST A, Line E, and WKST A-8-2
ICU–Inpatient Revenue	($7,500,000), WKST C
ICU–Salary Expense	$1,200,000, WKST A, Line F
ICU–Employee Benefits	$120,000, WKST A, Line B
ICU–Supply Expense	$350,000, WKST A, Line G
ICU–Profession Fees	$50,000, WKST A, Line G, and WKST A-8-2
ICU–Other Expenses	$100,000, WKST A, Line G
ICU–Drugs	$50,000, WKST A, Line T
Operating Room–Inpatient Revenue	($5,000,000), WKST C
Operating Room–Outpatient Revenue	($10,000,000), WKST C
Operating Room–Salary Expense	$1,800,000, WKST A, Line H
Operating Room–Employee Benefits	$200,000, WKST A, Line B
Operating Room–Supply Expense	$400,000, WKST A, Line I
Operating Room–Other Expenses	$200,000, WKST A, Line I
Operating Room–Implants	$600,000, WKST A, Line I, and WKST A-6
Operating Room–Drugs	$50,000, WKST A, Line T
Operating Room–CRNA Expense	$200,000, WKST A, Line I, and WKST A-8
Laboratory–Inpatient Revenue	($4,000,000), WKST C
Laboratory–Outpatient Revenue	($3,000,000), WKST C

(Continued)

Table 8.1 (Continued) Trial Balance for County Hospital: Fiscal Year 1

Laboratory–Salary Expense	$800,000, WKST A, Line K
Laboratory–Employee Benefits	$90,000, WKST A, Line B
Laboratory–Supply Expense	$300,000, WKST A, Line L
Laboratory–Other Expense	$200,000, WKST A, Line L
MRI–Inpatient Revenue	($5,000,000), WKST C
MRI–Outpatient Revenue	($3,000,000), WKST C
MRI–Salary Expense	$1,100,000, WKST A, Line M
MRI–Employee Benefits	$110,000, WKST A, Line B
MRI–Supply Expense	$350,000, WKST A, Line N
MRI–Other Expenses	$120,000, WKST A, Line N
MRI–Professional Fees	$15,000, WKST A, Line N, and WKST A-8-2
ER–Inpatient Revenue	($2,000,000), WKST C
ER–Outpatient Revenue	($5,000,000), WKST C
ER–Salary Expense	$400,000, WKST A, Line O
ER–Employee Benefits	$40,000, WKST A, Line B
ER–Supply Expense	$900,000, WKST A, Line P
ER–Other Expenses	$1,120,000, WKST A, Line P
Physical Therapy–Inpatient Revenue	($5,000,000), WKST C
Physical Therapy–Outpatient Revenue	($3,000,000), WKST C
Physical Therapy–Salary Expense	$900,000, WKST A, Line Q
Physical Therapy–Employee Benefits	$90,000, WKST A, Line B
Physical Therapy–Supply Expense	$400,000, WKST A, Line R
Physical Therapy–Loss on Sale of Medical Equipment	$500,000, WKST A, Line R, and WKST A-8
Physical Therapy–Other Expenses	$200,000, WKST A, Line R
Administration–Rental Income	($1,000,000), WKST A-8
Administration–Cafeteria Sales	($1,500,000), WKST A-8
Administration–Salary Expense	$7,000,000, WKST A, Line S
Administration–Contractual Expense	$40,000,000, EXCLUDED
Administration–Bad Debt Expense	$5,000,000, EXCLUDED

(Continued)

Table 8.1 (Continued)   Trial Balance for County Hospital: Fiscal Year 1

Administration–Employee Benefits	$200,000, WKST A, Line B
Administration–Other Expenses	$1,200,000, WKST A, Line U
Administration–Depreciation–Building	$2,000,000, WKST A, Line U, and WKST A-6
Administration–Depreciation–Equipment	$3,000,000, WKST A, Line U, and WKST A-6
Medical Records–Salary Expense	$650,000, WKST A, Line V
Medical Records–Employee Benefits	$50,000, WKST A, Line B
Medical Records–Supply Expense	$200,000, WKST A, Line W
Medical Records–Other Expense	$125,000, WKST A, Line W
Maintenance–Salary Expense	$400,000, WKST A, Line X
Maintenance–Employee Benefits	$40,000, WKST A, Line B
Maintenance–Supply Expense	$100,000, WKST A, Line Y
Maintenance–Other Expense	$25,000, WKST A, Line Y
Pharmacy–Salary Expense	$200,000, WKST A, Line Z
Pharmacy–Employee Benefits	$50,000, WKST A, Line B
Pharmacy–Supply Expense	$100,000, WKST A, Line AA
Pharmacy–Other Expense	$25,000, WKST A, Line AA
Trial Balance Total	**$265,000 LOSS**

CRNA, certified registered nurse anesthetist; WKST, Worksheet.

Worksheet A-6

The purpose of Worksheet A-6 is to reclassify certain costs that are embedded in expenses reported on Worksheet A but need to be reclassed to a more appropriate grouping. The reclassifications in this worksheet should always sum to zero in that any addition to one grouping should be eliminated from another grouping. An example of an A-6 reclass would be the reclass of any depreciation expense recorded in Worksheet A that is not listed in the capital-related costs line item. This expense would be subtracted from another grouping and added to the capital line. Another example would be to reclass any radiology administration salary expense that may be embedded in one imaging department but responsible for managing all imaging departments. Using some allocation method such as a time motion study, the salary expense of the radiology manager would be allocated to all imaging departments based on percentage of time spent managing these departments. A more appropriate measure of cost allocation would be to use the number of hours spent managing, but that can be a difficult task because the supervisor may not have created a time log of hours spent managing each specific department. The allocation method that is used in Worksheet A-6 is pertinent to the cost report because auditors may ask to see the source data used to formulate the specific cost allocations. Another example of an A-6 reclass that is new in 2011 would be the reclass to the new line item "implantable devices charged to patients." Historically, these expenses were classified to medical supplies; however, the Form 2552-10 has created a new listing for this cost. Hospital accountants need to use the A-6 worksheet to reclass any implants used during surgery to the newly designated line item. The primary purpose of Worksheet A-6 is to make the appropriate cost reclasses to ensure that the hospital's cost structure is accurate.

CRITICAL ISSUE

Cost report auditors will ask for the source data and methodology used when costs are reclassified in Worksheet A-6.

Table 8.3 in the sample cost report lists three A-6 reclasses, which are moving depreciation from the administration department to the capital-related line item and reclassing implants from the operating room to its appropriate line item. The $600,000 of implant cost was previously listed in the operating room; however, this cost is now reclassed to the implantable device line. Also, $5,000,000 in depreciation expense is reclassed from the administration line to the capital line. These A-6 reclasses are embedded in column 4 of Worksheet A, and the net amount of the reclasses is equal to zero.

Worksheet A-8

The primary purpose of Worksheet A-8 (Table 8.4) is to eliminate the nonallowable costs listed in Worksheet A that are not directly related to patient care. Worksheet A-8 is often considered the most troublesome of all the cost report worksheets because there is not one all-inclusive source to what needs to be adjusted. *In Worksheet A-8, the costs that are not related to patient care are eliminated from the cost report so that they do not affect the cost-to-charge ratios needed to formulate the cost of patient care.* Different hospitals make different cost adjustments, but there are several A-8 adjustments that a majority of hospitals share. One example would be the cost of patient telephones and televisions in patient rooms. These expenses are common in almost all hospitals, but the federal government believes that these costs are not related to patient care and they should be eliminated from the cost report. The method to find these telephone/television costs may be time consuming, so it would be prudent for hospital staff to begin finding and tracking these expenses several months prior to the cost report deadline. Another common ledger item that is eliminated from the cost report are any gains or losses recorded during that fiscal year. These gains/losses usually relate to a sale of equipment or land that it is not related to patient care. A third type of cost that is eliminated relates to any marketing or advertising expenses, with the exception of "yellow page" advertising. The government will allow hospitals to include advertising expenses used in a phone book as long as it is not excessive. The government also allows a hospital to include any marketing or advertising expenses if they were used to promote a service that benefits the community. A gray area exists for this cost elimination because a hospital may pay for advertising to promote the benefits of prostrate screening but may also be soliciting patients to visit that hospital for other purposes. It is at the discretion of that hospital (and eventually the auditor) to determine if the marketing expense is truly for the promotion of the public's interest or the hospital's interest. A fourth type of expense that is eliminated is any lobbying fees paid by the hospital. Any contributions or donations made by the hospital are also removed in Worksheet A-8. Legal fees related to patient care are allowable, but most other legal expenses are not allowable. For example, if a hospital incurs legal expenses to purchase a physician practice or merge with another hospital, then these costs would not be allowed.

In Worksheet A-8, the largest component of expenses that need to be removed is the costs associated with producing nonoperating income. Such expenses would be for parking lot fees and cafeteria sales. *The methodology to remove these expenses can be done at either their cost or their revenue, whichever is easier to compute for the hospital.* In column 1 of Table 8.4, the basis code can be either 1 (cost) or 2 (revenue) to eliminate the items from the report. Another significant expense that is typically allowable is hospital interest expense. This operating expense is not included in the cost report if the borrowing is unnecessary, not related to patient care or incurred to make repayments to Medicare. The allowable interest cost included in Worksheet A-8 can be complicated in that if the hospital board of directors borrows money to add another building, then that interest expense would be included or allowable in the cost report. However, if that hospital already had sufficient funds to construct the building, then Medicare will state that the borrowing was unnecessary, and the interest expense cannot be included.

Lines 13, 15, and 26 in Worksheet A-8 (Table 8.4) list the revenue formulated from cafeteria sales, a gain on the sale of physical therapy equipment, and rental income. These amounts are carved out of the figures used to create a cost-to-charge ratio. The $3,000,000 in adjustments is also listed in column 6 of Worksheet A. In the sample cost report, the Worksheet A-8 reclasses are listed at their charge, not their cost (basis code of 2).

CRITICAL ISSUE

The significance of Worksheet A-8 is that certain nonallowable costs are eliminated from the cost report. The removal of costs is detrimental to the hospital because the more costs that are included in the report the higher the cost-to-charge ratio will be.

There are numerous other expenses that can be listed in Table 8.4 depending on the complexity of services used by a hospital. A common expense that needs to be eliminated is the employment or outsourcing of certified registered nurse anesthetists (CRNAs), which would be listed on line 22 (Table 8.4) of Worksheet A-8. For the mock cost report, $200,000 of CRNA fees are eliminated from the cost-to-charge computation. The expense can be substantial if a hospital performs a significant amount of surgeries. Another possible eliminating expense would be in line item 18 (Table 8.4), which lists any tuition or fees for a nursing school. This expense listing would only exist if a hospital employed a nursing school.

A significant component of the cost report is that correlating line items in Worksheet A must reference the line items in other worksheets. Column 4 in Worksheet A-8 references specific line items in Worksheet A. The elimination of $500,000 due to the sale of physical therapy equipment in A-8 is referenced in line 21, column 6, of Worksheet A. In addition, the rental income and cafeteria sales eliminated in A-8 are referenced in line 4, column 6, of Worksheet A. These line items must match throughout the entire cost report process.

CRITICAL ISSUE

A significant component of the cost report is that line items in Worksheet A must reference the correlating line items in other worksheets.

Worksheet A-8-1

The primary purpose of Worksheet A-8-1 is to list any related party transactions. The worksheet lists any information regarding the home office cost, which would be any corporate costs. Some healthcare systems have numerous hospitals in a consolidated umbrella, and they have a separate entity for corporate expenses, such as accounting, human resources, information technology, and other departments that are nonclinical in nature. If the corporate entity exists, then facilities are required to complete a separate *home office cost report* that needs to be filed with that hospital's MAC just like any other cost report. The home office cost report would have a trial balance just like any other hospital except there would not be any clinical revenues. Occasionally, there might be some nonoperating revenue, such as rental income in a corporate entity, but this amount should be offset by the cost. The expenses reported in the home office cost report would be allocated to the other hospitals in that healthcare system's structure based on some type of allocation method. For the sample cost report examined in this text, we assume that this county hospital is a stand-alone facility, and a separate home office cost report is not required.

Worksheet A-8-2

Worksheet A-8-2 (Table 8.5) is utilized to eliminate the Medicare Part B physician expenses because the government has already paid the doctor for the Part B services. The physician absorbed the cost of providing these services rather than the hospital. The issue with formulating these physician expenses is that it is often time consuming and difficult for a hospital to track all the correlating hours relating to each hospital physician's Part B expense. Medicaid (not Medicare) auditors will certainly look at Worksheet A-8-2 and ask for a log of the specific hours reported, so it would be prudent for a hospital not to estimate a figure. Medicaid will examine the A-8-2 worksheet in detail since most states are reimbursed at cost by Medicaid. Medicare auditors will probably not be concerned with the worksheet since Medicare is not cost reimbursed. A recent revision to the cost report is that medical directorships or medical director fees are included in the cost report computation. These directorship expenses are not directly attributable to a patient, and they are more administrative related, yet the federal government has allowed them to be included in the cost report, which will benefit a hospital.

CRITICAL ISSUE

Expenses related to medical directorships are included in the cost report; however, Part B physician-related expenses are excluded.

In Worksheet A-8-2 (Table 8.5) of the Medicare cost report, $135,000 of professional fees have been eliminated. These Part B physician expenses were listed in the hospital trial balance as professional fees, and the amounts are listed by department in Worksheet A-8-2. These expenses are also listed in column 6 of Worksheet A-8 (line items 13, 14, 15, and 19).

Worksheet A-7

Worksheet A-7 provides a reconciliation of balances; it represents more of a roll forward from previous years. Worksheet A-7 is primarily for informational purposes, and it does not affect the outcome of any cost-to-charge ratios. The three parts of the worksheet are the changes in capital asset balances, a reconciliation from Worksheet A, and a reconciliation of capital cost centers. Worksheet A-7 is not included in this text's sample cost report because it does not affect the final cost report computation.

Worksheet B-1

The purpose of Worksheet B-1 is to enter the statistical data needed to allocate the total expenses of the general service cost centers entered in Worksheet A, column 7 (line items 1–12). A cost driver must be chosen as a means to allocate the appropriate cost to the remaining cost centers. The statistical method used to allocate these overhead costs *cannot* be changed on a year-to-year basis without approval from the MAC. The reasoning for this is that auditors like to see consistency from year to year. A request to change the statistical method must be submitted no later than 90 days before the hospital's fiscal year end. The revised method must also support a more accurate way of allocating cost. The federal government does not provide a list of the criteria to allocate costs; however, a brief listing is given in Table 8.6.

Table 8.7 in the sample cost report is Worksheet B-1, which lists the statistical basis for each general service cost, and each column represents the total amount separated by cost center. In this sample cost report, we are assuming that 500,000 square feet exists for this hospital and that the engineering department in that facility measured the footage of each cost center to determine the appropriate size amounts. Columns 1, 2, and 5 of Worksheet B-1 list the square footage by cost grouping, which totals 500,000. Researching the total amount of square feet in a hospital is a tedious process due to the time and effort it takes. Many hospitals outsource this function to a third party, and the only updates to total square feet occur when significant transfers of space occur.

Table 8.6 Sample Cost Drivers

Expense	Cost Allocation Methodology
Equipment and buildings	Square footage
Housekeeping	Square footage
Laundry	Pounds used
Dietary	Meals served
Pharmacy	Drug requests

CRITICAL ISSUE

Worksheet B-1 only contains statistical information that is needed to allocate overhead costs to the appropriate cost centers.

Column 3 of Table 8.7 lists the employee benefit expense, which is usually allocated based on gross salary. Columns 10 and 11 list the pharmacy and medical record expenses, which are respectively pushed down using drug requests and time spent as cost drivers. These general service grouping costs are pushed or stepped down to other clinical groupings. A significant issue is that administrative/general expenses are allocated based on **accumulated cost**. The accumulated cost is the subtotal of the other general service cost groupings that are allocated after the other expenses have been allocated. In this sample cost report, we assume that accumulated cost consists of the depreciation and employee benefit expense. The treatment of the administrative/general expense exemplifies the "step-down" cost approach in that certain expenses must be allocated first before an accumulated total can be formulated.

The total salary expense that is listed in column 3, line 29, of Worksheet B-1 (Table 8.7) is formulated from column 1, line 29, of Worksheet A less the employee benefits ($17,450,000 = $19,040,000 − $1,590,000). This proportion-to-total figure will allocate the employee benefit expense to the appropriate cost grouping. For example, the total salary expense in adult/pediatrics (column 3, line item 13 of Table 8.7) is $2,000,000, which is 11.4613% ($2,000,000/$17,450,000) of the total salary expense amount. Therefore, the amount of employee benefit expense pushed down to the adult/pediatric cost center would be $182,235 (line 13, column 3) in Worksheet B Part 1. (0.114613 * $1,590,000).

CRITICAL ISSUE

A Medicare auditor will not spend much time on Worksheets A or B; a Medicaid auditor will spend a substantial amount of time reviewing the data. The reason is that Medicaid is primarily cost reimbursed. Medicare auditors will primarily concentrate on bad debt and DSH.

Worksheet B Part 1

Worksheet B Part 1 is an extension of Worksheet B-1 in that the overhead expenses are allocated to clinical departments based on the statistical figures entered in Worksheet B-1. The overhead amounts are pushed down to clinical areas based on a particular statistic, such as square footage. The figures in Worksheet B Part 1 are usually system generated by the cost report software, and they need not be keyed in to the report. This worksheet exhibits the cost-accounting aspect of the report in that the overhead costs used to maintain hospital operations are proportionately allocated to clinical cost groupings.

Table 8.8 represents the dollar values of the general service cost centers that need to be allocated to the appropriate clinical departments. In line 29, column 0, the $29,930,000 represents the total costs pulled from Worksheet A. The general service costs in lines 1 through 12 need to be pushed down to the other clinical cost centers (lines 13 through 28). The first items to be allocated are the depreciation expenses, which are located in columns 1 and 2 of Table 8.8. The total expenses of $2,000,000 and $3,000,000 are pushed down to the appropriate cost centers based on their listed square footage amount in Worksheet B-1. The third cost to be allocated is employee benefits, listed in column 3 of Table 8.8. The allocation method to push down these expenses is driven by the total salary costs listed in Table 8.7 or Worksheet B-1. Both the depreciation and the benefit expenses are subtotaled in column 4 before any additional allocations are made. The justification for this subtotal is that administrative and general expenses are often pushed down based on accumulated cost.

In column 5, line 4, of Table 8.8, the accumulated cost total of $6,587,822 is allocated to all other departments based on the figures accumulated in column 4. The $6,587,822 is a combination of the original $5,700,000 listed in column 0 and the additional stepped down costs of $100,000, $150,000, and $637,822 in columns 1, 2, and 3. The maintenance and repairs, pharmacy, and medical records figures listed in columns 6, 7, and 8 are allocated using a statistical base listed in Worksheet B-1; however, the pharmacy expense is only pushed down to line 24 "drugs charged to patients." These expenses are horizontally totaled, and the total amount in line 29 of column 9 should equal line item 29 in column 0. (In the sample cost report, it would be $29,930,000.)

CRITICAL ISSUE

The total expense figure in Worksheet A must equal the total expense figure in Worksheet B Part 1. The only difference between the two would be the allocation of overhead costs to clinical groupings. The total would not change.

The step down of administrative/general accumulated cost can be a difficult concept to grasp if the reader does not have an intermediate understanding of cost accounting. Each line item grouping is actually increasing as other general service costs are allocated. In addition, the general service costs that remain to be allocated (maintenance/repairs and medical records) will also increase before they are appropriately pushed down. In column 0, line item 11 of Table 8.8, the total medical records expense was $975,000; however, the expense figure increased to $1,472,892 (column 8) before it was actually pushed down. As previously stated, cost report software will automatically allocate these general service costs to the clinical groupings, so the hospital accountant need not be able to compute these figures manually.

Worksheet B Parts 2 and 3

Historically, the capital costs in a hospital were classified as either "new" or "old" capital. The purpose of Worksheet B Part 2 was to contain the new capital where Worksheet B Part 3 contained all old capital costs. This classification was pertinent in Centers for Medicare and Medicaid Services (CMS) Form 2552-96, but this has changed with the implementation of Form 2552-10. Beginning in 2011, the old and new capital designations were replaced by line items in Worksheet A.

Worksheet C

The purpose of Worksheet C of the Medicare cost report is to formulate a cost-to-charge ratio for hospital services. The starting point for Worksheet C is the gross patient revenue pulled from the trial balance; however, a crosswalk of gross to adjusted gross revenue must be formulated before any entries can be made. A significant weakness of Worksheet C is that a summary worksheet or crosswalk must be separately created because several charge reclasses must occur before a charge amount can be placed in the denominator of the cost-to-charge ratio. For example, all Part B physician *expenses* were removed in Worksheet A-8-2, but all Part B physician *charges* also need to be removed from the cost report. Columns 2 and 7 of Table 8.9 list the inpatient and outpatient professional fee charges related to physicians. These professional fee charges are embedded in the total charges listed in the trial balance, and they need to be eliminated from the cost report.

Professional Fees That Need to Be Removed from the Mock Cost Report in Worksheet C

Line Item	Revenue Detail	IP Charges	OP Charges
26 ER	Rev Code 981 Prof Fees ER	($100,000)	($110,000)
16 OR	Rev Code 960 Prof Fees CRNA	($400,000)	($200,000)

Note: ER, emergency room; IP, inpatient; OP, outpatient; OR, operating room; Prof, professional; Rev, revenue.

A majority of the professional fees that need to be eliminated from the cost report are found in UB-04 revenue codes 960 through 985 (Professional Fees). Additional adjustments in Worksheet C would be reclasses for drug charges, implant charges, or medical supply charges that are charged in one department or line item but need to be reclassed to another. A sample listing of these types of changes are listed below.

Line Item	Revenue Detail	IP Charges	OP Charges
13 Adult/Ped	Rev Code 250 Pharmacy General	($1,200,000)	
14 ICU	Rev Code 250 Pharmacy General	($750,000)	
16 OR	Rev Code 250 Pharmacy General ($200,000)	($400,000)	
19 MRI	Rev Code 250 Pharmacy General	($50,000)	($25,000)
20 Lab	Rev Code 250 Pharmacy General	($50,000)	($50,000)
26 ER	Rev Code 250 Pharmacy General	($150,000)	($500,000)
24 Drugs	Rev Code 250 Pharmacy General	$2,400,000	$975,000
16 OR	Rev Code 360 OR Services	($800,000)	
23 Implants	Rev Code 360 OR Services	$800,000	
Net		$0	$0

Note: ICU, intensive care unit; Ped, pediatric.

Columns 3 and 8 of Table 8.9 list all the drug charges located in clinical groupings that need to be reclassed to the "drugs charged to patients" line item ($2,400,000 to $975,000). The medical supply reclasses in columns 4 and 9 represent the transfer of the hip/knee implant charges from the operating room to the implantable device line item ($800,000). *Columns 5 and 10 of Table 8.9 represent the total inpatient and outpatient charges after adjustments; these figures are keyed into Worksheet C Part 1 of Table 8.10.* By making the appropriate reclassifications, each line item in Worksheet C contains the accurate amount of charges. These inpatient and outpatient gross charge figures are utilized to formulate a hospitalwide cost-to-charge ratio. The crosswalk or source data used to formulate the charge figures in Worksheet C must be maintained since cost report auditors will ask for the source data to determine how these net charge figures were formulated.

Once the source data for Worksheet C is compiled, the hospital accountant need only key in gross inpatient charges (column 6) and gross outpatient (column 7) charges from Table 8.9 into Table 8.10. The remainder of the worksheet will formulate the ratios automatically. The total cost by grouping ($29,930,000) will be in column 1, line 26, of Worksheet C Part 1, and this information is automatically pulled from Worksheet B Part 1. This cost figure consists of all variable and fixed expenses of patient care. Column 2 in Worksheet C Part 1 is classified as "Therapy Limit Adjustment," and this column is used if a hospital outsourced its therapy services to a third party at a substantial cost. Medicare placed a cap on the therapy cost outsourced, and this usually affects only small hospitals. Column 4 is the "RCE Disallowance," which is the cap limit placed by Medicare for physician salaries associated with Part A services. The amount of RCE allowance varies on the type of physician. A cost-to-charge ratio for each line item can be formulated once the inpatient and outpatient gross charge figures are entered. Column 11 of Table 8.10 lists the appropriate cost-to-charge ratio for each clinical grouping.

CRITICAL ISSUE

The Worksheets A through C encompass the cost-finding process of the Medicare cost report. These cost-to-charge ratios are used as a mechanism to determine the appropriate amount of cost to treat patients.

Worksheet D

The primary purpose of the documents in Worksheet D is to formulate an expected cost of providing service. Worksheets A through C were utilized to formulate a cost-to-charge ratio that can be multiplied against charges to find expected cost. The charges for Medicare services are derived from the government-issued *Provider Statistics and Reimbursement* (PSR) reports that list all the charges and payments for that particular hospital. Worksheet D-1 creates a per diem figure for the hospital services; this is formulated through the cost-reporting software. A hospital accountant would not have to enter any data in this worksheet. Worksheet D-1 is significant because in contrast to ancillary services, the cost of room and board groupings at a hospital are formulated through a "cost per day" formula rather than a cost to charge ratio. For this mock cost report we will assume in Table 8.12 that the program costs for adults/pediatrics, ICU and nursery are $6,971,017, $2,690,006 and $2,004,979. These figures are arbitrary amounts that do not tie back into any worksheets. For the purposes of this text, Worksheet D-1 is not formulated for the mock cost report.

Worksheet D-3 contains the cost-to-charge ratios formulated in Worksheet C Part 1 and the PSR report charges provided by the federal government. The PSR report will segregate charges and payments for both Medicare inpatient and outpatient services as well as any outlier payments. For this mock cost report, we assume that the MAC provided this hospital with the data in Table 8.11.

These charges represent all the charge information submitted by the hospital to the MAC for the cost report time period. They represent the gross charges and payments of providing hospital services. The inpatient charges are keyed into column 2 of Table 8.12 (Worksheet D-3), while the outpatient charges are entered into column 2 of Table 8.13 (Worksheet D-5). Worksheet D-3 is separated between routine service costs and ancillary service costs. The justification for this separation is that routine service costs or room and board costs are formulated using a per diem or cost per day formula. Ancillary service costs are formulated using the ratios created in Worksheets A through C. Column 3 of Worksheet D-3 computes an expected inpatient cost of providing hospital services; column 3 of Worksheet D-5 formulates an expected outpatient cost of providing hospital services. Both Table 8.12 and Table 8.13 list the identical cost-to-charge ratios formulated in Worksheet C Part 1. A significant difference in the Form 2552-10 cost report is that inpatient nursery charges are allowed in Worksheet D-3. This addition in 2011 was mainly for Medicaid

Table 8.11 PSR Report

Room and Board	Inpatient Charges	Outpatient Charges
Room and Board		
Adult/Pediatric	$12,349,012	
Intensive Care Unit	$6,469,470	
Ancillary		
Operating Room	$3,058,018	$9,060,000
MRI	$4,891,000	$2,944,500
Laboratory	$3,912,000	$2,718,000
Physical Therapy	$5,868,000	$3,011,000
Implantable Devices	$733,500	
Drugs Charged to Patients	$2,080,000	$906,000
Emergency Room	$2,445,000	$4,636,500
Subtotal	$41,806,000	$23,276,000
Medicare Operating Payments	$8,093,642	$4,422,440
Medicare Capital Payments	$650,128	
Medicare Deductible	$500,000	$2,000
Medicare Co-Insurance	$200,000	

patients. In Table 8.12, the total inpatient nursery charges were $7,459,000 (column 2, line 15), and this figure is not found within Medicare in the PSR report. Worksheet D-3 is also used for any pass-through payments for either nursing schools or paramedical education.

CRITICAL ISSUE

The purpose of Worksheet D is to formulate an expected cost of performing inpatient and outpatient services. Room and Board costs are formulated using a cost per day formula while ancillary services use cost to charge ratios.

The culmination of formulating costs ends in Worksheet D of the cost report. Worksheets A through C involve formulating a cost-to-charge ratio by clinical grouping; Worksheet D creates an actual cost of providing care. Most state-administered Medicaid agencies will examine Worksheet D because Medicaid reimbursement is often based on cost.

Worksheet E

The final worksheet in the cost report is Worksheet E, which calculates the settlement data. The purpose of Worksheet E is to compare what was actually paid to the hospital for services completed to what theoretically should have been paid. Worksheet E formulates a gap between payment and cost. Worksheet E-1 Part 1 lists any interim payments that were made to the hospital. Worksheet E Part A documents the inpatient Medicare settlement; Worksheet E Part B documents the outpatient Medicare settlement. Before Worksheet E can be calculated, an overview of bad debt and Medicare DSH needs to given.

Medicare Bad Debt

The federal government will reimburse hospitals for a proportion of their Medicare bad debts only if certain conditions are met. The bad debt must be related to patient deductible and coinsurance payments, and the hospital must be able to establish that reasonable collection efforts were made. The strict definition of reasonable collection efforts is that the hospital consistently attempted to collect the debt after 120 days from the date the first bill was mailed to the former patient. Basically, the 120-day clock begins when the first bill is mailed. A significant aspect of classifying Medicare bad debt is that collection policies must be consistent for all payers, not just Medicare patients (Medicare auditors will research this). Unfortunately, a hospital cannot claim the Medicare bad debt on the cost report after 120 days of reasonable collection efforts if they factor the accounts to a third party. Medicare's belief is that the hospital is still working on the account even though a collection agency is attempting to collect the debt. *Only after the hospital requests back the accounts from the collection agency after both parties have agreed the account is worthless can the hospital report the account as allowable bad debt.* Any bad debt recoveries received during that cost report time period must be used to reduce current period bad debts, and the MAC pays 70% of the bad debt reported on the cost report. In other words, Medicare reimburses 70 cents on the dollar for the deductible and coinsurance amounts not paid by Medicare beneficiaries after the hospital considers the figures to be worthless.

A problem with reporting Medicare bad debt lies in the 120-day window that must occur for a patient's unpaid bill to be classified as bad debt. For example, if 90 days pass and a patient has not made any payments on an account, yet on the 91st day the patient makes a payment, then technically the 120-day clock restarts. This 120-day window creates a gray area in that what if a patient paid $20 on a $1,000 balance? It is at the discretion of the hospital to determine if this $20 payment has or has not affected the 120-day window. Not only are traditional Medicare patients included in the bad debt computation but also any charity care patients that had unpaid deductibles or coinsurance.

CRITICAL ISSUE

The deductible and coinsurance payments owed by patients of Medicare health maintenance organizations (HMOs) are not included in the bad debt computation, but they can be independently negotiated with that particular Medicare HMO.

Medicare DSH Calculation

As stated in the Medicare chapter, hospitals receive add-on amounts to their blend rate for providing additional benefits to the public. The Medicare DSH add-on payment is given to hospitals for treating patients with minimal income. The Medicare DSH add-on is the total of the Medicare and Medicaid fractions calculated in Worksheet E Part A (Table 8.14) of the cost report, lines 30 through 34. For the mock cost report, we assume the following hospital statistics, which are listed in the S worksheets.

	Medicaid Days	*Total Days*
Adult and Pediatric	500	3,000
ICU	50	250
Nursery	125	300
Total	675	3,550

The Medicare fraction is provided by the federal government, and it is reported in line 30 of Table 8.14. For this mock cost report, we assume the figure is 8%. The Medicaid fraction is the proportion of Medicaid days divided by total days, which is 19% (675/3,550). The combination of these percentages results in 27% (8% + 19%), which is listed in line 32 of Table 8.14 (Worksheet E Part A). To formulate the actual add-on, the federal government has enacted the following for both the operating and the capital Medicare DSH add-on payment:

Operating Portion	
1.	If the combination of the Medicare/Medicaid fraction is less than 15%, then no operating DSH payment is calculated.
2.	If the combination of the Medicare/Medicaid fraction is between 15% and 20.2%, then the operating DSH payment = 2.5% + (0.65 * (Medicare DSH − 15%)).
3.	If the combination of the Medicare/Medicaid fraction is greater than 20.2%, then the operating DSH payment = 5.88% + (0.825 * (Medicare DSH − 20.2%)).
Capital Portion	
1.	This is 2.71828 raised to the power of (0.2025 * Medicare/Medicaid fraction) − 1.

Since our mock cost report example results in a Medicare/Medicaid fraction of 27%, we calculate the add-on at greater than 20.2%, which formulates to 11.49% (5.88% + (0.825 * (27% − 20.2%)). The 11.49% will be reported in line item 33 of Worksheet E Part A. This add-on percentage will be multiplied against the total operating payments provided by the federal government-produced PSR report, which is $8,093,642. The sum of this computation is $929,959 (0.1149 * $8,093,642), and it is reported on line 34 of Worksheet E Part A. The $8,093,642 in operating payments is reported in line 1, and when combined with line 32 totals to line 47 (Table 8.15) as $9,023,601 ($929,959 + $8,093,642).

The capital portion of the Medicare DSH add-on payment is formulated quite differently from the operating payment. A government figure of 2.71828 is raised to the power of (0.2025 * Medicare/Medicaid fraction) − 1. The calculation of the capital portion of the Medicare DSH add-on is usually a system-generated computation formulated by the software. This results in a computation of 4.46%, which is multiplied against the PSR-produced DRG capital payment of $650,128. The capital add-on amount of $28,995 (4.46% * $650,128) is reported in line 50 of Worksheet E Part A (Table 8.15), and the sum of the diagnosis-related group (DRG) payments received plus the operating and capital Medicare DSH add-on figures is reported in line 59.

CRITICAL ISSUE

The Medicare DSH add-on percentage is reported in Worksheet E Part A, and it is a combination of several equations created by the federal government.

Medicare DSH Add-On (for Mock Cost Report)

Operating Medicare DSH Add-on = 11.49%
Capital Medicare DSH Add-on = 4.46%
Total Medicare DSH Add-on = 15.95% (to be included in the Medicare blend rate)

Worksheet E Part A

Worksheet E Part A calculates the Medicare inpatient settlement of the cost report. The first component is in Table 8.14; the second half resides in Table 8.15. Lines 1 and 2 in Table 8.14 list the payments received from Medicare, which are found in the government-issued PSR report. This amount is added to the Medicare operating DSH adjustment reported on line 34. The combination of these figures is reported on line 47 of Table 8.15 as $9,023,601 ($8,093,642 + $929,959). The capital portion of the Medicare DSH add-on is then added in line 50 ($48,434) to form a subtotal in line item 59 of $9,072,035.

The subtotal in line 59 is adjusted by the deductible/coinsurance amounts that were billed and paid by Medicare beneficiaries. Lines 62 and 63 are the deductible and coinsurance amounts, respectively, provided by Medicare listed in the PSR report; these amounts need to be keyed in the cost report. This amount is then adjusted for the allowable bad debt for which a hospital is claiming reimbursement. Line 64 of Table 8.15 ($250,000) is the allowable amount multiplied by 70%, resulting in an actual Medicare bad debt settlement of $175,000. The subtotal in line 67 represents the combination of reimbursable bad debt ($175,000) plus the adjusted payments already received. This figure must be compared to any interim payments in line 71 (pulled from Worksheet E-1) to determine if a settlement is due to a hospital. Line 74 in Worksheet E Part A determines the gap of whether a hospital was over- or underpaid for Medicare services. In our sample cost report, the county hospital received $8,200,000 in interim payments from the government; however, the cost report states they should have been paid $8,547,035. The settlement figure of $347,035 (line 74) represents an underpayment to the county hospital for treatment of Medicare inpatients.

Worksheet E Part B

In comparison to Part A, the purpose of Worksheet E Part B is to calculate the outpatient Medicare settlement. The computation of the settlement is almost identical to Worksheet E Part B except the Medicare DSH add-on figure is not included in the computation. The deductibles and coinsurance payments are subtracted from the expected payments, which are added to the reimbursable bad debt amounts. Any interim Medicare payments are listed in E-1 Part 1.

CRITICAL ISSUE

The actual cost report settlement occurs in Worksheet E. The document formulates a gap between the actual and expected Medicare reimbursement.

Subprovider (Psychiatric and Rehabilitation)

Certain types of medical services are reimbursed separately from the traditional DRG methodology because they absorb a different amount of costs. Two types of these services are rehabilitation and psychiatric care; they are termed *subproviders* for cost report purposes. As an option, a hospital can choose to list a subprovider in the cost report if the facility offers those services. The hospital can also choose not to record a subprovider designation and include such psychiatric and rehabilitation services in a traditional inpatient prospective payment system (IPPS) methodology.

Some larger hospital systems offer rehabilitation services, and they are reimbursed on what is termed the inpatient rehabilitation facility (IRF) PPS. A separate DRG listing exists for rehabilitation services, and that hospitals specific Medicare blend rate is multiplied against this statistic much like any other clinical procedure. To qualify for this payment methodology, the hospital must attain the "75% rule" in that 75% of inpatient rehabilitation patients must qualify for 1 of the 13 specified medical rehabilitation conditions:

1. Stroke
2. Spinal cord injury
3. Congenital deformity
4. Amputation
5. Major multiple trauma
6. Fracture of femur
7. Brain injury
8. Neurological disorders
9. Burns
10. Knee or hip joint replacement
11. Active arthritis
12. Systemic vasculidites with joint inflammation
13. Severe or advanced osteoarthritis

If one of these medical criteria is met, then the hospital can be reimbursed using the IRF PPS rather than the traditional Medicare IPPS methodology. Instead of reviewing each rehabilitation case individually, the hospital uses what is called a compliance percentage to determine if the rehabilitation population meets 1 of the 13 conditions. An additional aspect of rehabilitation services is that patients must have a patient assessment instrument (PAI) completed at admission and discharge. Each patient is also assigned a case mix index based on the PAI.

In contrast to rehabilitation services are the services received by patients treated for psychiatric conditions. Currently, hospitals are reimbursed using the inpatient psychiatric facility (IPF) PPS, which has several different elements. Much like the IPF PPS methodology, a hospital can choose to be reimbursed using either the traditional PPS system or the specific psychiatric IPF PPS methodology. Prior to 2005, the reimbursement methodology for psychiatric patients was based on a *Tax Equity and Fiscal Responsibility Act* (TEFRA) rate, which was a cost-based reimbursement model. TEFRA reimbursement was based on a reasonable cost per case that was capped at a certain payment limit. As of 2010, hospitals are now reimbursed on a DRG model for psychiatric services. The federal government previously reimbursed hospitals using a per diem rate for psychiatric care; however, the reimbursement is now all prospectively DRG based.

CRITICAL ISSUE

Both psychiatric and rehabilitation services for inpatients are reimbursed using a separate DRG model; however, a hospital has the choice of whether to participate in that program. The hospital can choose to have psychiatric or rehabilitation services paid using the traditional DRG methodology.

For cost report purposes, the subprovider elements are formulated using information provided by the federal government. Much like the PSR reports provided to hospitals for other types of care, the government provides hospitals with PSR reports for subprovider services such as psychiatric and rehabilitative care. The PSR reports list the appropriate charges and payments for Medicare-reimbursed services.

Clinics

A freestanding clinic is a separate entity from the hospital; it bills for services using the traditional physician-based Resource-Based Relative Value Scale (RBRVS). A provider- or hospital-based clinic is a part of the hospital that is classified as an outpatient service, and it bills for services using an outpatient fee schedule. The provider clinic presents a patient with two bills: one from the hospital and one from the physician. *There are requirements to being a provider clinic since these costs are included in the cost report, and the freestanding clinic costs are not included.* The primary reason why a teaching facility would employ a provider clinic is so that resident physicians can make their rounds as part of the graduate medical education (GME) training. Historically, a provider clinic has a high population of indigent patients, with most qualifying for either Medicaid or charity care.

Conclusion

The cost report is a detailed financial document that is responsible for formulating and classifying the costs to treat hospital patients. The CMS is responsible for administering the report, and its structure is similar to a tax return. By isolating variable costs and allocating appropriate fixed costs, a cost-to-charge ratio is formulated that is multiplied against charges to create an expected cost. This expected cost is compared against payments received to determine if a positive or negative gap exists between cost and payment. This gap in Medicare cost/payment does not result in an additional asset/liability since the federal government reimburses hospitals using a DRG/APC (Ambulatory Payment Classification) methodology. For Medicaid, the cost figure that is produced represents the theoretical payment that should have been paid to the hospital. The information listed in the cost report is vital to both the state and federal governments in formulating the appropriate DRG weights and payments made to hospitals throughout the country. In addition, add-on percentages used in the Medicare blend rate, such as DSH, are formulated by the cost report data. A hospital accountant should have a thorough understanding of not only the purpose of the Medicare cost report but also the many components of how it is formulated.

Table 8.2 Form CMS-2552-10

County Hospital: Fiscal Year 1
Worksheet A

	Cost Center Descriptions	Salaries	Other	Total	A-6 Reclassifications	Reclassified Trial Balance	A-8 Adjustments	Net Expenses for Allocation
		1	2	3	4	5	6	7
	General Service Cost Centers							
1	Capital-Related Costs–Buildings and Fixtures				$2,000,000	$2,000,000		$2,000,000
2	Capital Related Costs–Movable Equipment				$3,000,000	$3,000,000		$3,000,000
3	Employee Benefits	B) $1,590,000		$1,590,000		$1,590,000		$1,590,000
4	Administrative and General	S) $7,000,000	U) $6,200,000	$13,200,000	($5,000,000)	$8,200,000	($2,500,000)	$5,700,000
5	Maintenance and Repairs	X) $400,000	Y) $125,000	$525,000		$525,000		$525,000
6	Housekeeping							
7	Dietary							
8	Nursing Administration							
9	Central Services and Supply							
10	Pharmacy	Z) $200,000	AA) $125,000	$325,000		$325,000		$325,000
11	Medical Records	V) $650,000	W) $325,000	$975,000		$975,000		$975,000
12	Social Service							

	Inpatient Routine Service Cost Centers							
13	Adult and Pediatrics	A) $2,000,000	C) $850,000	$2,850,000		$2,850,000	($50,000)	$2,800,000
14	Intensive Care Unit	F) $1,200,000	G) $500,000	$1,700,000		$1,700,000	($50,000)	$1,650,000
15	Nursery	D) $1,000,000	E) $420,000	$1,420,000		$1,420,000	($20,000)	$1,400,000
	Ancillary Service Cost Centers							
16	Operating Room	H) $1,800,000	I) $1,400,000	$3,200,000	($600,000)	$2,600,000	($200,000)	$2,400,000
17	Radiology–Diagnostic							
18	Computed Tomography (CT Scan)							
19	Magnetic Resonance Imaging (MRI)	M) $1,100,000	N) $485,00	$1,585,000		$1,585,000	($15,000)	$1,570,000
20	Laboratory	K) $800,000	L) $500,000	$1,300,000		$1,300,000		$1,300,000
21	Physical Therapy	Q) $900,000	R) $1,100,000	$2,000,000		$2,000,000	($500,000)	$1,500,000
22	Medical Supplies Charged to Patient				$600,000			
23	Implantable Devices Charged to Patients					$600,000		$600,000
24	Drugs Charged to Patients		T) $175,000	$175,000		$175,000		$175,000
	Outpatient Service Cost Centers							
25	Emergency	O) $400,000	P) $2,020,000	$2,420,000		$2,420,000		$2,420,000
26	Observation Beds							

(Continued)

Table 8.2 (Continued)   Form CMS-2552-10

County Hospital: Fiscal Year 1
Worksheet A

	Cost Center Descriptions	Salaries	Other	Total	A-6 Reclassifications	Reclassified Trial Balance	A-8 Adjustments	Net Expenses for Allocation
		1	2	3	4	5	6	7
27	Subtotal	$19,040,000	$14,225,000	$33,265,000		$33,265,000	($3,335,000)	$29,930,000
	Nonreimbursable Cost Centers							
28	Gift Shop							
29	Total	$19,040,000	$14,225,000	$33,265,000		$33,265,000	($3,335,000)	$29,930,000

Table 8.3 Form CMS-2552-10

County Hospital: Fiscal Year 1
Worksheet A-6

		Increases				Decreases				
Explanation of Reclassifications	Code	Cost Center	Line #	Salary	Other	Cost Center	Line #	Salary	Other	Wkst A-7 Ref
	1	2	3	4	5	6	7	8	9	10
1 Reclass depreciation to appropriate line item		Depreciation–Building	1		$2,000,000	Administrative and General	4		$5,000,000	
2 Reclass depreciation to appropriate line item		Depreciation–Equipment	2		$3,000,000					
3 Reclass implants to appropriate line item		Implantable Devices Charged to Patients	23		$600,000	Operating Room	16		$600,000	
4 Total					$5,600,000				$5,600,000	

Table 8.4   Form CMS-2552-10

County Hospital: Fiscal Year 1

Worksheet A-8

	Description	Basis/ Code	Amount	Expense Classification on Worksheet A to/ from which the Amount Is to Be Adjusted		Work-sheet A-7 Ref.
		1	2	3	4	5
1	Investment income					
2	Investment income					
3	Trade, quantity, and time discounts					
4	Refunds and rebates of expenses					
5	Rental of provider space by suppliers					
6	Telephone services					
7	Television and radio service					
8	Parking lot					
9	Provider-based physician adjustment	1	($135,000)	Worksheet A-8-2		
10	Sale of scrap, waste, etc.					
11	Related organization transactions					
12	Laundry and linen service					
13	Cafeteria employees and guests	2	($1,500,000)	Admin and general	4	
14	Rental of quarters to employees					
15	Sale of medical and surgical supplies	2	($500,000)	Physical therapy	21	
16	Sales of drugs to other than patients					

(Continued)

Table 8.4 (Continued) Form CMS-2552-10
County Hospital: Fiscal Year 1
Worksheet A-8

	Description	Basis/ Code	Amount	Expense Classification on Worksheet A to/ from which the Amount Is to Be Adjusted		Work-sheet A-7 Ref.
		1	*2*	*3*	*4*	*5*
17	Sale of medical records and abstracts					
18	Nursing school					
19	Vending machines					
20	Depreciation: buildings					
21	Depreciation: movable equipment					
22	Non-physician anesthetist	1	($200,000)	Operating room	16	
23	Physician assistants					
24	Adjustment for speech pathology cost in excess of limitation					
25	Adjustment for occupational therapy cost in excess of limitation					
26	Miscellaneous income: rent	2	($1,000,000)	Admin and general	4	
27.01						
28.02						
	Total		($3,335,000)			

Admin, administration.

Table 8.5   Form CMS-2552-10

County Hospital: Fiscal Year 1
Worksheet A-8-2

Wkst A Line #	Cost Center Physician Identifier	Total Remuneration	Professional Component	Provider Component	RCE Amount	Physician/Provider Component Hours	Unadjusted RCE Limit	5% of Unadjusted RCE Limit
1	2	3	4	5	6	7	8	9
13	Adults and Pediatrics	$50,000	$50,000					
14	ICU	$50,000	$50,000					
15	Nursery	$20,000	$20,000					
19	MRI	$15,000	$15,000					
Total		$135,000	$135,000					

Table 8.7 Form CMS-2552-10

County Hospital: Fiscal Year One
Schedule B-1
Statistical Basis

Cost Center Description	Capital-Related Costs Buildings/Fixtures (Square Feet)	Capital-Related Costs Movable Equipment (Square Feet)	Employee Benefits (Gross Salaries)	Administrative and General (Accumulated Cost)	Maintenance and Repairs (Square Feet)	House-keeping	Dietary	Nursing Administration	Central Service and Supply	Pharmacy (Drug Requests)	Medical Records (Time Spent)	Social Service
	1	2	3	4	5	6	7	8	9	10	11	12
General Service Cost Centers												
1 Capital Related Costs–Buildings and Fixtures												
2 Capital Related Costs–Movable Equipment												
3 Employee Benefits												
4 Administrative and General	25,000	25,000	$7,000,000		25,000							
5 Maintenance and Repairs	11,000	11,000	$400,000		11,000							
6 Housekeeping												
7 Dietary												
8 Nursing Administration												

(Continued)

Table 8.7 (Continued) Form CMS-2552-10

County Hospital: Fiscal Year One
Schedule B-1
Statistical Basis

	Cost Center Description	Capital-Related Costs Buildings/Fixtures (Square Feet)	Capital-Related Costs Movable Equipment (Square Feet)	Employee Benefits (Gross Salaries)	Administrative and General (Accumulated Cost)	Maintenance and Repairs (Square Feet)	House-keeping	Dietary	Nursing Administration	Central Service and Supply	Pharmacy (Drug Requests)	Medical Records (Time Spent)	Social Service
		1	2	3	4	5	6	7	8	9	10	11	12
9	Central Services and Supply												
10	Pharmacy	14,000	14,000	$200,000		14,000							
11	Medical Records	10,000	10,000	$650,000		10,000							
12	Social Service												
Inpatient Routine Service Cost Centers													
13	Adult and Pediatrics	220,000	220,000	$2,000,000		220,000						10,000	
14	Intensive Care Unit	25,000	25,000	$1,200,000		25,000						2,500	
15	Nursery	10,000	10,000	$1,000,000		10,000						1,250	
Ancillary Service Cost Centers													
16	Operating Room	50,000	50,000	$1,800,000		50,000						5,000	
17	Radiology–Diagnostic												
18	Computed Tomography (CT Scan)												

#	Cost Center										
19	Magnetic Resonance Imaging (MRI)	20,000	20,000	$1,100,000		20,000				20,000	
20	Laboratory	35,000	35,000	$800,000		35,000					
21	Physical Therapy	30,000	30,000	$900,000		30,000				250	
22	Medical Supplies Charged to Patient										
23	Implantable Devices Charged to Patients										
24	Drugs Charged to Patients	20,000	20,000			20,000			400,000		
	Outpatient Service Cost Centers										
25	Emergency	30,000	30,000	$400,000		30,000				1,000	
26	Observation Beds										
27	Subtotal										
	Nonreimbursable Cost Centers										
28	Gift Shop										
29	Total	500,000	500,000	$17,450,000		500,000			400,000	20,000	

Table 8.8 Form CMS-2552-10

County Hospital: Fiscal Year 1
Worksheet B Part 1

	Cost Center Description	Net Expenses for Cost Allocation	Capital-Related Costs Buildings/Fixtures	Capital-Related Costs Movable Equipment	Employee Benefits	Subtotal	Administrative and General	Maintenance and Repairs	Pharmacy	Medical Records	Total
		0	1	2	3	4	5	6	7	8	9
General Service Cost Centers											
1	Capital-Related Costs: Buildings and Fixtures	$2,000,000	$2,000,000								
2	Capital-Related Costs: Movable Equipment	$3,000,000		$3,000,000							
3	Employee Benefits	$1,590,000			$1,590,000						
4	Administrative and General	$5,700,000	$100,000	$150,000	$637,822	$6,587,822	$6,587,822				
5	Maintenance and Repairs	$525,000	$44,000	$66,000	$36,447	$671,447	$189,501	$860,948			
6	Housekeeping										
7	Dietary										
8	Nursing Administration										

#											
9	Central Services and Supply										
10	Pharmacy	$325,000	$56,000	$84,000	$18,223	$483,223	$136,379	$25,977	$645,580		
11	Medical Records	$975,000	$40,000	$60,000	$59,226	$1,134,226	$320,111	$18,555		$1,472,892	
12	Social Service										
	Inpatient Routine Service Cost Centers										
13	Adult and Pediatrics	$2,800,000	$880,000	$1,320,000	$182,235	$5,182,235	$1,462,573	$408,208		$736,446	$7,789,462
14	Intensive Care Unit	$1,650,000	$100,000	$150,000	$109,341	$2,009,341	$567,093	$46,387		$184,112	$2,806,933
15	Nursery	$1,400,000	$40,000	$60,000	$91,117	$1,591,117	$449,058	$18,555		$92,056	$2,150,786
	Ancillary Service Cost Centers										
16	Operating Room	$2,400,000	$200,000	$300,000	$164,011	$3,064,011	$864,751	$92,775		$368,223	$4,389,760
17	Radiology: Diagnostic										
18	Computed Tomography (CT Scan)										
19	Magnetic Resonance Imaging (MRI)	$1,570,000	$80,000	$120,000	$100,229	$1,870,229	$527,832	$37,110			$2,435,171
20	Laboratory	$1,300,000	$140,000	$210,000	$72,894	$1,722,894	$486,249	$64,942			$2,274,086
21	Physical Therapy	$1,500,000	$120,000	$180,000	$82,006	$1,882,006	$531,155	$55,665		$18,411	$2,487,237

(Continued)

Table 8.8 (Continued)   Form CMS-2552-10

County Hospital: Fiscal Year 1
Worksheet B Part 1

	Cost Center Description	Net Expenses for Cost Allocation	Capital-Related Costs Buildings/Fixtures	Capital-Related Costs Movable Equipment	Employee Benefits	Subtotal	Administrative and General	Maintenance and Repairs	Pharmacy	Medical Records	Total
		0	1	2	3	4	5	6	7	8	9
22	Medical Supplies Charged to Patient	$600,000									
23	Implantable Devices Charged to Patients	$600,000				$600,000	$169,337				$769,337
24	Drugs Charged to Patients	$175,000	$80,000	$120,000		$375,000	$105,836	$37,110	$645,580		$1,163,525
	Outpatient Service Cost Centers										
25	Emergency	$2,420,000	$120,000	$180,000	$36,447	$2,756,447	$777,947	$55,665		$73,645	$3,663,704
26	Observation Beds										
27	Subtotal	$29,930,000	$2,000,000	$3,000,000	$1,590,000	$29,930,000	$6,587,822	$860,948	$645,580	$1,472,892	$29,930,000
	Nonreimbursable Cost Centers										
28	Gift Shop										
29	Total	$29,930,000	$2,000,000	$3,000,000	$1,590,000	$29,930,000	$6,587,822	$860,948	$645,580	$1,472,892	$29,930,000

Table 8.9 Form CMS-2552-10

County Hospital: Fiscal Year 1
Worksheet C Source Data

	Inpatient Charges from Trial Balance	Eliminate Professional Fees	Drugs Charged Reclass	Medical Supply Reclass	Adjusted Inpatient Charge Total	Outpatient Charges from Trial Balance	Eliminate Professional Fees	Drugs Charged Reclass	Medical Supply Reclass	Adjusted Outpatient Charge Total	Adjusted Total Charges
	1	2	3	4	5	6	7	8	9	10	11
13 Adult and Pediatrics	$15,000,000		($1,200,000)		$13,800,000						$13,800,000
14 Intensive Care Unit	$7,500,000		($750,000)		$6,750,000						$6,750,000
15 Nursery	$8,000,000				$8,000,000						$8,000,000
16 Operating Room	$5,000,000	($400,000)	($200,000)	($800,000)	$3,600,000	$10,000,000	($200,000)	($400,000)		$9,400,000	$13,000,000
17 Radiology–Diagnostic											
18 Computed Tomography (CT) Scan											
19 Magnetic Resonance Imaging (MRI)	$5,000,000		($50,000)		$4,950,000	$3,000,000		($25,000)		$2,975,000	$7,925,000
20 Laboratory	$4,000,000		($50,000)		$3,950,000	$3,000,000		($50,000)		$2,950,000	$6,900,000
21 Physical Therapy	$5,000,000				$5,000,000	$3,000,000				$3,000,000	$8,000,000

(Continued)

Table 8.9 (Continued)   Form CMS-2552-10

County Hospital: Fiscal Year 1
Worksheet C Source Data

		Inpatient Charges from Trial Balance	Eliminate Professional Fees	Drugs Charged Reclass	Medical Supply Reclass	Adjusted Inpatient Charge Total	Outpatient Charges from Trial Balance	Eliminate Professional Fees	Drugs Charged Reclass	Medical Supply Reclass	Adjusted Outpatient Charge Total	Adjusted Total Charges
		1	2	3	4	5	6	7	8	9	10	11
23	Implantable Devices Charged to Patients				800,000	$800,000						$800,000
24	Drugs Charged to Patients			$2,400,000		$2,400,000			$975,000		$975,000	$3,375,000
25	Emergency	$2,000,000	($100,000)	($150,000)		$1,750,000	$5,000,000	($110,000)	($500,000)		$4,390,000	$6,140,000
28	Gift Shop		($500,000)					($310,000)				
	Total	$51,500,000	($500,000)			$51,000,000	$24,000,000				$23,690,000	$74,690,000

Table 8.10   Form CMS-2552-10

County Hospital: Fiscal Year 1
Worksheet C Part 1

	Total Cost from Wkst B Part 1	Therapy Limit Adjustment	Costs			Charges			Cost or Other Ratio	TEFRA IP Ratio	PPS IP Ratio
			Total Costs	RCE Dis-allowance	Total Costs	Inpatient	Outpatient	Total			
Cost Center Descriptions	*1*	*2*	*3*	*4*	*5*	*6*	*7*	*8*	*9*	*10*	*11*
Inpatient Routine Service Cost Centers											
13 Adult and Pediatrics	$7,789,462		$7,789,462		$7,789,462	$13,800,000		$13,800,000			0.5645
14 Intensive Care Unit	$2,806,933		$2,806,933		$2,806,933	$6,750,000		$6,750,000			0.4158
Coronary Care unit											
Burn Intensive Care Unit											
Surgical Intensive Care Unit											
Other Special Care											
Subprovider IPF											
Subprovider IRF											

(Continued)

Table 8.10 (Continued)   Form CMS-2552-10

County Hospital: Fiscal Year 1
Worksheet C Part 1

		Cost Center Descriptions	Total Cost from Wkst B Part 1	Therapy Limit Adjustment	Costs				Charges					
					Total Costs	RCE Dis-allowance	Total Costs	Inpatient	Outpatient	Total	Cost or Other Ratio	TEFRA IP Ratio	PPS IP Ratio
			1	2	3	4	5	6	7	8	9	10	11
		Subprovider											
15		Nursery	$2,150,786		$2,150,786		$2,150,786	$8,000,000		$8,000,000			0.2688
		Skilled Nursing Facility											
		Nursing Facility											
		Other Long-Term Care											
Ancillary Service Cost Centers													
16		Operating Room	$4,389,760		$4,389,760		$4,389,760	$3,600,000	$9,400,000	$13,000,000			0.3377
		Recovery Room											
		Labor Room and Delivery Room											
		Anesthesiology											
		Radiology–Diagnostic											

	Radiology–Therapeutic									
	Radioisotope									
	Computed Tomography (CT) Scan									
19	Magnetic Resonance Imaging (MRI)	$2,435,171	$2,435,171	$2,435,171		$4,950,000	$2,975,000	$7,925,000		0.3073
	Cardiac Catheterization									
20	Laboratory	$2,274,086	$2,274,086	$2,274,086		$3,950,000	$2,950,000	$6,900,000		0.3296
	PBP Clinical Laboratory Services									
	While Blood and Packed Red Blood Cells									
	Blood Storing, Processing, and Trans									
	Intravenous Therapy									
	Respiratory Therapy									
21	Physical Therapy	$2,487,237	$2,487,237	$2,487,237		$5,000,000	$3,000,000	$8,000,000		0.3109

(Continued)

Table 8.10 (Continued)   Form CMS-2552-10

County Hospital: Fiscal Year 1
Worksheet C Part 1

| | Total Cost from Wkst B Part 1 | Therapy Limit Adjustment | Costs | | | Charges | | | Cost or Other Ratio | TEFRA IP Ratio | PPS IP Ratio |
| | | | Total Costs | RCE Dis-allowance | Total Costs | Inpatient | Outpatient | Total | | | |
	1	2	3	4	5	6	7	8	9	10	11
Cost Center Descriptions											
Occupational Therapy											
Speech Pathology											
Outpatient Service Cost Centers											
Electro-cardiology											
Electro-cephalography											
Medical Supplies Charged to Patients											
23 Implantable Devices Charged to Patients	$769,337		$769,337		$769,337	$800,000		$800,000			0.9617
24 Drugs Charged to Patients	$1,163,525		$1,163,525		$1,163,525	$2,400,000	$975,000	$3,375,000			0.3447
Renal Dialysis											

ASC								
Other Ancillary								
Rural Health Center								
Federally Qualified Health Center								
Clinic								
25 Emergency	$3,663,703	$3,663,703	$3,663,703	$1,750,000	$4,390,000	$6,140,000		0.5967
Observation Beds								
Gift Shop								
26 Total	$29,930,000	$29,930,000	$29,930,000	$51,000,000	$23,690,000	$74,690,000		0.4007

Table 8.12   Form CMS-2552-10

County Hospital: Fiscal Year 1
Worksheet D-3

	Description	Ratio of Cost to Charges	Inpatient Program Charges	Inpatient Program Costs
		1	2	3
	Routine Service Cost Center			
13	Adults and Pediatrics		$12,349,012	$6,971,017
14	Intensive Care Unit		$6,469,470	$2,690,006
15	Nursery[a]		$7,459,000	$2,004,979
	Ancillary Service Cost Centers			
16	Operating Room	0.3377	$3,058,018	$1,032,693
17	Radiology–Diagnostic			
18	Computed Tomography (CT) Scan			
19	Magnetic Resonance Scan (MRI)	0.3073	$4,891,000	$1,503,004
20	Laboratory	0.3296	$3,912,000	$1,289,395
21	Physical Therapy	0.3109	$5,868,000	$1,824,361
	Medical Supplies Charged to Patients			
23	Implantable Devices Charged to Patients	0.9617	$733,500	$705,407
24	Drugs Charged to Patients	0.3447	$2,080,000	$716,976
	Outpatient Service Cost Centers			
25	Emergency	0.5967	$2,445,000	$1,458,932
	Observation Beds			
26	Total Ancillary and Outpatient Costs	0.3711	$22,987,518	$8,530,768

Note: Inpatient program charges were pulled from the government-produced PSR report.

[a] Total nursery inpatient charges of $7,459,000 are not found in the PSR report. This figure predominantly represents the charges for Medicaid patients.

Table 8.13   Form CMS-2552-10

County Hospital: Fiscal Year 1

Worksheet D-5

	Description	Ratio of Cost to Charges	Outpatient Program Charges	Outpatient Program Costs
		1	2	3
	Routine Service Cost Center			
13	Adults and Pediatrics			
14	Intensive Care Unit			
15	Nursery			
	Ancillary Service Cost Centers			
16	Operating Room	0.3377	$9,060,000	$3,059,562
17	Radiology–Diagnostic			
18	Computed Tomography (CT) Scan			
19	Magnetic Resonance Scan (MRI)	0.3073	$2,944,500	$904,845
20	Laboratory	0.3296	$2,718,000	$895,853
21	Physical Therapy	0.3109	$3,011,000	$936,120
	Medical Supplies Charged to Patients			
23	Implantable Devices Charged to Patients	0.9617		
24	Drugs Charged to Patients	0.3447	$906,000	$312,298
	Outpatient Service Cost Centers			
25	Emergency	0.5967	$4,636,500	$2,766,600
	Observation Beds			
26	Total Ancillary and Outpatient Costs	0.4007	$23,276,000	$8,875,277

Note: Outpatient program charges were pulled from the government-produced PSR report.

Table 8.14   Form CMS-2552-10

County Hospital: Fiscal Year 1

Worksheet E Part A

		Part A Inpatient Hospital Services Under PPS	1
1		DRG amounts other than outlier payments	$8,093,642
2		Outlier payments for discharges	
3		Managed care simulated payments	
4		Bed days available divided by number of days in cost report period	
		Indirect Medical Education Adjustment Calculation for Hospitals	
5		FTE count for allopathic and osteopathic programs ending 12/31/1996	
6		FTE count for allopathic and osteopathic programs that meet criteria for add-on	
7		Adjusted FTE count for allopathic and osteopathic programs for affiliated programs	
8		Reduced direct GME FTE cap	
9		Sum of lines 5 through 7 plus/minus 8	
10		FTE count for allopathic and osteopathic programs	
11		FTE count for residents in dental and podiatric programs	
12		Current year allowable FTE	
13		Total allowable FTE count for the prior year	
14		Total allowable FTE count for the penultimate year	
15		Sum of lines 12 through 14 divided by 3	
16		Adjustment for residents in initial years of the program	
17		Adjustment for residents displaced by program	
18		Adjusted rolling average FTE count	
19		Current year resident-to-bed ratio	
20		Prior year resident-to-bed ratio	
21		Enter the lesser of line 19 or 20	
22		IME payment adjustment	
		Indirect Medical Education Adjustment for the Add-on	
23		Number of additional allopathic and osteopathic IME FTE resident cap slots	

(Continued)

Table 8.14 (Continued) Form CMS-2552-10
County Hospital: Fiscal Year 1
Worksheet E Part A

		Part A Inpatient Hospital Services Under PPS	1
24	IME FTE resident count over cap		
25	If the amount on line 24 is greater than 0 then enter lower of line 23 or 24		
26	Resident to bed ratio		
27	IME payments adjustment		
28	IME adjustment		
29	Total IME payment (lines 22 and 28)		
	Disproportionate Share Adjustment		
30	Percentage of SSI recipient patient days to Medicare Part A patient days		8.00
31	Percentage of Medicaid patient days to total days reported on Worksheet S-3 Part 1		19.00
32	Sum of lines 30 and 31		27.00
33	Allowable disproportionate share percentage		11.49
34	Disproportionate share adjustment		$929,959

Table 8.15   Form CMS-2552-10

County Hospital: Fiscal Year 1
Worksheet E Part A

	Part A Inpatient Hospital Services Under PPS	*1*
	Additional Payment for High Percentage of ESRD Discharges	
40	Total Medicare discharges on Worksheet S-3 Part 1 excluding certain discharges	
41	Total ESRD Medicare discharges	
42	Divide line 41 by line 40	
43	Total Medicare ESRD inpatient days	
44	Ratio of average length of stay to 1 week	
45	Average weekly cost for dialysis treatments	
46	Total additional payment	
47	Subtotal (operating Medicare DSH + payments listed on PSR)	$9,023,601
48	Hospital-specific payments	
49	Total payment for inpatient operating costs	$9,023,601
50	Payment for inpatient program capital	$48,434
51	Exception payment for inpatient program capital	
52	Direct graduate medical education payment	
53	Nursing and allied health managed care payment	
54	Special add-on payments for new technologies	
55	Net organ acquisition cost	
56	Cost of teaching physicians	
57	Routine service other pass-through costs	
58	Ancillary service other pass-through costs	
59	Total	$9,072,035
60	Primary payer amounts	
61	Total amount payable for program	$9,072,035
62	Deductibles billed to program beneficiaries (found in PSR report)	$500,000
63	Coinsurance billed to program beneficiaries (found in PSR report)	$200,000
64	Allowable bad debts	$250,000

(Continued)

Table 8.15 (Continued)   Form CMS-2552-10
County Hospital: Fiscal Year 1
Worksheet E Part A

	Part A Inpatient Hospital Services Under PPS	*1*
65	Adjusted reimbursable bad debts (Medicare pass-through payment)	$175,000
66	Allowable bad debts for dual-eligible beneficiaries	
67	Subtotal	$8,547,035
68	Credits received from manufacturers for replaced devices applicable to MS-DRG	
69	Outlier payments	
70	Other adjustments	
71	Amount due provider	$8,547,035
72	Interim payments (from E-1 Part 1)	$8,200,000
73	Tentative settlement	
74	Balance due provider (sum of lines 71 minus 72 and 73)	$347,035
75	Protested amounts	

Note: ESRD, end-stage renal disease.

Chapter 9

Statement of Operations (Income Statement)

Introduction

The statement of operations is a financial report used by not-for-profit and governmental hospitals while the income statement is primarily used by for-profit hospitals. The items formulated in these statements are recorded on an accrual basis, and the structure of the reports are commonly listed as revenue less expenses equals net income. Regardless of the hospital structure, the overall purpose of the report is to state the profitability of the hospital in an *interval or period of time*. The interval of time may be 1 month, 3 months, or 1 year, and this document is often formulated at both a facility and a department level. Of all the financial reports formulated by accounting, the statement of operations or income statement is typically considered the most significant because of its effect on performance evaluation. The time interval component should be contrasted against the moment-of-time aspect utilized in the statement of financial position. The revenue and expense balances listed in the statement of operations are classified as nominal accounts in that they are closed at fiscal year end to real or permanent accounts. In the case of a for-profit hospital, the total income or loss is closed to a retained earnings account. A significant benefit of both of these statements is that monthly variance analysis can be performed, which has the ability to identify positive and negative variations from budget.

Gross Revenue

The operations statement used by hospitals is similar to the financial reports used by companies in other industries; however, there are some differences. The basic income statement formula of revenue less expense exists, but the computation from gross to net revenue may require some additional explanation. In hospital financial statements, the gross revenue consists of all inpatient and outpatient revenues listed before any deductions or subtractions occur. These revenue figures can be very detailed depending on the nature of the services performed at that hospital. Some larger

Table 9.1   Listing of Gross Revenue

Inpatient revenue	$25,000,000
Outpatient revenue	$10,000,000
Total gross revenue	$35,000,000

facilities may offer cardiac and neurological services, whereas some smaller hospitals may only employ basic healthcare services. The formula for gross revenue is *price multiplied by quantity,* and a sample gross revenue figure is listed in Table 9.1.

Basically, any patient who has been admitted is classified as an inpatient; as all other patient services are classified as outpatient. Services for home health care and observation days are also included in outpatient revenue. A significant issue in gross revenue is that, regardless of the patient's insurance or ability to pay, the facility will charge the same price for hospital services. A hospital cannot raise its prices if a wealthy patient is admitted or lower charges when a homeless patient is treated in the emergency room (ER). The gross charges are uniform no matter what the payer classification.

CRITICAL ISSUE

A hospital will price its services the same regardless of the insurance provider or the patient's ability to pay.

Hospitals follow the basic accounting principle that revenue is recorded when realized or realizable; however, this method can be difficult to implement due to the various types of services that exist in a healthcare environment. The primary source of revenue is from treating patients, but additional revenue can be from capitated contracts that are negotiated with insurance carriers. In the case of healthcare, revenue is usually classified based on the payer type or service rendered. Any additional revenue classification that is not clearly stated can be explained in the notes to the financial statement.

Net Revenue

The reduction of gross revenue to net revenue takes place through the use of what is termed contractual or reserve analysis. Often considered the most crucial aspect of hospital accounting, the calculation of the reserve/contractual is an *estimate* based on what the hospital expects the third party will pay for services. The basic premise for the entry is to reduce the gross receivable/revenue to what is expected to be collected. *The reduction or credit to the receivable would be the reserve, while the reduction or debit to the revenue is called the contractual.* Much like any other business, a hospital may charge for a certain amount of services, but it realistically expects to receive only a smaller portion. This is crucial in hospital accounting because different insurance plans reimburse hospitals at different amounts. An example of the ledger entries for the gross revenue and accounts receivable are listed for a typical commercially insured patient who hypothetically had a cardiac procedure priced at $50,000 at a county hospital. On discharge from the hospital, the general ledger records will dictate a debit to a receivable and a credit to revenue.

| Commercial receivable | $50,000 | |
| Commercial revenue | | $50,000 |

This $50,000 figure represents the uniform gross charges that a hospital would charge for services. It is simply calculated as units multiplied by price. Historically, the county hospital has tracked that this specific commercial insurance plan only pays 75% of what is charged for this type of procedure. Therefore, the accounting staff at the county hospital will reduce the patient's account to the realistic and expected amount of $37,500 (75% * $50,000). The following adjusting entry would be made to the ledger to debit the contractual and credit the reserve:

| Commercial contractual | $12,500 | |
| Commercial reserve | | $12,500 |

The actual receivable and revenue are not actually adjusted, but two separate accounts now act as "contra" accounts that offset the $50,000 in gross charges. Table 9.2 provides a better description that details the net balances of the patient.

This elementary example reveals the basic fundamentals of the reserve/contractual journal entry; however, the formulation of the actual reduction from gross to net may be difficult to estimate for some hospitals. This adjustment is paramount to financial personnel because the $12,500 figure affects both the statement of financial position (balance sheet) and the statement of operations (income statement). The $12,500 not only reduces the receivable balance but also more significantly flows through the income statement as a reduction to net income. Auditors will spend a substantial amount of due diligence determining if these estimates are conservative and accurate since they can be manipulated to affect net income positively. Table 9.3 is an example of the gross-to-net revenue presentation in an income statement/statement of operations.

Since it would not be feasible to adjust every patient's account manually, hospitals often employ software that systematically reduces the gross figure to a realizable amount. After discharge, the software can formulate a contractual or reserve based on a preprogrammed collection percentage for that service provided for that particular payer. Even though a system-generated reduction from gross to net occurs, the accounting department must make additional adjustments to the net receivable. The net balances have been reduced to their expected amount, but additional adjustments need to be performed to take into account the time a third party pays a hospital. For

Table 9.2 Calculation of Net Receivable/Net Revenue

Commercial receivable $50,000	Commercial revenue $50,000
Commercial reserve ($12,500)	Commercial contractual ($12,500)
Net receivable $37,500	Net revenue $37,500

Table 9.3 Presentation of Net Revenue

Inpatient revenue	$25,000,000
Outpatient revenue	$10,000,000
Total gross revenue	$35,000,000
Contractual adjustments	$20,000,000
Net revenue	$15,000,000

simplicity, hospitals lump the patient balances into payer buckets, such as Medicare, Medicaid, Blue Cross/Blue Shield, and self-pay. These payer buckets are consolidated into an aging schedule, and additional reserve/contractual entries are formulated for both inpatients and outpatients based on payer and time frame. An example of a typical aging schedule for inpatient services is listed in Table 9.4.

The collection percentages represent the proportion of patient balances that a hospital plans to collect from that payer after a certain point in time. The accounts receivable balances of all patients who were discharged and billed are grouped into these buckets based on the age of the uncollected balances. Notice in Table 9.4 that the collectability of the balances decreases over time. The justification for this is that the hospital will not expect to receive payment for services as time elapses. Often called "100% reserved," a hospital will value a receivable at zero as time progresses and payment has not been received.

CRITICAL ISSUE

Most hospitals reserve 100% of the total patient balance after 1 year regardless of the payer. In other words, if a hospital has not received payment for services after 1 year, then no payment is expected, and the receivable is valued at zero.

Table 9.4 Aging Schedule

	Age of Uncollected Balance (days)				
Payer	*1–30*	*31–60*	*61–90*	*91–120*	*121–150*
Medicare	90%	85%	50%	0%	0%
Medicaid	90%	90%	75%	60%	0%
VA hospital	95%	95%	95%	95%	50%
Managed care	95%	80%	75%	50%	25%
Self-pay	10%	5%	0%	0%	0%
Workers' compensation	90%	80%	60%	50%	30%

Note: The collection percentages used in the aging schedule were formulated after the patient balances were reserved to their net balances.

A significant attribute of calculating reserves for hospitals is that a certain portion of patients has not been discharged. Examples would be patients still in hospital beds at the end of the month and those patients who have been discharged but their bill has not been sent because of other issues. These accounts receivable balances are referred to as either in house (still in a bed) or discharged not final billed (DNFB). These figures are commonly classified by payer in the 1- to 30-day aging bucket. These patient accounts are reserved very slightly, if at all, since they are technically still receiving care from the hospital.

An additional step in examining receivables is to carve out certain high-dollar accounts. As in other industries, the 80/20 rule applies to healthcare (80% of the receivable issues are caused by 20% of patient accounts). These high-dollar accounts can be identified by establishing a threshold, such as $100,000 or $200,000, for all net patient balances. These individual accounts must be isolated and reviewed for accuracy before they are aged since they have such significant balances. Examples of high-dollar accounts could be patients who had excessive lengths of stay for high-acuity procedures. In some cases, patients may stay at hospitals for months before being discharged. Representatives in the billing department must properly review these accounts in detail to find an approximate net figure after consulting the patient's insurance provider. Hospitals can better maintain ratios such as receivables and the days in accounts receivable by addressing high-dollar accounts as soon as the patients are discharged.

An interesting concept that is specific to healthcare is the presentation of charity care revenue. Charity care represents patient care that is given with the hospital not expecting any payment or reimbursement. Since all revenue is recorded on an accrual basis, the actual recording of charity care gross revenue is recorded just like that for any other insurance provider; however, the contractual amount for charity care is made equal to the gross revenue to ensure that the net revenue is zero. *A hospital does not expect to receive any cash from a charity care patient; therefore, the net revenue figure for charity care is always zero.* Assume from the previous example that the $50,000 cardiac procedure was performed on a patient who qualified for charity care (see Table 9.5).

Charity care is a revenue classification given to those patients who are classified between Medicaid and self-pay. In other words, the patient is not indigent enough to qualify for Medicaid but still lacks the necessary funds to pay for hospital services. Each hospital throughout the country employs an internally unique charity care policy. To be eligible for the charity care classification, registration personal (front-end operations) must ensure that patients provide necessary information such as tax forms to verify lack of income or assets. In the financial statements, the monthly charity care revenue/contractual figures are netted against each other to ensure that net revenue is zero. Table 9.6 lists a sample loss from treating a typical patient who qualified for charity care.

Other Revenue

In addition to inpatient and outpatient revenue, a healthcare facility records non-patient-related revenue, such as rental income or cafeteria sales. Since this revenue is technically patient related

Table 9.5 Presentation of Charity Care

Charity receivable	$50,000	Charity revenue	$50,000
Charity reserve	($50,000)	Charity contractual	($50,000)
Net receivable	$0	Net revenue	$0

Table 9.6   Loss from Treating Charity Care Patient

Revenue	$50,000
Contractual	($50,000)
Net revenue	$0
Salary expense	$10,000
Fringe benefit expense	$2,500
Supply expense	$8,000
Other expense	$4,000
Total variable costs	$24,500
Contribution margin	($24,500)
Estimated fixed costs	$6,000
Net income	($30,500) loss

Table 9.7   Presentation of Total Revenue

Inpatient revenue	$25,000,000
Outpatient revenue	$10,000,000
Total gross revenue	$35,000,000
Contractual adjustments	$20,000,000
Net revenue	$15,000,000
Other revenue	$3,000,000
Total revenue	$18,000,000

but not patient driven, it is classified below the net revenue line. Occasionally, small packets of other revenue are reserved, but a majority of this income does not require a reduction from gross to net. Other types of revenue that would be classified as nonoperating revenue would be proceeds from the gift shop and any cash from parking lot fees. A presentation of the total revenue in an income statement/statement of operations is given in Table 9.7.

Operating Expenses

The cost of doing any business results in the creation of operating expenses. These expenses can range from the cost of paying employees to the cost of supplies used for clinical services. In a hospital setting, the salary and supply expenses represent a majority of the operating expenses used to treat patients. A common misconception is that all physicians are employed by hospitals. In some cases, a hospital will employ a physician, but a majority of doctors have *privileges* to refer or treat

Table 9.8 Partially Complete Income Statement/Statement of Operations

Revenue	
Inpatient revenue	$25,000,000
Outpatient revenue	$10,000,000
Total Gross revenue	$35,000,000
Contractual adjustments	$20,000,000
Net revenue	$15,000,000
Other revenue	$3,000,000
Total revenue	$18,000,000
Expenses	
Salary expense	$5,000,000
Benefit expense	$1,200,000
Supply expense	$4,500,000
Total expense	$10,700,000

patients at a hospital. The physician is not employed by the hospital but is contracted to perform surgeries, procedures, or other medical services. A physician will have a charge nurse who records what services the physician performs on the patient, and that individual will receive a separate bill from that physician. The salary expenses that a hospital predominantly incurs would be those of the registered nurses (RNs), surgical technicians, and other clinical personnel. Examples of supply expenses would be the syringes, bandages, surgical implants, and pharmaceuticals used to treat patients. An additional expense that is associated with salaries are the fringe benefits that a hospital provides employees as an added benefit. Examples of fringe benefits would be health insurance, dental insurance, and disability benefits. Historically, these added benefits represent an additional 24%–25% of the salary expense at a hospital. Table 9.8 is a partially complete income statement/statement of operations that lists the revenue and expenses of a hypothetical hospital.

CRITICAL ISSUE

Physicians are occasionally employed by a hospital, but often they have independent practices with privileges to use the hospital to treat patients.

Bad Debt

The concept of bad debt is often misunderstood because of the complexities that exist in the healthcare accounting field. Bad debt is an operating expense that arises because the patient has

Table 9.9 Formulating the Cost of Bad Debt

Inpatient revenue	$25,000,000
Outpatient revenue	$10,000,000
Total revenue	$35,000,000
Estimated bad debt percentage	8%
Bad Debt Expense Reported	
Within the income statement	$2,800,000 (0.08 * $35,000,000)
Actual Cost of Bad Debt	
Hospital cost-to-charge ratio	35% (pulled from cost report)
Cost of bad debt	$980,000 (0.35 * $2,800,000)

the ability to pay for services but chooses not to do so. For a majority of hospitals, bad debt represents the cash that is not expected to be collected from the *patient portion* of the bill. The patient portion represents the deductible and coinsurance figures that are not paid by the insurance company but are the responsibility of the patient. A significant concept in hospital reimbursement is distinguishing between bad debt and charity care. *Charity care is the classification given to hospital patients who do not have the ability to pay for services; bad debt represents those patients who have the ability but choose not to pay.* Much like Medicaid, if a patient qualifies for a hospital's charity care policy, then the patient would not have to pay any portion of the bill, including deductibles and coinsurance.

The definition of bad debt is a debated topic in the healthcare accounting field due to how it is reported in the annual cost report. Most not-for-profit hospitals record bad debt as an operating expense in the income statement; however, the figure is commonly listed as a charge amount rather than an expense. For example, the monthly bad debt amount listed in the income statement is usually a fixed percentage of gross charges. To estimate the cost of bad debt, a hospitalwide cost-to-charge ratio needs to be multiplied against the bad debt charge figure. Table 9.9 provides an example of formulating the actual cost of bad debt.

From the example in Table 9.9, the hospital has reported $2,800,000 in bad debt expense in its financial statements. The amount is reported as an operating expense that reduces net income. The actual cost of the bad debt is formulated by multiplying the hospitalwide cost-to-charge ratio against the bad debt estimate. The $980,000 represents the cost of hospital patients not paying their portion of the bill.

Responsibility Accounting

The primary function of the statement of operations or income statement is to list the revenue and correlating expense for the entire hospital; however, the financial report is also used at a departmental level for budgeting and performance evaluation. The hospitalwide statement represents a compilation of all the clinical and nonclinical departments that exist in the facility. In contrast, the departmental statement (ER, intensive care unit [ICU], and maintenance) usually lists only

Table 9.10   Laboratory Department: Gross Revenue

Inpatient revenue Medicare	$300,000
Inpatient revenue Medicaid	$200,000
Inpatient revenue commercial	$100,000
Inpatient revenue self-pay	$50,000
Inpatient revenue charity	$50,000
Inpatient revenue other	$10,000
Outpatient revenue Medicare	$100,000
Outpatient revenue Medicaid	$60,000
Outpatient revenue commercial	$40,000
Outpatient revenue self-pay	$15,000
Outpatient revenue charity	$10,000
Outpatient revenue other	$10,000
Total gross revenue	$945,000

the gross revenue and variable costs of that particular department. The justification for this is that the departmental manager can control these figures, whereas fixed costs and contractual adjustments are beyond his or her control. An example of the revenue in a statement of operations for the laboratory department is listed in Table 9.10.

Not all hospitals segregate inpatient and outpatient revenue in this manner, but this increased classification allows the departmental manager to view the appropriate payer mix of those patients being serviced by the laboratory. The revenues that are listed in the departmental statement are gross figures, *not* net amounts. The reasoning is that the manager should only be responsible for items that are in his or her span of control. Departments list revenue and expense in their monthly statements, but they do not view any liabilities or receivables because it is the function of the hospital rather than the department to pay invoices and collect cash. Therefore, contractual/reserve amounts are excluded because the lab manager is not responsible for collecting patient balances, and the lab manager cannot influence the types of insurance carriers that are serviced by the lab. The departmental manager's job duties are to perform lab services in an effective and efficient manner.

Much like revenue, the operating expenses that exist in a departmental statement consist of only the items that a departmental supervisor can influence. The variable expenses consist of not only salary and supply expenses but also other miscellaneous expenses that may or may not move with volume but are at the discretion of the manager. Table 9.11 is a sample listing of the variable expenses that are in a typical laboratory department.

The reason why revenue and expense figures are segregated into departments is to assign accountability and management responsibility. Departmental managers are given not only the duty of formulating their budgets but also the added responsibility of monitoring the positive and negative revenue/expense variances that occur on a monthly basis. Expenses are often differentiated between *discretionary* and *nondiscretionary* to distinguish what amounts are controllable.

Table 9.11 Laboratory Department: Expenses

Salary expense–general/administration	$80,000
Salary expense–technician/specialist	$400,000
Salary expense–other	$50,000
Subtotal salary expense	$530,000
Medical supplies	$600,000
Pharmaceuticals	$50,000
Office supplies	$25,000
General supplies	$10,000
Outside services	$120,000
Equipment rental	$30,000
Books and subscriptions	$5,000
Training and education	$5,000
Subtotal supply/other expenses	$845,000
Total expenses	$1,375,000

Discretionary expenses represent costs that can be adjusted or influenced; nondiscretionary or mandatory expenses are costs that are a necessity, and they need to be incurred. In hospital accounting, discretionary spending cuts are often implemented during the creation of the annual budget. Typical discretionary expenses would be training/education, employee recognition, and meals/entertainment. These departmental expenses can be reduced and not affect the quality of patient care given.

CRITICAL ISSUE

Responsibility accounting means that costs and revenues are allocated to the individual manager or managers who are responsible for making decisions about those items.

A key aspect of responsibility accounting is the actual reporting mechanism used to monitor these departments. The distribution of the monthly departmental reports is a function of month-end close, which is produced by the accounting department. The driving reason why these monthly reports are issued is to identify and explain variances from the budget.

Variance Analysis

Variance analysis is a process in which actual revenues and expenses are compared to the budgeted amounts, often on a monthly basis. Usually, departmental managers research the

Table 9.12 Revenue Variance

Nursery April YTD	YTD Budget	YTD Actual	Variance
Inpatient revenue	$5,000,000	$5,100,000	$100,000
Deliveries	2,000	2,000	0

variances that exist, but accounting personnel can also perform this duty. The review of budget variances is a *form of control* that checks to make sure that the hospital is on course to meet its goals and objectives. Prior to each fiscal year, hospital personnel budget each department's revenues and expenses. These departmental totals flow within the hospitalwide statement of operations/income statement, which helps formulate the other financial statements. Budgeted revenue and expense figures are predominantly formulated by the departmental manager, who should be aware of what is being spent and how many patients are being serviced. A revenue variance occurs when there is either a *price variance* or a *volume variance*. A price variance occurs when the price for services either rises or falls compared to what was budgeted. This rarely happens in the hospital accounting field since all prices are uniform no matter who the payer; however, certain clinical issues could arise in which a medical procedure that was currently not billed is now being billed. An example would be the circumcision procedure that occurs in the nursery when a child is delivered. Most hospitals formerly did not charge for this procedure. It was included in the cost of care, and hospitals absorbed this expense with no correlating revenue. Some hospitals have begun to bill for this procedure, and some payers have agreed to pay and some have not. The nursery departmental revenue of a sample hospital is listed Table 9.12. This increase in revenue is driven by an unforeseen change in a rate increase that was not budgeted.

From this example, the hospital is over budget by $100,000 in revenue in the nursery department. Imagine that the hospital decided to bill an additional $200 for the circumcision procedures beginning in April, and the total charge for a delivery was $2,500 ($5,000,000/2,000). Assume the fiscal year of the hospital begins in January, which means that January, February, and March should have correct revenue figures, but April revenue should be higher than what was budgeted due to the new charges. Also, assume that 500 deliveries occurred each month during the first 4 months of the year. In Table 9.12, the 4-month YTD (year-to-date) actual revenue figure is higher than that of the budget but not by an excessive figure. *The additional $100,000 in revenue is driven by an increase in price that is independent of volumes.* Through proper research and knowledge of hospital accounting, the employee reviewing the variance can determine that the increase in April revenue is driven by a price variance ($200 additional charge per procedure * 500 procedures incurred during the month of April). The volumes were constant, which means that somehow a charge increase occurred.

A volume variance exists when the budgeted statistical volumes do not match what actually occurred. Using the same nursery department example, assume that the charge per case is still $2,500; however, the amount of patients serviced varied from what was budgeted for the fiscal year (see Table 9.13).

In April, the 4-month actual inpatient revenue figure was $500,000 less than what was budgeted. Assume that the previously mentioned circumcision rate increase did not occur, which means that the reduction in revenue is driven by a decrease in patient volumes. The actual variance in revenue ($500,000) is the summation of the charge per delivery and the volume variance (200 * $2,500). Identifying a volume variance is usually much easier than identifying a price variance.

Table 9.13 Revenue Variance

Nursery April YTD	YTD Budget	YTD Actual	Variance
Inpatient revenue	$5,000,000	$4,500,000	($500,000)
Deliveries	2,000	1,800	(200)

The causation of this volume variance could be due to numerous factors, and the nursery manager needs to be informed of this issue. The problem could simply be that the department overbudgeted for the month, or maybe an OB/GYN (obstetrics/gynecology) physician has decided to take his or her patients to another facility. The proper identification and analysis of revenue variances is the result of an efficient and effective hospital environment.

Payroll

At year end, the payroll department must formulate all the wage earnings statements, that not only list the amounts paid to employees but also any federal and state withholding figures as well as other payroll-related benefits. Examples of additional amounts would be the employer and employee HSA (healthcare savings account) contributions, mileage reimbursement, and pretax contributions for long-term disability. All of these data are accumulated into a W-2 statement, which is provided to the employee so he or she can file annual tax returns. The data in the W-2 is not something that is easily formulated. The payroll staff must plan several months before the calendar year end to determine how to find, report, and reconcile all of these data.

Conclusion

The statement of operations is a report specific to those who have received tax-exempt status, and it is formulated by reporting the revenues and expenses that exist throughout a hospital. A for-profit hospital would use an income statement, and there are minor differences between the two documents. Both of the financial statements are primarily used for budgeting purposes and performance evaluation. The departmental statement contains only items that the departmental supervisor can control. These revenues and expenses are examined and reviewed each month using variance analysis not as a means to assign blame but to identify possible inefficiency. The primary purpose of both the income statement and statement of operations is to list what was earned during a period of time. The financial reports also list the resources used to provide services; however, they do not list any cash that was disbursed. A hospital accountant should be well versed on how to formulate and analyze both an income statement and statement of operations.

Chapter 10

Statement of Financial Position (Balance Sheet)

Introduction

Of the three types of hospitals discussed in this text, only for-profit hospitals would utilize the traditional balance sheet. The balance sheet is a commonly used financial statement that is formulated not only in healthcare accounting but also in virtually every other industry. It is a compilation of ledger account balances that provides financial information about a company's assets, liabilities, and equity. The balance sheet represents the basic accounting equation in that assets equal liabilities plus owner's equity. This equation is the fundamental aspect of accounting that reflects the proprietary theory that the remaining owner's interest is the result of subtracting liabilities from assets. In comparison, both not-for-profit and governmental hospitals use a statement of financial position, which basically substitutes net assets for equity. The statement of financial position segregates the balances within net assets and contains notes that explain or describe additional information. Both financial statements list the hospital's data at a moment in time rather than an interval of time and they assist decision makers examining the company's financial flexibility.

Cash

Of all the accounts in each financial statement, the cash balance is by far the most critical regardless of the industry. Cash is needed for numerous purposes, including but not limited to compensating employees for their services as well as paying vendors for supplies purchased. The cash asset is consistently evaluated and examined to determine if the appropriate balance is being sustained. Many ratios are pulled strictly from cash since a hospital's operations depend on its existence. The phrase "cash is king" is true in that a hospital can record all the revenue it desires, but without the appropriate cash balance, the facility will not be able to operate. The three main reasons why a hospital needs cash are as a medium of exchange, speculation, and a precautionary measure. The medium of exchange aspect of cash is required so employees and vendors can be paid for their services. Cash is speculative in that it is held to act on an investment that needs to be made quickly. Cash is also used as a precautionary measure in that companies may not foresee all the necessary expenses or financial issues that may occur in the future. Having satisfactory cash balances allows hospitals the comfort of having some security to account for unpredictable circumstances. Due to the numerous bank accounts that a hospital employs, a member of the accounting staff is usually responsible for completing a monthly *bank reconciliation,* which compares the hospital's cash balance to the balance listed on the bank statements. The staff accountant will reconcile the cash on the bank statement by adjusting for outstanding checks, deposits in transit, and bank fees.

Cash is classified as a current asset, and it also contains any cash-equivalent items, which are liquid assets that have maturities of 3 months or less. Examples of cash equivalents would be any short investments, such as treasury bills, commercial paper, or money market holdings. Either within a balance sheet or a statement of financial position, a hospital may classify an asset as restricted cash, which is cash used for special purposes, such as a bond sinking fund. The nature and use of this cash will determine when and if it will be used.

Accounts Receivable

Receivables represent money that is owed to the hospital for a variety of both clinical and nonclinical services. Accounts receivable usually represents the second-largest asset in a hospital; however, the balance does not provide any benefit unless it is transformed into cash. Hospitals will often present patient balances by payer rather than individual account. *Whether it be a balance sheet or a statement of financial position, the amount of receivables is always presented at their net balances or net realizable value.* In addition, healthcare facilities will often separate the receivables based on whether they are derived from treating a patient or another clinical function. For example, a statement of financial position will list patient receivables at net, but a separate line item for "other receivables" may exist that contains any Medicare/Medicaid cost report settlements. These settlement figures can be significant, depending on the status of filed cost reports. The revenue recorded to provide hospital services is recorded at its gross amount, and the correlating receivable is contractually adjusted to formulate an expected collection amount. The chapter on the statement of operations addresses the process of reducing a gross receivable to a net amount. The classification of receivables is recorded on an accrual basis, and it is listed as a current asset. A sample current assets listing in a statement of financial position or balance sheet is given in Table 10.1.

Table 10.1 Listing of Current Assets

Assets	2011	2010
Current Assets		
Cash and cash equivalents	$25,000	$20,000
Patients accounts receivable, net	$250,000	$245,000
Other receivables	$75,000	$70,000
Total current assets	$350,000	$335,000

Table 10.2   Example of Factoring

A collection agency charges a 7% factor fee and 10% interest on all account balances that are sold. In addition, the collection agency charges a 5% reserve for all balances. The total amount to be sold is $2,000,000, and it is due for collection in 90 days. The amount of cash to be received by the hospital for selling its accounts receivable is calculated as follows:

Amount of receivables factored	$2,000,000
Reserve 5%	($100,000)
Factor fee 7%	($140,000)
Subtotal	$1,760,000
Interest (10% on 90 days)	($44,000)
Amount to be received	$1,716,000

$44,000 = (90/365 * $1,760,000) * 0.10

Much like other businesses, healthcare organizations will sell their receivables to collection agencies. Termed *factoring*, a hospital will sell uncollected patient balances to a third party that specializes in collecting cash. The advantages of factoring are that the costs of collection are minimized, and the collection agency can collect payment more efficiently than the hospital. The disadvantage of factoring is that the reduction in costs from having to collect on patient accounts may not offset the fees and interest charged by the collection agency. The amount that is factored usually represents the patient portion of the hospital bill (bad debt) rather than the insurance company's portion. Unfortunately, when factoring receivables the removal of unpaid patient balances from the general ledger is not a simple process. Besides a factoring fee, a hospital must also take into account a possible reserve percentage and interest amount. An example of this journal entry is given in Table 10.2.

The total cash that a hospital would receive based on these assumptions would be $1,716,000. The benefits of outsourcing these receivables must be balanced against the cost. In this sample, the cost of factoring the receivable is $284,000 ($100,000 + $140,000 + $44,000); however, the reserve figure of $100,000 may or may not be absorbed by the collection agency.

The hospital accounts receivable balance is listed as an asset, but its consistent growth can be negative for a hospital in that the higher the receivable, the less cash is collected. Auditors and other parties will dissect receivable balances to determine if they need to be adjusted or additionally reserved. The maintenance of hospital receivables can be a cumbersome process since many payers take weeks and even months to pay hospitals. This lag in payment is an inherent weakness of hospital reimbursement that must be monitored and minimized. Proper protocols implemented by the business office/collections department can decrease the amount of time it takes for the numerous payers to reimburse hospitals for services rendered.

CRITICAL ISSUE

The receivables recorded in the balance sheet statement of financial position are listed at their net balances, in other words, what is expected to be collected or converted to cash.

Inventories

Due to patient needs and unexpected volumes, a hospital must keep a satisfactory amount of inventory on site. Inventory is not a desirable asset for a business because it represents an unnecessary cost. This amount must be minimized through proper supply chain distribution and inventory control. Typical hospital inventory items can range from medical supplies used for surgery to gasoline used to service facility vehicles. Inventory is different from a capital asset in that it is not depreciated. Inventory represents items that will be consumed in the near future, and they will not be resold. The valuation of inventory can be a complex accounting process, and certain methods such as LCM (lower of cost or market), LIFO (last in, first out), or FIFO (first in, first out) are often used. The notes to the financial statements will explain which inventory valuation method is being used.

CRITICAL ISSUE

Inventory or supplies are not classified as fixed assets or depreciated since they are consumed in the day-to-day operations of the hospital.

Investments

Regardless if a hospital is incorporated as for-profit or not-for-profit, the facility will make the appropriate investments to obtain additional cash. For presentation purposes in a balance sheet, a for-profit hospital will classify investments in three different groupings: held-to-maturity (HTM) securities, trading securities, and available-for-sale (AFS) securities. *HTM securities* are investments made by a hospital with the intent to hold until they mature. These investments usually provide dividends to a hospital, and they are presented in a balance sheet at what is termed *amortized cost*. Investments that are made to be sold in the short term are classified as *trading securities,* and they are reported in the balance sheet at fair value. Since these investments are recorded at fair value (usually at month end), there will be additions and subtractions to this investment balance based on fluctuation in the market. A for-profit hospital needs to record these changes in fair value as unrealized holding gains or losses in earnings. A final investment type is classified as *AFS*, and these financial instruments represent any investment that cannot be classified as a trading or HTM security. Much like trading securities, AFS securities are recorded at fair value in the balance sheet; however, changes in fair value are recorded in a separate component of the equity. This classification of investments into trading, HTM, or AFS is utilized not only in healthcare but also in other industries outside the healthcare realm.

Not-for-profit hospitals, in contrast, record all investments at fair value in the statement of financial position, and all unrealized holding gains or losses are reported as changes in net assets. All investment return that is not subject to donor restriction is classified in unrestricted net assets. Any return that is subject to restriction is classified as either temporarily restricted or permanently restricted.

A significant problem for both for-profit and not-for-profit hospitals is how to account for a substantial decline in investment value that is other than temporary. The fair value of an investment could decline for various reasons, but healthcare accounting personnel must test for what is

Table 10.3   Impairment Example

Investment A: $100,000 purchased on January 1, 2011	
January 31, 2011: The fair value of Investment A is $75,000, and management does not believe this reduction is temporary.	
Loss on impairment of investment	$25,000
Contra holding account investments	$25,000
Investment A: Balance sheet value on January 1, 2011	$100,000
Impairment	($25,000)
Investment A: Balance sheet value on January 31, 2011	$75,000

termed *impairment.* The two major indicators that an asset is in serious trouble are that fair value is below cost and the decline is consistent over an extended time period. Approximations to what is considered an "extended time period" could range from 6 months to 1 year. Additional impairment factors are that the condition of the third party that sold the investment has deteriorated or the investment security has been downgraded by an agency. The act of impairing an investment should not be taken lightly since once the asset is written down, it cannot be reversed. An example of an impairment entry is given in Table 10.3.

As mentioned, this $25,000 reduction is permanent, and it is recorded as a loss. Even if the fair value of Investment A rises above $75,000, the hospital cannot record a holding gain because of the impairment entry on January 31, 2011. The $25,000 loss is not recorded as an extraordinary item but instead is listed as operating expense.

CRITICAL ISSUE

The process of impairing an investment should be researched extensively since once the asset is written down it cannot be reversed (generally accepted accounting principle [GAAP] rule).

A sample current assets listing in a statement of financial position or balance sheet is given in Table 10.4.

Property and Equipment (Fixed Assets)

Hospitals use various types of equipment, which can range in cost from several thousand to several million dollars. Examples of fixed hospital equipment would be a magnetic resonance imaging (MRI) machine, surgical lasers/robots, computers, and the building itself. These numerous types of assets are classified into groupings often called land, land improvements, buildings, major movable equipment, and minor equipment. All of these asset groupings are totaled into one total fixed-asset sum. Fixed assets are unique in that they are depreciated over time, so that a portion of the historical cost of the asset can be allocated to periods that they benefit. The concept of depreciation is fundamental to the accounting profession, and it is usually one of the first concepts addressed

Table 10.4   Listing of Current Assets

Assets	2011	2010
Current Assets		
Cash and cash equivalents	$25,000	$20,000
Patients accounts receivable, net	$250,000	$245,000
Other receivables	$75,000	$70,000
Inventories	$45,000	$40,000
Investments (current portion)	$10,000	$15,000
Total current assets	$405,000	$390,000

in accounting student tests. There are numerous depreciation methods that can be used to allocate cost; however, most companies use the straight-line method because of its ease of use and simplicity. The basic straight-line formula is

Straight Line Depreciation = Historical Cost less Salvage Value/Useful Life

The historical cost is the amount paid for the piece of equipment plus any installation costs, testing costs, shipping costs, and sales tax. The salvage value is the estimated value of the equipment at the end of the useful life (very seldom do hospitals estimate a salvage value). The useful life of the asset is at the discretion of the hospital; however, the AHA (American Hospital Association) publishes a useful guideline for estimated useful lives for property and equipment utilized by hospitals. An example of a common depreciation adjusting entry is given in Table 10.5.

The monthly depreciation expense that is debited flows through the income statement or statement of operations and reduces net income. *Depreciation is an operating expense that is presented much like salary and supply expense even though no cash has been disbursed.* The process of

Table 10.5   Depreciation Example

X-ray equipment purchased on January 1, 2011, for $120,000.		
Salvage value is $20,000 and estimated useful life is 10 years.		
Adjusting depreciation expense recorded on February 1, 2011 = ($120,000 –$20,000)/10 = $10,000 per year, $833.33 per month (12 months in the year, 10,000/12 = 833.33).		
The entry to record the purchase of the X-ray equipment on January 1, 2011:		
X-ray equipment (historical cost)	$120,000	
Cash		$120,000
The entry to record the monthly depreciation expense on February 1, 2011:		
Depreciation expense	$833.33	
Accumulated depreciation		$833.33

depreciation is not used to reduce the asset amount but to allocate systematically the cost of utilizing the fixed asset. Another benefit of using depreciation is that it formulates a net book value figure for each fixed asset purchased. For example, the X-ray machine purchased on January 1, 2011, had a balance sheet value of $120,000; however; the net book value on February 1, 2011, is now $119,167.

X-ray historical cost	$120,000
Accumulated depreciation	($833)
Net book value	$119,167

The accumulated depreciation account balance is termed a *contra account* because it offsets the balance of another account rather than being added to or subtracted from it. The accumulated depreciation credit of the monthly adjusting entry affects the balance sheet or statement of financial position in that it reduces the value of the equipment without affecting the historical cost. A significant aspect of capitalizing an asset is that the item can possibly be sold in the future. By depreciating an asset, the hospital can formulate a net book value amount that allows the facility to record either a gain or a loss if the item is sold.

A hospital may have other assets that are not tangible but still need to be listed on a financial statement. These nonfinancial items are classified as *intangible assets,* and they have no physical form. Examples of intangibles would be patents, copyrights, and trademarks. Instead of being depreciated, these assets are amortized over a period of time.

Table 10.6 provides a list of current and noncurrent assets in the statement of financial position or balance sheet.

Accounts Payable

The presentation of a liability for either for-profit or not-for-profit hospitals is very similar to that of any other business with the exception of a few ledger accounts. The liability section of a balance sheet/statement of financial position predominantly represents what is owed by the hospital, and much like the asset section, it is segregated into either current or noncurrent liabilities. The current section contains all liabilities that are due in 1 year or less. Outside healthcare in other industries such as manufacturing, the current portion of the liability section might contain accounts that are less than 1 year or what is termed the operating cycle. The *operating cycle* is the sum of the days that inventory is held before it is sold plus the number of days that accounts receivable is held before collection less the number of days accounts payable outstanding (1).

A common liability would be accounts payable that represent the balance owed to vendors or suppliers for goods and services. This liability account exists because of the time lag between receiving the goods or services and actually paying for them. *The accounts payable account reflects the need for the use of credit as a payment for goods in not only the healthcare accounting field but all industries.* Unlike bonds payable or notes payable, interest is not accrued on accounts payable, and the balance is reduced by every check run. The accounts payable balance represents the amount due for both medical and nonmedical supplies such as surgical implants, equipment repairs, or printer cartridges. The supply chain methodology for how these items are ordered is different for

Table 10.6   Listing of Total Assets

Assets	2011	2010
Current Assets		
Cash and cash equivalents	$25,000	$20,000
Patients accounts receivable, net	$250,000	$245,000
Other receivables	$75,000	$70,000
Inventories	$45,000	$40,000
Investments (current portion)	$10,000	$15,000
Total current assets	$405,000	$390,000
Property and equipment (gross)	$1,400,000	$1,200,000
(Accumulated depreciation)	($510,000)	($500,000)
Property and equipment (net)	$890,000	$700,000
Investments (noncurrent portion)	$20,000	$25,000
Total noncurrent assets	$910,000	$725,000
Total assets	$1,315,000	$1,115,000

each facility, and many hospitals have begun to employ popular accounts payable/inventory methods such as JIT (just in time) to decrease costs. The following is an example of a typical accounts payable ledger entry:

a) Medical supplies expense	$25,000	
a) Accounts payable		$25,000

The entry follows the accrual method of double-entry accounting in that expenses are recorded when they are incurred. The purchase of the medical supplies was made (a) because a particular clinical department needed the item for medical services. Once the particular hospital pays the vendor/supplier for services, the following entry is recorded:

b) Accounts payable	$25,000	
b) Cash		$25,000

In the balance sheet/statement of financial position, the payment of cash (b) has reduced the accounts payable balance to zero, and the cash balance has been reduced by the payment to the vendor. The medical supply expense entry flows through the income statement or statement of operations and reduces net income.

Medical Supply Expense	Accounts Payable		Cash	
a) $25,000	b) $25,000	a) $25,000	b) $25,000	
$25,000				$25,000

Another entry to record expense within a department is to reduce inventory for an item that has already been purchased by the hospital. The hospital previously purchased $25,000 worth of medical supplies; however, the product was not utilized. (c) These supplies are classified as inventory in the financial statements. The following entry would reclass the supplies if they were requested by a department for use in the hospital:

d) Medical supplies expense	$25,000	
d) Inventory		$25,000

Inventory		Medical Supply Expense
c) 25,000	d) 25,000	d) $25,000

Another example of a current liability would be patient refunds. Due to the numerous insurance companies that exist, a healthcare facility may be overpaid for services provided. This money is owed to the appropriate third parties. Appropriate billing protocols can minimize the balance in the liability; however, patient refunds cannot be completely eliminated. Overpayments occur in hospitals regardless of size or services offered, and there will always be cases of a possible refund on a hospital bill. A hospital usually determines that a refund is needed when there is a credit balance in a patient's account. After the billing representative reviews the account for accuracy, the credit balance figure is reclassed to a patient refund account, where it remains until a check run occurs. An example of a typical patient refund entry is

b) Patient accounts receivable balance	$5,000	
b) Patient refund		$5,000

The patient had a credit balance of $5,000 (a) in his or her account, which usually means that an overpayment occurred. To zero out this account, the patient's accounts receivable balance was debited for $5,000, and the correlating credit to the patient's refund (liability) account is $5,000 (b):

c) Patient refund	$5,000	
c) Cash		$5,000

The patient or patient's insurance company will then receive a refund check of $5,000 for the overpayment of hospital services (c). Often, patient refund balances are classified under "other current liabilities."

Patient Balance		Patient Refund		Cash	
	a) $5,000	c) $5,000	b) $5,000	c) $5,000	
b) $5,000				$5,000	

Much like other service industries, a majority of the expenses in a hospital are driven by salary costs. Nurses, surgical technicians, and other healthcare personnel are responsible for approximately 35% to 40% of the total cost in a typical hospital. These employees are compensated not only with salaries but also with fringe benefits such as holiday pay, vacation pay, and sick pay. Often referred to as *paid time off* (PTO), this expense/liability must be accrued just like any other employee expense. For a hospital to accrue an employee expense such as vacation pay, four criteria must be met:

1. The employee's right to receive compensation is based on services already performed.
2. The employee's right to receive compensation is vested.
3. It is probable that the compensation will be paid.
4. The amount can be reasonably estimated.

If *all four* of these criteria are met, then a member of the accounting staff would accrue an expense and a correlating liability for the appropriate sick, holiday, or vacation pay. An example of a sample PTO entry is as follows:

Paid time off expense	$200,000
Paid time off liability	$200,000

The estimation and recording of this expense/liability is usually provided by the payroll department of the hospital since it has access to employee pay rates and vested PTO amounts. Another liability that relates to employees is postretirement benefits for those employees who qualify for pensions. Hospitals are required to identify and disclose the amount of net periodic pension costs attributable to that period and the net amount of the entire pension plan. The formulation of this entry is complex and beyond the nature of this text, but hospitals are typically required to present this liability much like other companies.

Table 10.7 provides a list of the current liabilities in a sample statement of financial position or balance sheet.

Table 10.7 Listing of Current Liabilities

Liabilities	2011	2010
Current Liabilities		
Accrued salaries and benefits	$55,000	$50,000
Accounts payable	$35,000	$40,000
Other current liabilities	$12,000	$14,000
Total current liabilities	$102,000	$104,000

Long-Term Debt

Hospitals require large sums of cash not only to expand operations but also to upgrade buildings and other facilities. The primary source of financing for hospitals is long-term debt since neither governmental nor not-for-profit hospitals have retained earnings or the ability to issue stock. A significant benefit of being a 501(c)(3) hospital is that the hospital can qualify for tax-exempt long-term debt, which offers a longer maturity period and a lower interest cost. The majority of tax-exempt debt issued by hospitals is revenue bonds, which are secured by the hospital's revenues. Most, if not all, hospitals cannot issue bonds by themselves, so a financing authority is needed that issues the bonds to the public on behalf of the healthcare organization. The bond obligation is reported both as a current liability (12 months of debt) and a long-term liability (remaining balance) in the balance sheet/statement of financial position. As a requirement of tax-exempt bond financing, hospitals must keep what is termed a *bond covenant* during the tenure in which the debt is held. These bond covenants vary, but a majority require a certain amount of cash to be restricted, and certain financial ratios must be maintained.

Hospitals often restructure debt over time due to new capital projects, cash management issues, or other operating issues. New debt is occasionally reissued for the purpose of replacing existing debt, and it is termed *advance refunding*. Advance refunding allows hospitals to restructure long-term liabilities either to take advantage of declining interest rates or to eliminate troublesome bond covenants. Sometimes, the use of advance refunding involving tax-exempt debt can be subject to arbitrage rules. A hospital may incur a higher return on a tax-exempt bond than the stated interest rate on the bond. In this scenario, an arbitrage rebate liability occurs, and the excess of the interest is recorded as a liability that must be paid to the U.S. Treasury for the hospital to retain tax-exempt status.

Other Liabilities

Other businesses incur lawsuits based on patents, copyrights, or product negligence. The healthcare field also incurs a tremendous amount of lawsuits, but the lawsuits are predominantly restricted to medical malpractice. Patients often sue hospitals for what they believe is negligence or carelessness. There are cases when hospitals are truly liable, such as the administration of incorrect medication; however, some medical malpractice claims are brought about by unscrupulous lawyers who are looking for a substantial portion of the damages that were supposedly inflicted on their client. It is the duty of the hospital to either employ or outsource a legal department that is capable of defending the hospital against such claims. It is the duty of the hospital's accounting department to ensure that the potential lawsuits are recorded and presented appropriately.

The total amount accrued as a liability in the financial statements includes all costs associated with litigating or settling claims. The amount is recorded when the incidents that give rise to these lawsuits occur, not when the lawsuit is resolved or settled. *The lawsuit is accrued only if it is probable and reasonably estimated.* If the legal staff in the hospital believes that the loss from the lawsuit is remote, then the amount is not accrued, but it is disclosed in the notes to the financial statements. In estimating the probability of lawsuit outcomes, the hospital may develop a monetary range. It is at the discretion of the legal staff to determine if a lawsuit is either probable or remote; however, when formulating a range of dollar amounts, the conservative accrual would be the least-optimistic estimate. Most lawsuits against hospitals are detrimental and require the accrual of a loss; however, some lawsuits may be due to litigation against another party. In these instances, the accrual of a gain is not permitted even if the amount is probable and reasonably estimated. The gain is recorded when the lawsuit is resolved rather than when the incident occurred. A typical accrual of an unfavorable lawsuit reasonable estimated at $500,000 is

Lawsuit expense	$500,000
Lawsuit liability	$500,000

The hospital has credited a liability account for the expected unfavorable lawsuit and has debited an expense for the correlating amount. The lawsuit expense will flow through the income statement or statement of operations as a reduction to net income.

CRITICAL ISSUE

Medical malpractice lawsuits against a hospital are accrued when the incident occurs, and the amount is probable and reasonably estimated.

Table 10.8 lists the current and noncurrent liabilities in a sample statement of financial position or balance sheet.

Net Assets

A significant difference between a for-profit and a not-for-profit hospital is the reporting of net assets in the financial statements. Net assets are somewhat similar to equity that is reported by for-profit entities to describe accumulated capital. Due to its tax-exempt status, a not-for-profit hospital has to segregate net assets into three distinct groupings, and the fundamental reason for this process is that the hospital can monitor compliance with donor restrictions and maintain fiscal accountability. The primary net asset grouping and usually the largest of the three is termed

Table 10.8   Listing of Total Liabilities

Liabilities	2011	2010
Current Liabilities		
Accrued salaries and benefits	$55,000	$50,000
Accounts payable	$35,000	$40,000
Other current liabilities	$12,000	$14,000
Current portion of long-term debt	$60,000	$60,000
Total current liabilities	$162,000	$164,000
Noncurrent Liabilities		
Long-term portion of debt	$1,000,000	$1,060,000
Other liabilities	$200,000	$250,000
Total liabilities	$1,362,000	$1,474,000

unrestricted net assets. These assets are those contributions given to a hospital at which the discretion of use for these funds is given to the nonprofit facility. An example of an unrestricted net asset would be someone giving money to a nonprofit with no stipulations on use of the funds. The donor receives a tax deduction for the donation, and the hospital administrators can use the money as they please. The only restriction to the use of unrestricted net assets can be traced to the bylaws or articles of incorporation for that facility. The funds should be used to enhance hospital operations or serve the needs of the community.

The distinction between temporarily and permanently restricted net assets is more complex but is primarily based on the nature of the donor's restriction. *Temporarily restricted net assets* have considerations that are dictated by time or the purpose of the donation. Examples of a temporarily restricted net asset would be a donor giving $1 million to a hospital and specifying that the amount be used for vaccinations in an economically challenged community for 5 years. After 5 years, if any balance remains, the hospital may use the funds at its discretion. In other words, the remaining balance is transferred to unrestricted net assets. *Permanently restricted net assets* are similar to temporarily restricted net assets except the restrictions are not removed by the passage of time or the actions of the hospital. An example would be a donor giving $1 million to a hospital and specifying that money be invested and interest from this investment be used for vaccinations for the poor. This example would be classified as a permanent endowment fund.

Information regarding the nature and amount of these net asset figures can be found either in the notes to the financial statements or within the statement of changes in net assets. All funds that are donated to a 501(c)(3) hospital must be classified in these three groupings. Much like a not-for-profit hospital, a governmental healthcare organization would also be required to segregate donations into these groupings.

CRITICAL ISSUE

The classification of donated funds is critical to hospital accounting. The amounts must be classified as unrestricted, temporarily restricted, or permanently restricted.

Statement of Changes in Net Assets

Even though the total amount of net assets is listed in the statement of financial position, the breakdown and classification of the increases and decreases of fund balances are listed in a separate financial statement. Also known as the statement of changes in net assets, this financial document emphasizes aggregated information about the entity as a whole rather than the individual funds. An example of the statement of changes in net assets is given in Table 10.9.

Table 10.9   Statement of Changes in Net Assets

	Unrestricted	Temporarily Restricted	Permanently Restricted	Total
Balance as of December 31, 2008	$450,000	$55,000	$10,000	$515,000
Revenue and gains over expenses/loss	$50,000			$50,000
Contribution and grants		$5,000	$1,000	$6,000
Net assets released from restrictions	$10,000	($10,000)		
Increase/decrease in net assets	$60,000	($5,000)	$1,000	$56,000
	Unrestricted	Temporarily Restricted	Permanently Restricted	Total
Balance as of December 31, 2009	$510,000	$50,000	$11,000	$571,000
Revenue and gains over expenses/loss	$30,000			$30,000
Contribution and grants		$8,000	$2,000	$10,000
Net assets released from restrictions	$5,000	($5,000)		
Increase/decrease in net assets	$35,000	$3,000	$2,000	$40,000
Balance as of December 31, 2010	$545,000	$53,000	$13,000	$611,000

The statement of net assets is a self-explanatory document that primarily lists the donations given to a hospital and the movement of those from restricted to unrestricted. The financial statement gives a comparative analysis of the last 2 years' net asset amounts. The net assets statement is specific to businesses that have qualified for 501(c)(3) status. *If a hospital is classified as for profit, then the statement of net assets would not be created.* Instead, a statement of changes in equity would be formulated, which lists not only hospital profit/loss but also total comprehensive income. *Comprehensive income* can be a confusing term, but it is primarily the sum of net income and other financial items that have not been realized, such as foreign currency translation gains/losses. The goal of reporting comprehensive income is to list all the operating and financial events that have affected the equity of the for-profit hospital.

Statement of Cash Flows

The statement of cash flows is a financial document that virtually every for-profit or not-for-profit business reports because of its classification and division of cash. The statement reflects the flow of cash for that particular period, and it is divided into three different sections: operating, investing, and financing. The operating cash activities are generated from patient services, while investing cash activities relate to either debt or capital purchases. Financing activities primarily relate to restricted income, contributions, or other debt issues. The statement of cash flows pulls information from other statements as well as other sources in the general ledger. This document is commonly reviewed by a select few in hospital management, and it is examined to determine how much cash is being collected/dispersed and from what sources. The statement of cash flows is not a measure of performance evaluation, and most hospital personnel outside accounting rarely examine the document. An example statement of cash flows is given in Table 10.10.

The statement of cash flows can be a complex document to formulate if someone is not skilled in the debits and credits of financial accounting. For the purpose of this text, only a broad overview of the classification of cash is given.

Financial Statement Notes

The notes are considered part of the financial statements, and they are not used to correct mistakes or improper presentations. The notes to the financial statements usually include a description of the entity and a summary of the accounting policies used to formulate the statements. The notes also provide supporting detail to many of the amounts listed. Accounting issues such as inventory valuation, contingencies, and depreciation methods would be the types of disclosures written in the notes to the financial statements. In hospital reimbursement, the total amount of charity care is usually disclosed in the notes to the financial statements.

Conclusion

The statement of financial position is a document that is vital to the healthcare accounting field because it reveals the financial condition of the hospital. Comparable to a balance sheet, this financial statement reflects a "snapshot" or single moment of time for that facility. Usually, both of the statements are formulated on a monthly/annual basis, with occasional reporting occurring

Table 10.10 Statement of Cash Flows

	Year 2	Year 1
Cash Flows from Operating Activities		
Increase in net assets	$100,000	$75,000
Gain on sale of equipment	$25,000	$20,000
Increase in patient accounts receivable	($75,000)	($60,000)
Decrease in other liabilities	$10,000	$12,000
Depreciation	$45,000	$45,000
Net cash provided by operating activities	$105,000	$92,000
Cash Flows from Investing Activities		
Additions to property and equipment	($25,000)	($22,000)
Termination of swap investment	($2,000)	($500)
Net cash provided by investing activities	($27,000)	($22,500)
Cash Flows from Financing Activities		
Payments of long-term debt	($10,000)	($10,000)
Payments of capital leases	($1,000)	($1,000)
Net cash provided by financing activities	($11,000)	($11,000)
Net increase/decrease in cash and cash equivalents	$67,000	$58,500
Cash and cash equivalents, beginning of year	$20,000	$23,000
Cash and cash equivalents, end of year	$87,000	$81,500

on a quarterly basis. A weakness of these financial documents is that many items reported are listed as estimates, such as net receivables and accumulated depreciation. These values are subject to change; however, conservative ledger entries should minimize any misinformation presented. The statement of net assets is a report that is essential to a not-for-profit hospital because of its classification of the numerous donations that a tax-exempt facility receives. The statement of cash flows is an additional report that accumulates and segregates both outgoing and incoming cash for the healthcare facility, and it is formulated by a hospital regardless if the facility is classified as for-profit or not-for-profit. The primary purpose of formulating these numerous financial statements is to assist hospital management in making the appropriate operational decisions.

Reference

1. Loth, Richard. 2011. Operating performance ratios: operating cycle. http://investopedia.com.university/ratios/operating-performance/ratio3.asp (accessed November 26, 2011).

Chapter 11

Coding

Introduction

The coding of a patient's medical chart is a technical, complex process that is unique to healthcare. Also referred to as medical records or health information management (HIM), coding is often perceived as the most perplexing aspect of the hospital revenue cycle due to the various terminology and jargon used to transform what was performed on the patient into a billable invoice. Coding is a vital component of hospital reimbursement since capturing the appropriate amount of revenue significantly affects the hospital's ability to maintain operations. Each hospital maintains a specific charge description master (CDM) for hospital services, and the formula to code a patient's chart varies on the clinical treatment received. The coding process has been shaped and improved by recent technology as the introduction of the electronic medical record (EMR) attempts to improve quality of care and minimize redundancy. Unfortunately, it is not feasible to detail the actual coding of a medical record in this text, but an overview of the concepts and methodology is given.

Charge Description Master

The pricing of hospital services is derived from a catalog of services known as a charge description master. The CDM is the charge listing for all hospital services, and it represents the "menu" of procedures, supplies, and services that a hospital offers. Depending on the size and capability, some hospitals may have significantly larger CDMs than others, and each CDM is specific to a hospital. The CDM contains not only the description and charge for the service but also any federally mandated billing codes. The CDM itself is a computer file that typically contains approximately several thousand line items. One of these codes is the UB-04 or Uniform Billing Code, which is used to identify the service and create uniformity. *The CDM or simply "charge master" basically represents the selling price of all services.* Much like any other business, a hospital offers a price; however, in healthcare the payment received is significantly different. The CDM is used as a reference tool when negotiating contracts with third parties, and hospital charges are sometimes benchmarked against other facilities that perform similar services. Even though a hospital provides a variety of services and procedures, the facility must charge all patients an equal amount even though the facility is reimbursed a different amount by each payer. The CDM creates uniformity and transparency in that regardless of whether the patient was insured by Medicare or Blue Cross/ Blue Shield, the price of the service does not change. In other words, the CDM basically creates a gross amount used to generate the patient's bill. The layout of each CDM varies from hospital to hospital, but generally each file has a group of core data elements. The price of each procedure is accompanied by a specific code that consists of both an FIM (financial item master) and a SIM (service item master) code. The *FIM code* is a hospital-specific number that is used not only for billing purposes but also to ensure that each department receives revenue for services provided. Within each FIM code is a *SIM code* that identifies the numerous procedures or services that are performed at the hospital. Some hospitals term the combination of both the FIM and SIM codes as a procedure charge code; however, the SIM code itself is always a component of the FIM code. In the following hypothetical example, a CDM code for a cardiac procedure is used.

FIM Number	UB Code	Description	Price
1000-12345	0480	Cardiac procedure	$20,000

The SIM code in the FIM would be 12345 for this sample listing. Also in the CDM are revenue codes that are uniform for all hospitals. A national committee with various regional components formulates a listing of four-digit codes used to report types of services provided. The purpose of this UB code is to identify the service for ease of comparison both locally and nationally; however, the MAC (Medicare administrative contractor) in that state or region decides which UB codes should be utilized. It often reflects where the service was provided. An example of a revenue code would be 0450, which would mean emergency room services were utilized. The national UB-04 codes are used significantly throughout the cost-reporting process as gross revenue is reclassed from department to department. Sample revenue codes used in a UB-04 are listed in Table 11.1.

Table 11.1 Sample UB-04 Revenue Codes

0200	Intensive Care
0210	Coronary Care
0220	Special Charges
0230	Incremental Nursing Care
0240	All Inclusive Ancillary
0250	Pharmacy
0260	IV Therapy
0270	Medical/Surgical Supplies
0280	Oncology
0290	Durable Medical Equipment

Note: A full list of all the UB-04 revenue codes is given in Appendix A.

Usually, hospitals employ a CDM coordinator whose purpose is to maintain the CDM so that a clean claim is produced the first time. The CDM is also needed not only for compliance issues but also to identify patterns and trends that exist in the facility. The process of coding is often separated between hard coding and soft coding. *Hard coding* is the systematic coding completed by the CDM, and it occurs in approximately 99% of all outpatient medical records. *Soft coding* is the manual coding completed by hospital employees, and it occurs in 99% of all inpatient medical records. The justification for these differences is that the *International Classification of Diseases, Ninth Revision* (ICD-9) codes are not built in the CDM. The CDM consists of only Healthcare Common Procedure Coding System (HCPCS) level 1 and 2 codes. Medical advancements and improvements in technology have made the coding process a dynamic field that needs to be monitored consistently as new services and procedures are introduced.

Inpatient Coding

If a patient is admitted to a hospital, then he or she will be given inpatient status. A large portion of those who are admitted to a hospital are the elderly (Medicare), and hospitals are reimbursed for services based on the inpatient prospective payment system (IPPS) model. Many other insurance providers have used this reimbursement method as a basis to pay hospitals; however, certain components of the diagnosis-related group (DRG) model may be modified or altered. Approximately 750 DRGs were applicable as of 2011, and they are driven by two separate principle diagnosis and principle procedure codes. All inpatients regardless of insurance provider are assigned an *ICD-9-CM* (*International Classification of Diseases, Ninth Revision, Clinical Modification*) diagnosis code. It is the responsibility of the hospital coders to determine which ICD code best represents the inpatient stay. *A patient may have been admitted for numerous conditions, and he or she may be assigned numerous codes, but each patient can only have one principle* ICD-9-CM *diagnosis code and one principle* ICD-9-CM *procedure code.* Through the use of these two principle codes, a DRG can be formulated. A patient does not need both a principle diagnosis/principle procedure to formulate a DRG. It may occur, but usually it is either one or the other. The principle diagnosis code drives the medical portion the DRG, while the principle procedure code drives the surgical portion of the DRG (see Table 11.2).

The principle diagnosis is the condition established "after study" that is responsible for the hospital admission. The after-study component is significant because it is not always the admitting diagnosis but rather the diagnosis after clinical tests that proves to be the reason for admission. The *ICD* codes are formulated, updated, and maintained by the World Health Organization (WHO). There are approximately 14,000 different *ICD-9-CM* codes; however, this figure will expand with the introduction of *ICD-10-CM*. Much like the change from a DRG to MS-DRG (Medicare Severity-DRG) structure described in the Medicare chapter, the WHO has updated the

Table 11.2 Formulation of DRG

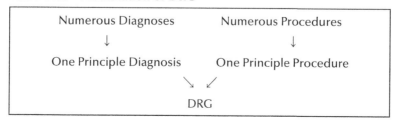

Table 11.3   ICD-10-CM Codes

Chapter	Codes	Description
1	A00–B99	Certain Infectious and Parasitic Diseases
2	C00–D48	Neoplasms
3	D50–D89	Diseases of the Blood and Blood-Forming Organs
4	E00–E90	Endocrine, Nutritional, and Metabolic Diseases
5	F00–F99	Mental and Behavioral Disorders
6	G00–G99	Diseases of the Nervous System
7	H00–H59	Diseases of the Eye and Adnexa
8	H60–H95	Diseases of the Ear and Mastoid Process
9	I00–I99	Diseases of the Circulatory System
10	J00–J99	Diseases of the Respiratory System
11	K00–K93	Diseases of the Digestive System
12	L00–L99	Diseases of the Skin and Subcutaneous Tissue
13	M00–M99	Diseases of the Musculoskeletal System
14	N00–N99	Diseases of the Genitourinary System
15	O00–O99	Pregnancy and Childbirth
16	P00–P96	Certain Conditions Originating in the Perinatal Period
17	Q00–Q99	Congenital Malformations and Deformations
18	R00–R99	Symptoms and Signs of Abnormal Laboratory Findings
19	S00–T98	Injury, Poisoning, and Other Causes
20	V01–Y98	External Causes of Morbidity
21	Z00–Z99	Other Factors Influencing Health Status
22	U00–U99	Codes for Special Purposes

ICD codes from a ninth edition to a tenth edition to better capture more health-related conditions. Table 11.3 presents a block grouping of all the *ICD-10-CM* codes.

The official use of the *ICD-10-CM* codes begins on October 1, 2013; however, this date is subject to delay. All hospitals that comply with the Health Insurance Portability and Accountability Act (HIPAA) regulations must use the *ICD-10-CM* methodology. The monetary affect of changing from the ninth edition to the tenth edition cannot be determined without performing a comprehensive analysis since so many variables affect the *ICD* codes. The new listing incorporates greater specificity and detail, which should result in improved quality. Some diseases have been reclassified, while some chapters have been restructured. Hospital management must be aware of the change to the *ICD-10-CM* methodology because of its impact on the revenue cycle.

The inpatient diagnosis codes are three digits with a decimal point separating the fourth and fifth digits; procedure codes are two digits followed by two additional numbers. *ICD-9-CM* diagnosis codes contain a minimum of three digits and a maximum of five. In coding, it is important that all diagnoses must be coded to the highest level of specificity, meaning that as many digits as allowed must be used to code a diagnosis. Certain codes, termed V and E codes, are subsets used in inpatient coding that describe a circumstance other than the diagnosis. A V code would be used if a patient had a communicable disease, a need for isolation, or other potential health hazards. An E code would be used to describe external causes of injury, such as an auto accident or poisoning. Coding departments often employ an assigned DRG coordinator whose responsibility is to review each DRG-reimbursed chart before it is submitted for processing. An essential element of the coding process is that the doctor only document the numerous diagnosis and procedures that relate to the patient. *If only a nurse documents a patient's chart, then medical records employees cannot use this information for coding purposes. A doctor/physician must document the patient's condition for the information to be relevant to coding.* Clinical personnel do not have the ability to determine the actual codes that are created from the numerous medical procedures and services. This segregation of duties improves the integrity of coding a patient's medical chart.

CRITICAL ISSUE

Coders, not nurses or doctors, classify the appropriate reimbursement figures that affect a hospital's profitability.

Outpatient Coding

Unlike inpatient reimbursement, the outpatient setting is significantly different due to the lack of time spent in a hospital environment. Many third parties have adopted the Medicare APC (Ambulatory Payment Classification) as a payment methodology for outpatient services. The APC model is different from the DRG reimbursement methodology in that a fee schedule rather than a unique blend rate is used. *A patient may have numerous APC designations but can only have one DRG.* The Centers for Medicare and Medicaid Services (CMS) implemented the APC methodology in the year 2000 as an attempt to control growing costs, and numerous other insurance providers have decided to mimic this system. There are approximately 850 APCs for services that can vary from magnetic resonance imaging (MRI) to the removal of a wart. Much like the DRG system, there is an outlier payment for some outpatient services, and each APC is driven by two different levels in what is termed the *HCPCS* (Healthcare Common Procedure Coding System) (Table 11.4).

The HCPCS model is uniform to all hospitals to ensure transparency with healthcare suppliers, insurance companies, and the government. The HCPCS code determines the APC assignment, and it drives the reimbursement under the outpatient prospective reimbursement methodology. Within the HCPCS methodology are the CPT-4 (Current Procedural Terminology) codes, which are virtually the same as HCPCS level 1 codes. The CPT-4 codes are the services performed by physicians to the patient, and they are maintained by the AMA (American Medical Association).

Table 11.4   HCPCS Level 1 and 2

Level 1 HCPCS (reports procedures performed): Consists of CPT-4 (Current Procedural Terminology) codes that are owned and maintained by the American Medical Association. These codes are updated annually, and they are linked to UB revenue codes.
Level 2 HCPCS (reports services provided): Additional HCPCS not included in level 1, such as durable medical equipment and ambulance services. These level 2 codes are owned and maintained by CMS and updated quarterly, and they are also linked to UB revenue codes.

CPT-4 codes are five digits long with a possible two-digit modifier. The modifier allows a physician's service to be altered based on a circumstance. In some cases, the CPT code is the preferred code when both a CPT and an HCPCS code exists for the same service. Even though some insurance companies pay hospitals using the APC system, others may simply utilize the HCPCS/CPT methodology because of the differentiation of one procedure from another similar procedure. The level 2 HCPCS codes were created to supplement the CPT codes, which did not include coding for non-physician-related issues, like wheelchairs or other medical supplies. The HCPCS methodology can be built as a fee-for-service model that companies like Blue Cross/Blue Shield utilize because it is simpler to use, and it avoids the bundling of codes that occurs in the APC methodology.

CRITICAL ISSUE

Level 1 HCPCS codes and CPT-4 codes are used for the same purpose. They are complimentary coding classification systems.

A noteworthy method to influence APC reimbursement is that providers are paid 100% on each primary procedure and 50% on each secondary procedure. Proper classification of each APC can possibly result in higher reimbursement for a healthcare facility. For example, if a patient had outpatient surgery for a bone spur but also had a wart removed, then the hospital would be reimbursed 100% for the bone spur and 50% for the wart removal. This process is significant because Medicare auditors will look closely to determine if hospital personnel are coding this correctly so that the more expensive outpatient procedure is not classified as primary.

Pricing

Overall, hospitals price their services based on cost and expected reimbursement. The Medicare cost report is usually a good starting point when formulating costs; however, these estimated cost figures exclude many other operating expenses that are essential for maintaining hospital operations. Hospitals may still resort to using these figures as base amounts when applying some type of markup percentage that can range anywhere from 200% to 400%. The issues when using a cost-plus markup percentage is that some services need to be marked up differently from others. Some inexpensive supplies like gauze or bandages may have high markups, whereas expensive items such as implants or pacemakers have lower markup percentages. The justification for this is that most hospitals have a minimum charge for services. For example, assume a facility has a minimum charge of $35 for hospital services. If the cost of a hospital supply item is $5, then it will result in a 700% markup calculation. If the cost is greater than $5,000, then a particular hospital may use a markup of only 200% ($10,000 charge in CDM). A majority of all hospitals will not even charge for a supply if it is used on at least 75% of that hospital's patient population. The justification for this is that the cost is already included in the room-and-board charges. The charge in the CDM is unique and outside the costs that are typically consumed by a patient. Each year, a hospital will increase its overall charge structure by an inflationary adjustment such as 3% or 4%. This annual charge increase is applied to all CDM charges.

CRITICAL ISSUE

A majority of hospitals will not charge for a supply if the item is used on 75% or more of the patient population. These costs are already embedded in either the room-and-board charge or the emergency room level charge.

Some healthcare facilities may base their prices on expected payment of services, and Medicare usually is the benchmarked payer. In theory, Medicare is the only payer that hospitals know the expected payment in advance of service because of the DRG blend rate and APC fee schedule. The issue that occurs in this strategy is that some commercial insurance providers, such as Cigna or United Healthcare, reimburse at a much higher rate than Medicare. The hospital may be under-pricing for its services if it only uses expected Medicare payments.

The pricing of hospital services is a decision of both senior management and the board of directors, which affects not only the financial statements but also the goodwill of the hospital. Consumers are aware of hospital prices, and their choice of competing hospital systems may hinge on a facility's pricing structure. Many, if not all, patients are unaware of the complexity of hospital reimbursement, so they may base their financial decision simply on price alone. Hospitals should not price their services by comparing their charges against competing hospitals since this would be a form of price fixing.

Charge Flowchart

Before a patient's bill is sent to a third party for payment, there is a systematic course of events that must occur. The medical record must be documented, reviewed, and examined by several different departments before it can be considered a "clean claim." Table 11.5 is a flowchart of a typical hospital patient charge as it transforms into a billable invoice.

In each clinical department, there is charge nurse who is responsible for collecting and recording information on whatever is performed on a patient. This information is logged in the patient's chart, which is keyed into some type of EMR system. The EMR information is transferred to medical records, where then the patient's chart is coded based on the diagnosis and procedures. The job duties of a medical records coder and a unit charge nurse should always be independent of one another. Once medical records codes the patient's chart, this information is transmitted to the hospital financial system, which creates a gross patient balance based on the medical records code and the CDM charge. A majority of this process is done electronically and in real time. The progression of hospital revenue from the charge nurse to billing is a large component of the hospital

Table 11.5 Flowchart of Patient Charge

Service keyed by charge nurse

↓

Transferred into electronic medical record

↓

Transferred electronically to medical records (HIM)

↓

Transferred electronically to financial system

↓

Bill is sent to third party

revenue cycle that needs to be monitored and controlled by HIM. To decentralize the charge entry process, hospital systems are employing *computerized physician order entry* (CPOE), which allows hospital personal to enter patient charge information directly. Previously, the specified charge nurse was solely given the ability to enter patient charges or orders. By using CPOE, the physician or other hospital employee can decrease delay in order completion while possibly decreasing mistakes generated from handwriting or transcription errors.

A significant component of this process is the use of the EMR, which is the result of the federal government's attempt to reform health care. This legislation is part of the American Recovery and Reinvestment Act of 2009, which promoted the use of EMRs not only for hospitals but also for all other healthcare facilities. This unified electronic patient record will cross all components (physician practice, hospital, nursing homes), and competing hospitals will be able to access patient records regardless of the service. The EMR will create a national data repository where all patient information will be stored, and other healthcare providers can access this information to improve patient care. The purpose behind the EMR is that it may reduce duplication and redundancy of medical services. One hospital may not have to perform an MRI if the results of that patient's most recent MRI completed at another facility are available electronically. The additional MRI that would have been requested is now eliminated. The implementation of the EMR has the ability to mitigate unnecessary medical procedures that were previously performed on a patient. Regardless of the facility, hospital staff will have the ability to access patient records to determine what imaging tests, lab work, and other services were performed on the patient. The EMR will also save the physician time because the physician can make hospital rounds in the morning and does not have to call the nurses in the afternoon to see how the patient is doing since it can be done electronically. The EMR also has the ability to automate clinical results and improve outcomes by identifying errors or omissions of tests.

Coding Accuracy

In addition to maintaining an effective medical records department, hospitals often purchase software that examines or proofreads a patient's chart to ensure it is accurate. Another purpose is possibly to obtain additional reimbursement by identifying missed charges. Certain types of decision support software can retrospectively review each patient's bill to determine if certain charges need to be added, amended, or omitted. Coders use CAC (computer-aided coding) software as they review the medical record, but occasionally mistakes may occur. Some software uses heuristic processing based on an extensive set of predetermined rules that are customized to a hospital's CDM. The criteria for coding a patient's chart is based on CCI (Correct Coding Initiative) and LMRP (licensed medical review policies). The CMS created these initiatives to promote a nationally correct coding methodology to minimize improper coding. Hospitals often purchase software programs that essentially "scrub" the patient's bill to make sure the invoice is clean and the hospital will be reimbursed accordingly. This type of proofreading software is used not only to verify coding information but also to identify any patient access or billing errors.

A significant issue that occurs when implementing these proofreading modules is that the billing system will not release a patient record if it believes an error has occurred. If the software finds an error, then the patient's chart is automatically remitted to medical records rather than being billed to a third party. By not releasing the patient's record, the hospital revenue cycle has been lengthened since these patient charts must be examined and coded for a second time. *The more time medical records reviews a patient's chart, the longer it takes to bill an insurance provider and receive payment.* An example of a typical error would be the normal delivery of a child; however, the gender of the patient giving birth is classified as male. This error needs to be corrected before it can leave the medical records department because a third-party payer will reject the claim since the mother is listed as male rather than female. Also, reworked accounts often result in a lengthened *DNFB (discharged not final billed) statistic.* This DNFB figure must be closely monitored by hospital management since it has the ability to increase the ratio of days in accounts receivable. Before any "scrubbing" or "proofreading" software can be implemented, the hospital must perform cost-benefit analysis to determine if the software will be either a benefit or a detriment to a facility.

If a billing scrubber is utilized, then instead of remitting all flagged patient charts to medical records, the hospital should employ a group of internal auditors to examine the system-generated errors. This protocol would allow hospital personnel to dissect and analyze the list of all errors and manually review each of the given patient accounts to determine if the errors are accurate. A significant issue is that the internal audit department usually does not have the resources to review each medical record error since there could be hundreds of errors produced on a monthly basis. The internal audit staff should pull individual patient records that they believe will result in additional charges based on the acuity of the procedure and the precedence of the rule being violated. A negative by-product of using these bill-scrubbing software programs is that false positives are occasionally produced. These types of false errors must be eliminated from the software so they do not flag incorrect accounts. An example of a typical false-positive violation would be *if* a patient was admitted for hip surgery *then* accompanying lab, imaging, and implant charges should be expected on the bill. The software may state that a hospital missed certain charges; however, the insurance provider could have been billed correctly due to charges being embedded in another hospital charge code such as "miscellaneous" or "other." This may possibly occur when a charge nurse incorrectly inputs a charge to an inappropriate line. Another issue is that some software programs may believe that certain additional services are required, yet they are not applicable. The software may review all diagnosis codes in the patient's account regardless of the principle diagnosis. If a patient was admitted for asthma but previously sustained a broken ankle, then the software will state that an imaging charge is expected. This methodology is erroneous because the patient was treated for asthma rather than a broken bone. Medical records, information technology, and financial personnel need to work in conjunction to ensure that appropriate internal control measures are implemented to ensure that the coding of the patient's medical record is accurate.

Conclusion

The coding of a patient's medical chart is a process unique to healthcare that requires an abundant amount of training and expertise. Often, HIM personnel have some type of certification and possibly a master's degree in the field. The process is vital to the hospital revenue cycle because the appropriate code often determines the gross charge for that patient. The goal of HIM is to enhance or improve patient care by accurately coding a chart the first time. The length of a hospital's revenue cycle often hinges on the effectiveness and efficiency of the medical records department. In addition, the pricing of hospital services determines the gross revenue for clinical services, and this markup percentage has a profound impact on the community. Many consumers, suppliers, competing hospitals, and even the government will review and examine hospital charges to determine their accuracy. Inpatient coding is generated from an *ICD-9-CM* code, whereas outpatient coding is driven by the HCPCS methodology. Hospital systems also have the option of purchasing software that proofreads or scrubs the patient's bill to determine if it is accurate and complete. A hospital accountant need not have the expertise actually to code a patient's medical record; however, a comprehensive understanding of coding principles and methods is needed.

Chapter 12

Managing the Month-End Close Process

Each month accountants, accounts payable clerks, and payroll technicians all work at a hectic pace to formulate month-end financial statements. These statements are typically the departmental income statement, actual-to-budget comparisons, and other miscellaneous documents created through the numerous reclasses, interfaces, and accruals formulated during the month-end close process. A primary role of the director of accounting is to plan and organize this chaotic process and to ensure that financial reports are completed in a timely and consistent manner. Central to month-end close is the coordination and motivation of accounting personnel, who have varying levels of education and experience. Certain staff may be driven by extrinsic rewards, whereas others are motivated through intrinsic benefits, such as challenging job duties. Traditionally, supervisors have used either coercive or reward techniques to increase performance, and in the short run, both approaches are somewhat effective. However, a growing trend in the hospital accounting profession is the use of a participatory management style that emphasizes input and feedback from employees in formulating goals. A manager can significantly improve departmental procedures and overall morale by giving employees additional planning and control over their duties and assignments.

In most health care organizations, the accounting department is usually defined as a decision support mechanism that provides financial information to those with decision-making authority. *The primary goal of the month-end close process is to produce financial statements that assist management in making relevant decisions.* This process can take several days, depending on the size and staff of the hospital. Typical month-end entries range from recording depreciation to accruing expensing to estimating a contractual. Typically, each member of the accounting staff is designated an assigned number of journal entries with the correlating balance sheet reconciliations. A paramount issue for the accounting manager is how to motivate employees to complete assigned entries and reconciliations within specified timelines. To meet these deadlines, a majority of supervisors employ two distinctive management styles. One style is often referred to as the directive approach while a contrasting style is called the participative approach. Historically, most accounting managers have employed the directive management style, which is a top-down approach that uses either fear or rewards to influence performance. The accounting supervisor uses his or her authority to motivate employees to perform duties without listening to their input or suggestions. Often called the "carrot-or-stick" technique, this method usually results in decreased morale and poor communication. This approach typifies the theory X model formulated by Douglas McGregor in that managers believe employees are inherently lazy, dislike work, and have little desire to succeed (1). The directive style is necessary under certain conditions; however, it is not well suited for the month-end close process. The result of the directive approach is that employees will feel as if their opinions do not matter, and they will have little incentive to improve performance. Absenteeism and turnover may increase, while creative thinking will decline.

A style that is opposite to the directive approach and is gaining increased acceptance is the participative style of management. Also referred to as *management by objectives* (MBO), the basic premise behind this managerial style is that the supervisor includes lower-level staff in departmental planning and scheduling. The accounting director would elicit the opinions and advice of accounting staff in devising not only the month-end close process but also any other relevant issues. Benefits of this approach are increased morale, better communication, and an improved work environment. Another benefit is that employees might have more extensive knowledge of operational details and accounting data that may not be evident to management. Accounts payable clerks may have valuable ideas about cash management since they process invoices on a daily basis, while payroll clerks may have helpful ideas regarding the interface of payroll data. Some of this knowledge may be unknown to the accounting supervisor since he or she does not have the necessary time to analyze the massive amounts of data that flow through an accounting department. Management gives staff the opportunity to improve the work environment by allowing employees to provide input into their jobs and their department. This approach often leads to increased employee motivation, while turnover and absenteeism decline.

The participative management style can be applied in the following manner: The process begins with the accounting manager meeting with each employee on an individual basis to discuss that person's role in the month-end process. The manager would define each journal entry or reconciliation precisely and discuss possible approaches to complete these duties; both parties would agree on the optimal method to meet the outcome. The employee is given an opportunity to explain how he or she would best complete the task, and the supervisor is present to coach or guide the employee. *This is the essential principle behind the participatory style. The supervisor is jointly working with a subordinate to discuss methods to achieve departmental goals.* The involvement of lower-level staff will also increase the understanding of and commitment to company goals. This form of upward communication adheres to McGregor's theory Y model in that managers believe employees are ambitious, are motivated, and like to work (1). Granted, not all requests and suggestions from employees can be implemented. The four essential elements of the participative approach are

1. Establishment of tasks by both manager and employee
2. Specification of objectives and methods to be used
3. Specification of time frame in which goals should be met
4. Provision of ongoing feedback to monitor or adjust performance

Throughout these four elements, the process of communication is critical to success. The acid test of the participatory style occurs when an employee strongly believes his or her methods are superior to the accounting supervisors. At this point, the manager can either coach the employee to change behavior or allow the individual to proceed and fail on his or her own. It is at the discretion of the accounting supervisor to determine which practice would fit better; however, managers must be wary that each employee should be treated on an individual case-by-case basis. What may seem logical to one staff member may seem insulting to another. The accounting director needs to stress goal congruence in that everyone should work together to ensure that the company is reaching its goals.

A possible and beneficial result of employing a participatory management approach may be *job enrichment*. The learning curve for most accounting entries is like any other discipline in that the material is often initially difficult, but the activity becomes easier as repetition occurs. Over time, the employee may find the work mundane, which may lead to decreased motivation and possibly attrition. The participatory method allows employees to provide feedback to how the department can be run more effectively, which may result in the creation of new duties and activities. These new job duties have the capability to improve or enrich the employee's job. Another possible result of a participative approach could be *job rotation*. Some employees may not desire a duty that requires a higher skill; however, they may wish to perform new duties. Accounts payable clerks can be given different vendors, while staff accountants can rotate specific journal entries. The result is that employees perform similar but different job duties. Before implementing a job rotation system, the employees should be consulted to determine what new duties they wish to learn and what old assignments they wish to discard. This process will increase departmental motivation as well as morale. This cross training of hospital employees could eventually resemble a lean manufacturing work cell in that the accounting staff is trained to do other employee duties, ensuring that the month-end process will not cease when an individual is absent.

The participatory management style does not have to be limited to internal employees. The month-end close process can be frustrating since many journal entries rely on information from sources outside the department's control. Staff accountant entries may be dependent on data from outside billing agencies or statistical data from off-site cost centers. This information may be inconsistently received due to time constraints, different technology, or simply lack of effort. The accounting supervisor can improve this process by personally contacting the respective third party and eliciting input on how this information can be better sent or received. The third party should also be informed on why accounting uses the data and the specific time frame in which it needs to be received. *The outside party will be better motivated to provide the data if he or she understands why it is needed and how the material affects the goals of the hospital.* This two-way communication process is always better received if the accounting supervisor requests rather than commands or instructs the third party. The tone and manner of how someone is addressed are extremely important as well as the chosen communication channel. Many entities outside accounting may not see the significance of financial statements, or they may view those in the accounting department as merely a bunch of "number crunchers" or "bean counters." These perceptions can largely be eliminated by not only improving lines of communication but also allowing outside entities to provide feedback.

Thus, all the effort and devotion used to formulate statements is useless unless the material is provided to management in a timely and reliable manner. The validity of the data will be questioned if they are not consistently received. Traditionally, month-end reports were physically provided to the supervisor; however, the advancement of technology has allowed the accounting function to send documents electronically to the necessary personnel. Electronic mail has created a more efficient mode of communication that adds the benefit of providing written confirmation; however, the sender does not know if the message intended was the message received. *A significant disadvantage of using e-mail is that it does not provide feedback.* Despite advances in technology, accounting staff must constantly strive to improve communication between the department and the rest of the hospital. This can be accomplished by utilizing a participatory approach with departmental managers. Communicating with coworkers should not be significantly different from dealing with subordinates in that the accounting supervisor should meet with clinical staff to determine what sources and types of financial data are desired. The two parties need to agree jointly on the desired outcome and work together to discuss possible approaches or methods. The end result needs to be a process that both parties agree on. The director of accounting should build stable relationships with supervisors not only by providing relevant and reliable data but also through improved communication. Departmental managers should be given the opportunity to decide how they want month-end reports provided to them. Obviously, not all requests can be granted, but managers should be given the opportunity to voice their opinions.

The month-end financial statements that are formulated by hospital staff are intended to be used by those who have a reasonable understanding of accounting information. Usually, department managers have a satisfactory knowledge of revenues and expenses; however, their ability to dissect and analyze financial data is sometimes limited. An accounting director can utilize a participative approach to determine if a manager needs any additional assistance or education on month-end reporting functions. Historically, most clinical supervisors are solely concerned with negative variances that affect their bottom line, and they are quick to send e-mails when revenues are lower or expenses are higher than expected. An ancillary role of the accounting director is to educate and inform personnel about the intricacies involved with financial data. The director should volunteer to meet with the department manager on an "as-needed" basis to determine if the manager has any concerns or questions. This process should not only give the departmental supervisor the ability to inquire about financial methods but also provide any suggestions to improve the process. A participative approach requires the accounting department to be more willing and able to meet with any members of the hospital who have questions regarding financial material. *It should be a secondary goal of the finance department not only to inform but also to educate fellow hospital employees.* Some staff members may be exceptional nurses, yet they have no comprehension about the concept of accrual-based accounting. Words such as *capitalize* and *depreciation* may seem common to accountants but are part of a foreign language to others. There is a misconception that the accounting department is an isolated, academic function that does not work well with others. This perception can be drastically improved by communicating to both internal and external personnel in a more effective and efficient manner. Through the use of a participative or open management style, other hospital departments not only can provide input but also can be better informed on the duties and policies of the accounting division.

In conclusion, the month-end close process can be an extremely hectic procedure that involves input from several different sources. It is the role of the director of accounting to coordinate this process and to ensure that the material is provided in a consistent and reliable manner. One effective way to improve departmental morale and communication is to employ a participatory style of management. By employing this approach, the director can improve motivation both internally and externally. The participatory management style can also benefit hospital managers by allowing them to provide input and feedback on month-end reports. By creating open lines of communication and soliciting feedback from all staff members, the accounting director can improve both morale and productivity.

Reference

1. Hindle, Tim. 2008. *The Economist Guide to Management Ideas and Gurus.* London: Profile Books.

Chapter 13

Calculating the Financial Impact of Hospital Length of Stay

Introduction

A significant issue that hospital administrators face is how to reduce the length of stay (LOS) for clinical services without sacrificing the quality of care given. The LOS statistic is defined as total patient days divided by inpatient (IP) cases, and it is a significant driver of hospital net income. In fact, many financial personnel consider it the most significant measure of the effectiveness and efficiency of a hospital. The overall theory is that the less time a patient remains under hospital care, the fewer the expenses that are consumed. This belief is driven by the premise that a majority of IPs are insured through Medicare, which pays a fixed rate regardless of the patient's LOS. The effort to reduce hospital patient days is a delicate process because the decline in the patient's stay must be carefully balanced against the quality of care that is administered. Excessive waste can be minimized through the proper execution of functional protocols; however, a patient's discharge status should never be influenced by financial considerations. Each hospital payer should be analyzed separately to determine the viability of reducing the LOS.

As described in previous chapters, the hospital accountant should be cognizant of the Medicare reimbursement methodology since this governmental payer represents a significant portion of both IP and outpatient volumes. The IP reimbursement methodology that is federally imposed by Medicare is prospectively set in that services provided to the patient are assigned a diagnosis-related group (DRG) that drives the payment to the hospital. The DRG weight is then multiplied by a hospital-specific relative weight that is adjusted for additional add-on payments such as indirect medical education (IME) or Disproportionate Share Hospital (DSH). The significance of the Medicare inpatient prospective payment system (IPPS) reimbursement methodology is that the maintenance of costs is shifted to the healthcare provider. A hospital is paid the same amount regardless if a patient has a 5- or 50-day patient stay (not taking into account outlier payments). The impact of this methodology is that clinical personnel have attempted to implement new protocols that would reduce the patient's time at the healthcare facility without damaging the quality

Table 13.1   Hospital Service Line (Only Governmental)

Medicare LOS	Total IP Net Revenue	Total IP Variable Costs	Total IP Fixed Costs	Total IP Net Income	Patient Days	IP Cases
12.5	$2,500,000	$2,000,000	$1,000,000	($500,000)	5,000	400
	Total IP Net Revenue per Day		Total IP Variable Cost per Day		Adjusted IP Variable Cost per Day	
	$500		$400		$300	

of care given to the patient. The desired result would be decreased costs with correlating increased net income.

It is the responsibility of hospital management to determine not only the feasibility but also the financial benefit of reducing the LOS before any clinical protocols are amended. Analysis can be performed that calculates how much cost savings would occur if a healthcare provider reduced patient days for clinical services. Unfortunately, all payers cannot be viewed equally since each insurance carrier may have a different reimbursement model. *The best practice to determine the monetary impact of decreasing patient days is to separate the governmental and nongovernmental payers.* The justification for the separation is that the revenue received from a payer such as Medicare will not change as days decrease; however, many managed care payers may reimburse on a per diem basis or a percentage of charges. The reduction in days for these nongovernmental payers may decrease not only variable costs but also net revenue. The use of sensitivity analysis in both the governmental and nongovernmental payer buckets for an isolated procedure or service will generate an approximate cost reduction figure. To best illustrate this analysis, a hypothetical service line is presented in Table 13.1 with the appropriate accounting data for Medicare IP patients only.

Most of the data is self-explanatory except for the figure for adjusted IP variable cost per day, which is 75% of the total IP variable cost per day ($300 = 0.75 * $400). This reduction in cost is utilized because fewer expenses will be incurred toward the final days of a patient's admission. A majority of the lab work, imaging, and other high-dollar services are performed in the initial 1 to 2 patient days. This element is critical for understanding the overall LOS analysis. The adjusted IP variable cost per day figure approximates the final days in an IP admission to be only 75% of what the average cost would be.

CRITICAL ISSUE

A majority of the expenses consumed during a patient's stay occur in the first 1 to 2 days. These expenses are typically any lab and imaging services.

The next step is to reduce the IP day figure hypothetically until a desired LOS statistic is determined. This trial-and-error approach is obviously best suited when using some sort of a spreadsheet (see Table 13.2).

By decreasing the days from 5,000 to 4,600, the LOS has decreased by exactly 1 day. The reduction in cost is formulated by multiplying the decrease in days (400) by the adjusted variable cost

Table 13.2 Governmental Impact of Day Reduction

IP Days	IP Cases	Change in LOS	Reduction in Days	Revenue Reduction	Cost Reduction	Net Affect
4,600	400	11.5	400	N/A	$120,000	$120,000

per day ($300). Revenue is not affected because of the IPPS methodology employed by Medicare. *Determining the financial benefit of decreasing the governmental payer LOS is straightforward because the lone component is the impact of the IP variable costs.* Neither revenue nor fixed costs is affected by the decrease in the patient days. The reduction in days has improved governmental net income by $120,000. For simplicity purposes, other payer buckets such as Medicaid, self-pay, and charity care can be included in this model in the same manner as Medicare.

Contrary to the governmental reimbursement methodology, providers such as Blue Cross/Blue Shield or United Healthcare, have an added component because the reduction of variable must be contrasted against the reduction of net revenue. Similar financial data for the hypothetical service line are utilized; however, only nongovernmental IP payer data are used (see Table 13.3).

Much like the governmental LOS analysis, the adjusted IP variable cost per day is 75% of the total IP variable cost per day ($450 = 0.75 * $600). The next step is to reduce the IP day figure manually until a desirable LOS calculation is determined (see Table 13.4).

By decreasing the days from 2,000 to 1,800, the LOS has decreased by exactly 1 day. The reduction in revenue is formulated by multiplying the decrease in days (200) by the IP net revenue per day ($750); the cost reduction is calculated by multiplying the decrease in days (200) by the adjusted IP variable cost per day ($450). Contrary to governmental LOS analysis, the decrease in days actually *worsens* nongovernmental net income from a loss of ($200,000) to ($260,000) (Table 13.5). The result of this analysis is that the reduction of the LOS can possibly have a negative impact when services are reimbursed from third-party payers who use a per diem or percentage-of-charge model.

Table 13.3 Hospital Service Line (Non-Governmental)

LOS	Total IP Net Revenue	Total IP Variable Costs	Total IP Fixed Costs	Total IP Net Income	Patient Days	IP Cases
10.0	$1,500,000	$1,200,000	$500,000	($200,000)	2,000	200
	Total IP Net Revenue per Day		Total IP Variable Cost per Day		Adjusted IP Variable Cost per Day	
	$750		$600		$450	

Table 13.4 Non-Governmental Impact of Day Reduction

IP Days	Change in LOS	Reduction in Days	Revenue Reduction	Cost Reduction	Net Affect
1,800	9.0	200	$150,000	$90,000	($60,000)

Table 13.5 Net Effect of Decreasing a Service Line LOS by One Day

	Net Income Prior to LOS Change	Revenue Reduction	Cost Reduction	Net Income After LOS Change
Government	($500,000)	$0	$120,000	($380,000)
Nongovernment	($200,000)	$150,000	$90,000	($260,000)
Total	($700,000)	$150,000	$210,000	($640,000)

After the sensitivity analysis for each payer is completed, the revenue and cost reduction figures need to be combined to determine the total benefit of decreasing the LOS by 1 day for this particular clinical service. Table 13.5 provides a summary of the changes.

The governmental payers created a cost reduction of $120,000; the nongovernmental payer expenses declined by $90,000, resulting in a total cost reduction of $210,000. However, $150,000 of revenue was lost due to the per diem reimbursement of the nongovernmental payers. Overall, the elimination of *1 patient day* of this specific procedure's LOS would increase net income by $60,000 (loss of $700,000 decreased to $640,000).

CRITICAL ISSUE

It is *not* always beneficial to decrease the hospital LOS. Extensive analysis of reimbursement by payer must be addressed before any modifications are considered.

Thus, the reduction of patient days can possibly benefit a healthcare facility only after both governmental and nongovernmental payers have been separately analyzed. Financial personnel must also use current and accurate cost data when compiling variable expense figures. A general recommendation is that it would be beneficial if a hospital has a high Medicare or Medicaid payer mix to reduce the LOS substantially for all procedures. However, decreasing the LOS may be detrimental if a hospital has a large proportion of its reimbursement driven by per diem/percentage-of-charge reimbursing managed care payers. The best solution is to identify each payer separately to determine the appropriate payer mix and expense figures. Only through careful analysis of each service or procedure can a hospital accountant view the financial impact of altering clinical protocols to reduce excessive patient stays.

Hospitalist LOS

A significant part of the healthcare delivery system is the use of hospitalists in managing the care of admitted patients. A hospitalist is broadly defined as a physician whose primary focus is for the general medical care of patients (1). Hospitalist duties and activities extend across all service lines, and they are vital to a hospital's livelihood. A significant reason for the use of hospitalist care is that patient outcomes may be improved, and clinical efficiency could possibly be enhanced. Operational managers are usually responsible for tracking the clinical outcomes of hospitalist care; however, it is the duty of the accounting professional to document and benchmark the volumes of such physicians. By tracking the LOS of hospitalist physicians, the healthcare facility can determine if productivity goals are being achieved and costs are being minimized.

The term *hospitalist* has only been in existence for approximately 15 years; however, the profession has grown dramatically due to the increased demand placed on primary care physicians. A majority of hospitalists are general internists who cannot refer or admit patients. Their patient population is driven by other physician referrals or patients admitted through the emergency room (ER) who do not have a primary care physician. A substantial amount of these ER admits are high-acuity cases with a very poor payer mix. Typically, these cases result in excessive patient stays and very low reimbursement. It is the responsibility of the hospitalist to manage this difficult patient population without sacrificing the quality of care given.

The primary mechanism that a healthcare financial manager can use to monitor the patient population of hospitalists is to track the LOS for those individuals under their care. Healthcare providers should have the operational capability to monitor the IP cases and days of each physician. These statistics can often be extracted from a financial database using a nonprocedural language like SQL. A database can be formulated that matches all hospital physicians with three specific items:

1. Medicare IP cases
2. A principal diagnosis or DRG for each admission
3. Patient days for each admission

This database does not require any financial information, and only Medicare patients are listed for simplicity purposes. These three items can be listed for all hospital physicians and benchmarked against those physicians classified as hospitalists. Before any comparisons can be made, the acuity of services for all physicians must be addressed. It is not feasible to compare the LOS for physicians who perform orthopedic or cardiac procedures to those responsible for hospitalist care since their patients' medical issues are vastly different. To account for the variation in acuity, the healthcare accountant must carve out all surgical, cardiac, orthopedic, oncology, and renal/urology cases for both hospital physicians and hospitalists to get a more comparable population. *By backing out these specific cases, the patient population should be drastically reduced to reflect a data sample that is similar for all physicians.* A further step in making the cases more reflective of one another is to formulate the case mix index (CMI) for the remaining figures. Since only Medicare IP cases are used in this analysis, each DRG has an accompanying relative weight. (All DRGs and their appropriate weights are listed in Appendix B.) The CMI is formulated by multiplying each DRG's relative weight against the applicable IP cases. Once this summation is formulated, it must be divided by the total amount of IP cases to create an adjusted LOS (see Table 13.6).

The 5.56 figure represents the adjusted LOS after all outliers and service line acuity have been adjusted. *It is the most precise measure to be used when benchmarking hospitalist LOS against all other hospital physicians.* This statistic can now be used as a productivity measure to compare the efficiency of managing patient days. Table 13.7 provides a hypothetical example of two separate CMI totals for hospitalists and all other physicians.

In this example, the analysis reveals that the use of hospitalist care has resulted in a LOS that is approximately 1 day longer than the average LOS of all other physicians. The CMI is comparable since all the dissimilar cases have been carved out. A clinical manager should be made aware of this contrast in patient stay, and he or she should be educated that this analysis represents an "apples-to-apples" comparison.

Table 13.6 Formulation of Adjusted LOS

DRG	WEIGHT	IP CASES	DAYS	CMI	LOS
974	2.1382	6	75	12.83	12.5
975	1.5918	3	26	4.78	8.7
976	1.3357	3	19	4.01	6.3
		12	120	21.62	10.0

Note: Total CMI = 21.62/12 = 1.80

Adjusted LOS = 10.0/1.80 = 5.56

Table 13.7 Hospitalist LOS Compared to All Other Physician LOS

Hospitalist Medicare Volumes				All Other Physician Medicare Volumes			
IP Cases	Days	CMI	LOS	IP Cases	Days	CMI	LOS
963	8,462	1.57	8.79	3,270	23,310	1.57	7.13
Adjusted LOS			**5.60**	**Adjusted LOS**			**4.54**
8.79/1.57 = 5.60				7.13/1.57 = 4.54			

Conclusion

In conclusion, the employment of hospitalists has the possibility of managing patient care more effectively than if the attending physician were consistently on call. The hospitalist has the ability to improve patient outcomes and manage the LOS of high-acuity patients. By tracking and benchmarking hospitalist volumes, a healthcare facility can determine if productivity is being appropriately managed. The use of the CMI eliminates the comparability issues that exist with varying services and allows the accounting professional to better analyze the data. This data can be shared with not only clinical supervisors but also senior management to improve the overall effectiveness and efficiency of the healthcare facility.

Reference

1. Nabili, M.D., and M.P.H. Siamak. 2008. What is a hospitalist? http://www.medicinenet.com/script/main/art.asp?articlekey=93946 (accessed November 26, 2011).

Chapter 14

The Future of Healthcare Accounting

Introduction

Those who have chosen a career path in accounting have typically been classified as either audit or tax professionals. Historically, this segregation has been accurate since most accountants have pursued certified public accountant (CPA) licensure in these fields. However, the growth of certain industries, such as healthcare, has provided financial professionals the opportunity to pursue careers outside the audit and tax realm. A driving factor for this expansion is the federal government's enactment of healthcare reform in an attempt to extend insurance coverage as well as decrease costs. Another contributing factor is that new advancements in medical technology and pharmaceutical research are altering how health care is administered. People are beginning to live longer as cures are discovered, vaccines are formulated, and therapies are developed. As this progression continues, there is a correlating increase in demand for those who have accounting experience. The federal government has realized that the costs of the Medicare and Medicaid programs are increasing at an alarming rate, and mechanisms need to be implemented to curb this rising growth. New models, such as the accountable care organization (ACO), and bundled payment reimbursement have been introduced that focus on healthcare outcomes rather than costs.

Job Security

There are few industries or businesses that are truly recession proof; however, the healthcare field has proven to be the exception. Regardless of war, economic depression, or weather-driven catastrophe, the existence of a healthcare delivery system will always be present. As some point in all our lives, we will acquire some type of illness or medical issue that compels us to consult a physician, possibly require surgery, or in rare cases require an extended stay in a hospital. No matter what the extent of the illness or time frame of injury, there will always be a need for someone to maintain fiscal responsibility. Financial personnel are needed to bill the insurance company, post revenue, collect cash, estimate bad debt, process invoices, and formulate a budget—all within guidelines created by the state and federal governments. Billing methodologies must be adapted and collection techniques must be altered to meet the demand of new technology and national regulations. Due to these variables, the jobs in the healthcare accounting field are extremely secure. There may be times when late hours are worked and certain job duties may seem routine, but overall the healthcare accounting vocation is attractive to those who desire stability.

Historically, accountants have been perceived as boring, reclusive people who sit at a desk all day and have no personality. Occasionally, the day-to-day responsibilities of an accountant may become monotonous; however, the job duties are far from boring or mundane. Those who pursue a career in accounting are extremely analytical and highly motivated. Understanding double-entry accrual accounting is like learning a new language, and comprehending the trickle effect of each ledger entry takes years to truly master. The accountant's job is to create structure out of disorder. The practical aspects of the accounting field have been compared to other technical industries, such as manufacturing or engineering. *In other words, accounting is financial engineering.* It is not data entry, and it is not easy. The healthcare accountant's career is challenging, and it is constantly evolving. The primary reason why many people discontinue a vocation in accounting is not because they are not good with numbers but simply because they lack the necessary discipline and work ethic.

Since 2000, many colleges and universities have begun offering undergraduate healthcare accounting courses in response to the increased demand for the profession. The industry is even becoming more significant with the federal government's attempt to reform the United States healthcare system. There has never been a time when it would *not benefit* an aspiring financial professional to enter the healthcare industry. The healthcare accounting field has proven to be a rewarding, recession-proof industry that can offer substantial benefits and job security to those who have the applicable work ethic.

Accountable Care Organization

A recent trend in healthcare is the emergence of the ACO. The purpose of the ACO from the hospital perspective is to be a quality measure that can possibly improve the negotiation of rates with third parties. The purpose behind the ACO from the government's perspective is that teams of physicians, suppliers, and hospitals will work together to improve the care for traditional Medicare patients. ACOs will be rewarded if they meet performance standards on quality of care that are divided between patient experiences, care coordination, patient safety, preventive health, and elderly health populations. ACOs are a result of federal legislation, and hospital participation is voluntary. A concern with ACOs is that only Medicare patients are included, and there is no coordination between competing hospitals. A by-product of the ACO is the creation of the Independent Payment Advisory Board, which attempts to slow the growth of Medicare expenditures. This board has called for cuts in physician reimbursement and has researched ways to minimize administration expenses associated with Medicare. The Centers for Medicare and Medicaid Services (CMS) has proposed both a one-sided model and a two-sided model for shared savings, allowing the hospital to choose which one is a better fit. Whether or not the use of the ACO results in decreased costs or improved quality of care remains to be seen, but many hospital administrators are optimistic about the benefits it may provide.

Patient-Centered Care

As the topic of healthcare is consistently debated, consumers are becoming more educated about the different alternatives available to them. Patients can now use the Internet as a resource to determine the credibility not only of hospitals but also of individual physicians. Hospitals have responded to patients needs by expanding and improving the quality of care that is given to patients. Healthcare facilities have begun concentrating on patient safety and the timeliness/effectiveness of service provided. Patient safety is not only the clinical outcome of any procedure or service but also safety in regard to the patient's personal information (identity theft) and the patient's overall safety in the hospital (patient falling or being assaulted). Hospital management should implement new safety and security measures to prevent such incidents.

The quality of medical care that a patient receives at a hospital can be influenced by factors that are sometimes controllable by healthcare personnel but are occasionally not controllable. Examples of such factors would be the increase in chronic or fatal conditions, growing complexity of biotechnology, and misuse of information systems. The future of hospital accounting depends on the appropriate integration of clinical and nonclinical systems. An example of such an initiative would be the creation of the electronic medical record (EMR). Competing hospitals should work together to decrease costs by building supplier relationships and coordinating patient care. If a patient has services performed at numerous facilities, then each hospital should be aware of which services were provided and how this affects the clinical outcome. The implementation of the EMR has the ability to improve decision making and decrease overall costs. The patient's health needs to be at the core of all decisions made between competing hospitals.

A current weakness that exists in the hospital realm is the lack of a database or reporting system that tracks the occurrence and resolution of hospital errors. Other industries, such as the airline industry, have a mandatory national reporting system that tracks errors, and it is used for educational and training purposes. The Joint Commission on the Accreditation of Healthcare Organizations (JCAHO) is the closest regulatory body in healthcare that has set a national set of patient safety goals. These goals range from better patient identification measures to improving the safety of administering medication. JCAHO is also the regulatory body that periodically inspects hospital protocols to ensure that the quality of care given is appropriate. By using tracer methodology, JCAHO can determine what happens to the patient from admission to discharge. Both clinical and nonclinical protocols are reviewed to determine the effectiveness of hospital procedures. If the hospital is not adhering to standards, then JACHO has the authority to revoke the Medicare reimbursement of that hospital, which would basically shut down the entity. In addition to JCAHO regulations, the federal government enacted the Patient Safety and Quality Improvement Act of 2005, which encourages providers to identify and correct clinical errors. The act also created patient safety organizations (PSOs) to help create a network of patient safety databases. The Patient Safety Act is more of a work in progress since the legislation is voluntary rather than mandatory.

As a result of the emphasis placed on the quality of care, the federal government has enacted a pilot pay-for-performance (P4P) program for a select group of test hospitals throughout the country. Historically, most physicians and hospitals have been reimbursed for service regardless of the quality of care given. The P4P model creates targets or performance measures for achieving quality and providing effective care. The health systems are benchmarked against other providers to determine if they are operating efficiently. Medicare would reward these providers for meeting quality thresholds and penalize those facilities that did not meet performance initiatives. *The theory behind the P4P model is that giving healthcare providers the knowledge to improve and showing how they compare to others will increase quality.* The P4P initiative is still in a test phase, and participation is voluntary; however, the preliminary results have revealed that overall cost and mortality rates have been reduced.

The population is beginning to live longer as people stop smoking, medical technology improves, and healthier diets are consumed. The means and ability to treat this growing population can be a troubling thought; however, the landscape of medical care is evolving as the census increases. Technology is by far the most significant driving factor to bridge the quality gap. Imaging technology can diagnose diseases at an early stage, and decision support software can improve accuracy and eliminate redundancies. In the past, medical personnel have used evidence-based medicine as a method to treat ill patients, and this methodology is still used; however, new protocols and quality scorecards are being used to improve clinical outcomes. Healthcare facilities are now benchmarking their procedures against other facilities to determine the best outcome not only for the hospital but also for the patient. *A significant factor for the future of healthcare accounting is the unification of competing hospitals in providing patient care to the community.* By working together instead of competing against one another, hospitals can better utilize their economies of scale.

Bundled Payments

Recently, the federal government decided to research a bundling payment methodology to determine if this method could decrease Medicare expenditures. The theory behind the bundled payment is that one payment for total services will be given to the hospital for all services, including payments for physician services and postacute care. This continuum of treatment is sometimes referred to as an episode of care. Currently, if a Medicare patient is admitted to a hospital for a cardiac procedure, then the federal government would pay the hospital using the diagnosis-related group (DRG) model for the facility component of the procedure. In addition, the government pays each physician for the physician's professional component of the cardiac procedure. Part B Medicare physician fees for a cardiac procedure would be the payment to the cardiac surgeon, the anesthesiologist, the radiologist, and possibly a pulmonologist. The federal government also pays separate amounts if the patient was discharged to a nursing home or an independent rehabilitation hospital. The federal government pays numerous parties for the treatment of one patient. *The purpose behind the bundled payment model is that the federal government is propositioning the numerous parties to work in conjunction to formulate a single estimated reimbursement figure for all clinical services.* The bundled payment system is a hybrid of the fee-for-service and capitated payment methodology, and the possibility of cost savings is determined by which of the four models is chosen. The hope is that by working together the costs to service an episode of care will possibly decrease. The possible savings that occur by decreasing costs could be shared by all parties, including Medicare. The bundled payment initiative was created as a result of legislation, and hospitals have been given the choice of using four different models of care to structure their bundled payment (see Table 14.1).

As of 2011, the bundled payment system was only in the test phase, and certain hospitals can volunteer to participate in this experimental process. The integration of patient payments into one bundle is not a revolutionary idea, but it is the federal government's attempt to reduce the overall cost of care. A significant issue with this methodology is that outlier payments are still paid to the hospital if the Medicare patient absorbs an excessive amount of costs. The episode of care that pertains to a bundled payment would be for the traditional Medicare patient who did not classify into outlier status.

Table 14.1 Four Different Bundled Payment Models

Model 1: Only the acute hospital stay
Model 2: Acute care hospital stay plus associated postacute care
Model 3: Only postacute care service
Model 4: A prospective payment that encompasses all services for an inpatient stay

In 2010, the Patient Protection and Affordable Care Act (PPCA) was enacted, which is an attempt to reform the U.S. healthcare system. Significant provisions of the legislation are to increase healthcare coverage to the uninsured and eliminate preexisting conditions. To cover the costs of the uninsured, the federal government has proposed to expand Medicaid eligibility and create health insurance exchanges to make health insurance more affordable to citizens. *The PPACA has the possibility of expanding health coverage; however, the legislation may result in the reduction and possible elimination of the Medicaid Disproportionate Share Hospital (DSH) program.* Beginning in 2014, the funding for the Medicaid DSH program may be greatly reduced due to the enactment of other government programs aimed at the poor and uninsured. In addition, the government is moving toward a reimbursement system that pays hospitals based on clinical outcomes. This PPACA legislation was formulated in response to the government's belief that citizens should have a right to affordable healthcare coverage, and hospitals need to be more concerned with the quality of care given. The components and initiatives of the PPACA legislation are too broad to include in this text, and the legislation covers numerous areas outside a hospital system.

Conclusion

The healthcare accounting profession will always be in existence as long as there is an economy. Accountants understand fiscal matters that others may not comprehend, and hospitals will exist because people will always need medical care. Combining both accounting and healthcare creates a vocation that is desirable due to its job security, incentive for compensation, and evolving regulations. The federal government will continue to research methods to expand medical coverage and investigate alternatives to cutting patient-related costs. Current initiatives, such as the ACO, P4P reimbursement, and the bundled payment model may or may not achieve the desired outcomes; however, these ideas reiterate the government's belief that the healthcare system must be reengineered.

Chapter 15

Epilogue

Incorporating Faith in the Workplace

Several years ago, I had a conversation with a priest who stated that: "Being successful is not as important as being faithful." At the time, this statement did not mean much to me since I was just exiting college and entering the workforce. However, it has been numerous years since that memorable discussion, and only recently am I truly starting to comprehend the power of those words.

As we travel through life, the need for achievement, power, and increased compensation often outweighs such ideals as charity and stewardship. I am guilty of this just as much as anyone else. For many years, I would work long hours not because I had to but because I was driven by material wealth and self-satisfaction. This attitude is prevalent in today's society as many of us aspire to be the next Donald Trump or Bill Gates. By no means am I against people being ambitious or aspiring to be successful. As a matter of fact, it is a quality that I wish more people had. However, I believe we should find a sustainable balance between career goals and religious faith. Regardless of being Catholic, Protestant, Muslim, or Jewish, I believe everyone has the ability to implement his or her own faith in the workplace. Personally, as a Christian I always strive to incorporate the concepts of generosity and compassion into the healthcare accounting profession. I believe I am not alone when I state the importance of "treating others as you would like them to treat you." As I have matured and evolved, I have realized that financial achievement is important, but it should not be the sole motivating factor. I believe that a healthy balance of hard work and ethical decision making combined with religious beliefs will result in both happiness and success.

One easy way to incorporate one's religious faith into the workforce is simply to be friendly and kind. The simple act of complementing a coworker on personal appearance or praising a colleague for his or her efforts can improve someone's entire day. Effortless tasks like opening the door for others or saying "hello" to everyone you encounter may seem trivial, but these actions have lasting results. Performing random acts of praise, generosity, and kindness reiterate what Jesus stated in the Gospel of John 13:34: "Just as I have loved you, you should also love one another."

Another constructive approach to improve the workplace is to refrain from spreading the detrimental action of gossip. All of us have at one time been guilty of spreading negative information to make ourselves feel or look better. Jealousy and envy permeate all office environments, especially when promotions and bonuses are at stake. Despite the temptation to give in to these damaging habits, we must resist both external and internal influences. It is easy to be envious and jealous of someone if the person has achieved more than we have. As a Christian, I applaud those who are rewarded, and I try my best not to harbor any judgments. If others choose to spread gossip, then let them but do not join in their actions. *The best way to eliminate gossip is to ignore it.* Coworkers will see you as an example and possibly refrain from their slanderous actions. Gossip is carried through various informal communication channels, and its distribution can be minimized if employees simply refuse to pay attention to those who spread it.

A third method of incorporating one's spiritual beliefs into one's job is to use the gift of forgiveness. Regardless of our current stature, each of us at one time have been publicly ostracized or been the recipient of a cruel joke. By nature, we are hurt and offended by these actions. We sometimes envision wounding those who have insulted us so we can equalize the harm they have inflicted. This reaction is the easy way to respond to verbal abuse, and it often results in negative consequences. I believe the best action is to confront the coworker privately and explain to him or her, using polite words, how you have been offended. Usually, people are responsive when they are approached privately, and the issue is discussed in a logical and professional manner. If this method does not resolve the conflict, then a meeting with a supervisor should be scheduled. As a Christian, I try not to harbor any ill feelings against those who have damaged my psyche. It may be difficult to forget someone's actions, but we must forgive them. It takes strength and courage to let an offense go, and our true faith demands it. *However, the act of forgiveness does not require reconciliation.* It takes just one person to forgive, but two are needed for reconciliation. The act of forgiveness is driven by love, but it does not imply that we are responsible to fix a broken relationship. As a Christian, I am bound to explore the possibility of reconciliation, but it may not always occur. I believe Matthew 6:14 states it best: "For if you forgive others their trespasses, your heavenly Father will also forgive you, but if you do not forgive others, neither will your Father forgive your trespasses."

In conclusion, I believe God wants us to succeed in life by using all of the gifts he provided us, and we must do so by incorporating the appropriate themes. At times, we may find ourselves solely driven by financial rewards, and we may be tempted to act in unethical and unscrupulous ways. It is during these periods that we should rely on our spiritual beliefs for guidance. By simply being kindhearted to those around us and refraining from gossip, we can improve our workplace, while forgiving others brings us closer to God. Despite the lure of wealth and self-satisfaction, we must always remember that these benefits are temporary while the gift of salvation is eternal.

Appendix A

UB-04 Revenue Codes

0110	Room/Board Private	0550	Skilled Nursing
0120	Room/Board SP 2 bed	0560	Medical Social Services
0130	Room/Board SP 3–4 bed	0570	Home Health Aides
0140	Room/Board Private Deluxe	0580	Other Visits–HHA
0150	Room/Board Ward	0590	Units of Service
0160	Nursery	0600	Oxygen (Home Health)
0180	Leave of Absence	0610	Magnetic Resonance Imaging
0190	Sub-Acute Care	0620	Med-Surg Supplies Ext of 270
0200	Intensive Care	0630	Drugs Requiring Specific Identification
0210	Coronary Care	0640	Home IV Therapy
0220	Special Charges	0650	Hospice
0230	Incremental Nursing Care	0660	General Respite Care
0240	All Inclusive Ancillary	0670	Outpatient Special Residence
0250	Pharmacy	0700	Cast Room
0260	IV Therapy	0710	Recovery Room
0270	Medical/Surgical Supplies	0720	Labor Room
0280	Oncology	0730	EKG/ECG
0290	Durable Medical Equipment	0740	EEG
0300	Laboratory	0750	Gastro-Intestinal Services
0310	Laboratory–Pathology	0760	Treatment or Observation Room
0320	Radiology–Diagnostic	0770	Preventive Care Services

0330	Radiology–Therapeutic	0780	Telemedicine
0340	Nuclear Medicine	0790	Extra-Corporeal Shock Wave Therapy
0350	CT Scan	0800	Inpatient Renal Dialysis
0360	Operating Room Services	0810	Organ Acquisition
0370	Anesthesia	0820	Hemodialysis-Outpatient/Home
0380	Blood	0830	Peritoneal OPD/Home
0390	Blood Storage/Processing	0840	CAPD OPD/Home
0400	Other Imaging Services	0850	CCPD–Outpatient
0410	Respiratory Services	0880	Miscellaneous Dialysis
0420	Physical Therapy	0900	Behavioral Health Treatment
0430	Occupational Therapy	091X	Behavioral Health Treatment Ext of 900
0440	Speech-Language Pathology	0920	Other Diagnostic Service
0450	Emergency Room	0930	Medical Rehab Day Program
0460	Pulmonary Function	0940	Other Therapeutic Service
0470	Audiology	0960	Professional Fees
0480	Cardiology	0970	Professional Fees Reserved
0490	Ambulatory Surgery	0980	Professional Fees Reserved
0500	Outpatient Services	0990	Patient Convenience Items
0510	Clinic	1000	Behavioral Health Accommodations
0520	Free-Standing Clinic	2100	Alternative Therapy Services
0530	Osteopathic Services	3100	Adult Day Care
0540	Ambulance		

Appendix B

FYE 2010 Medicare MS-DRG Listing

MS-DRG	MS-DRG Title	Weights
001	HEART TRANSPLANT OR IMPLANT OF HEART ASSIST SYSTEM W MCC	24.8548
002	HEART TRANSPLANT OR IMPLANT OF HEART ASSIST SYSTEM W/O MCC	11.754
003	ECMO OR TRACH W MV 96+ HRS OR PDX EXC FACE, MOUTH & NECK W MAJ O.R.	18.2667
004	TRACH W MV 96+ HRS OR PDX EXC FACE, MOUTH & NECK W/O MAJ O.R.	11.1941
005	LIVER TRANSPLANT W MCC OR INTESTINAL TRANSPLANT	10.1358
006	LIVER TRANSPLANT W/O MCC	4.7569
007	LUNG TRANSPLANT	9.4543
008	SIMULTANEOUS PANCREAS/KIDNEY TRANSPLANT	5.0615
009	BONE MARROW TRANSPLANT	6.5419
010	PANCREAS TRANSPLANT	4.2752
011	TRACHEOSTOMY FOR FACE, MOUTH & NECK DIAGNOSES W MCC	4.7341
012	TRACHEOSTOMY FOR FACE, MOUTH & NECK DIAGNOSES W CC	3.0306
013	TRACHEOSTOMY FOR FACE, MOUTH & NECK DIAGNOSES W/O CC/MCC	1.8643
020	INTRACRANIAL VASCULAR PROCEDURES W PDX HEMORRHAGE W MCC	8.4392
021	INTRACRANIAL VASCULAR PROCEDURES W PDX HEMORRHAGE W CC	6.2068

MS-DRG	MS-DRG Title	Weights
022	INTRACRANIAL VASCULAR PROCEDURES W PDX HEMORRHAGE W/O CC/MCC	4.3765
023	CRANIO W MAJOR DEV IMPL/ACUTE COMPLEX CNS PDX W MCC OR CHEMO IMPLANT	4.9401
024	CRANIO W MAJOR DEV IMPL/ACUTE COMPLEX CNS PDX W/O MCC	3.2566
025	CRANIOTOMY & ENDOVASCULAR INTRACRANIAL PROCEDURES W MCC	4.8236
026	CRANIOTOMY & ENDOVASCULAR INTRACRANIAL PROCEDURES W CC	2.9421
027	CRANIOTOMY & ENDOVASCULAR INTRACRANIAL PROCEDURES W/O CC/MCC	2.0902
028	SPINAL PROCEDURES W MCC	5.109
029	SPINAL PROCEDURES W CC OR SPINAL NEUROSTIMULATORS	2.7768
030	SPINAL PROCEDURES W/O CC/MCC	1.6019
031	VENTRICULAR SHUNT PROCEDURES W MCC	4.5341
032	VENTRICULAR SHUNT PROCEDURES W CC	1.9186
033	VENTRICULAR SHUNT PROCEDURES W/O CC/MCC	1.3331
034	CAROTID ARTERY STENT PROCEDURE W MCC	3.19
035	CAROTID ARTERY STENT PROCEDURE W CC	2.0165
036	CAROTID ARTERY STENT PROCEDURE W/O CC/MCC	1.5744
037	EXTRACRANIAL PROCEDURES W MCC	2.919
038	EXTRACRANIAL PROCEDURES W CC	1.4783
039	EXTRACRANIAL PROCEDURES W/O CC/MCC	1.0033
040	PERIPH/CRANIAL NERVE & OTHER NERV SYST PROC W MCC	3.9518
041	PERIPH/CRANIAL NERVE & OTHER NERV SYST PROC W CC OR PERIPH NEUROSTIM	2.1249
042	PERIPH/CRANIAL NERVE & OTHER NERV SYST PROC W/O CC/MCC	1.6448
052	SPINAL DISORDERS & INJURIES W CC/MCC	1.4836
053	SPINAL DISORDERS & INJURIES W/O CC/MCC	0.8382
054	NERVOUS SYSTEM NEOPLASMS W MCC	1.5637
055	NERVOUS SYSTEM NEOPLASMS W/O MCC	1.0613
056	DEGENERATIVE NERVOUS SYSTEM DISORDERS W MCC	1.6952

MS-DRG	MS-DRG Title	Weights
057	DEGENERATIVE NERVOUS SYSTEM DISORDERS W/O MCC	0.9028
058	MULTIPLE SCLEROSIS & CEREBELLAR ATAXIA W MCC	1.5512
059	MULTIPLE SCLEROSIS & CEREBELLAR ATAXIA W CC	0.9581
060	MULTIPLE SCLEROSIS & CEREBELLAR ATAXIA W/O CC/MCC	0.7083
061	ACUTE ISCHEMIC STROKE W USE OF THROMBOLYTIC AGENT W MCC	2.9168
062	ACUTE ISCHEMIC STROKE W USE OF THROMBOLYTIC AGENT W CC	1.929
063	ACUTE ISCHEMIC STROKE W USE OF THROMBOLYTIC AGENT W/O CC/MCC	1.5187
064	INTRACRANIAL HEMORRHAGE OR CEREBRAL INFARCTION W MCC	1.8258
065	INTRACRANIAL HEMORRHAGE OR CEREBRAL INFARCTION W CC	1.158
066	INTRACRANIAL HEMORRHAGE OR CEREBRAL INFARCTION W/O CC/MCC	0.8223
067	NONSPECIFIC CVA & PRECEREBRAL OCCLUSION W/O INFARCT W MCC	1.3335
068	NONSPECIFIC CVA & PRECEREBRAL OCCLUSION W/O INFARCT W/O MCC	0.8593
069	TRANSIENT ISCHEMIA	0.7289
070	NONSPECIFIC CEREBROVASCULAR DISORDERS W MCC	1.7919
071	NONSPECIFIC CEREBROVASCULAR DISORDERS W CC	1.1027
072	NONSPECIFIC CEREBROVASCULAR DISORDERS W/O CC/MCC	0.7616
073	CRANIAL & PERIPHERAL NERVE DISORDERS W MCC	1.2939
074	CRANIAL & PERIPHERAL NERVE DISORDERS W/O MCC	0.838
075	VIRAL MENINGITIS W CC/MCC	1.667
076	VIRAL MENINGITIS W/O CC/MCC	0.8336
077	HYPERTENSIVE ENCEPHALOPATHY W MCC	1.6245
078	HYPERTENSIVE ENCEPHALOPATHY W CC	0.9822
079	HYPERTENSIVE ENCEPHALOPATHY W/O CC/MCC	0.7359
080	NONTRAUMATIC STUPOR & COMA W MCC	1.1461
081	NONTRAUMATIC STUPOR & COMA W/O MCC	0.7113
082	TRAUMATIC STUPOR & COMA, COMA > 1 HR W MCC	2.013
083	TRAUMATIC STUPOR & COMA, COMA > 1 HR W CC	1.3031

MS-DRG	MS-DRG Title	Weights
084	TRAUMATIC STUPOR & COMA, COMA > 1 HR W/O CC/MCC	0.8532
085	TRAUMATIC STUPOR & COMA, COMA < 1 HR W MCC	2.0572
086	TRAUMATIC STUPOR & COMA, COMA < 1 HR W CC	1.2098
087	TRAUMATIC STUPOR & COMA, COMA < 1 HR W/O CC/MCC	0.7815
088	CONCUSSION W MCC	1.4741
089	CONCUSSION W CC	0.9298
090	CONCUSSION W/O CC/MCC	0.6818
091	OTHER DISORDERS OF NERVOUS SYSTEM W MCC	1.5465
092	OTHER DISORDERS OF NERVOUS SYSTEM W CC	0.9167
093	OTHER DISORDERS OF NERVOUS SYSTEM W/O CC/MCC	0.6691
094	BACTERIAL & TUBERCULOUS INFECTIONS OF NERVOUS SYSTEM W MCC	3.4161
095	BACTERIAL & TUBERCULOUS INFECTIONS OF NERVOUS SYSTEM W CC	2.2416
096	BACTERIAL & TUBERCULOUS INFECTIONS OF NERVOUS SYSTEM W/O CC/MCC	1.7927
097	NON-BACTERIAL INFECT OF NERVOUS SYS EXC VIRAL MENINGITIS W MCC	3.0233
098	NON-BACTERIAL INFECT OF NERVOUS SYS EXC VIRAL MENINGITIS W CC	1.7985
099	NON-BACTERIAL INFECT OF NERVOUS SYS EXC VIRAL MENINGITIS W/O CC/MCC	1.2084
100	SEIZURES W MCC	1.4778
101	SEIZURES W/O MCC	0.7577
102	HEADACHES W MCC	0.9772
103	HEADACHES W/O MCC	0.6355
113	ORBITAL PROCEDURES W CC/MCC	1.7702
114	ORBITAL PROCEDURES W/O CC/MCC	0.8825
115	EXTRAOCULAR PROCEDURES EXCEPT ORBIT	1.1589
116	INTRAOCULAR PROCEDURES W CC/MCC	1.1418
117	INTRAOCULAR PROCEDURES W/O CC/MCC	0.6914
121	ACUTE MAJOR EYE INFECTIONS W CC/MCC	1.0006

MS-DRG	MS-DRG Title	Weights
122	ACUTE MAJOR EYE INFECTIONS W/O CC/MCC	0.6713
123	NEUROLOGICAL EYE DISORDERS	0.7153
124	OTHER DISORDERS OF THE EYE W MCC	1.1843
125	OTHER DISORDERS OF THE EYE W/O MCC	0.6627
129	MAJOR HEAD & NECK PROCEDURES W CC/MCC OR MAJOR DEVICE	2.0661
130	MAJOR HEAD & NECK PROCEDURES W/O CC/MCC	1.2054
131	CRANIAL/FACIAL PROCEDURES W CC/MCC	2.0146
132	CRANIAL/FACIAL PROCEDURES W/O CC/MCC	1.1355
133	OTHER EAR, NOSE, MOUTH & THROAT O.R. PROCEDURES W CC/MCC	1.5884
134	OTHER EAR, NOSE, MOUTH & THROAT O.R. PROCEDURES W/O CC/MCC	0.8166
135	SINUS & MASTOID PROCEDURES W CC/MCC	1.852
136	SINUS & MASTOID PROCEDURES W/O CC/MCC	0.9015
137	MOUTH PROCEDURES W CC/MCC	1.4004
138	MOUTH PROCEDURES W/O CC/MCC	0.7458
139	SALIVARY GLAND PROCEDURES	0.808
146	EAR, NOSE, MOUTH & THROAT MALIGNANCY W MCC	2.1291
147	EAR, NOSE, MOUTH & THROAT MALIGNANCY W CC	1.2345
148	EAR, NOSE, MOUTH & THROAT MALIGNANCY W/O CC/MCC	0.6995
149	DYSEQUILIBRIUM	0.6293
150	EPISTAXIS W MCC	1.3363
151	EPISTAXIS W/O MCC	0.6194
152	OTITIS MEDIA & URI W MCC	0.9396
153	OTITIS MEDIA & URI W/O MCC	0.6084
154	OTHER EAR, NOSE, MOUTH & THROAT DIAGNOSES W MCC	1.3872
155	OTHER EAR, NOSE, MOUTH & THROAT DIAGNOSES W CC	0.8823
156	OTHER EAR, NOSE, MOUTH & THROAT DIAGNOSES W/O CC/MCC	0.6201
157	DENTAL & ORAL DISEASES W MCC	1.4763
158	DENTAL & ORAL DISEASES W CC	0.9235
159	DENTAL & ORAL DISEASES W/O CC/MCC	0.5949

MS-DRG	MS-DRG Title	Weights
163	MAJOR CHEST PROCEDURES W MCC	4.9549
164	MAJOR CHEST PROCEDURES W CC	2.5164
165	MAJOR CHEST PROCEDURES W/O CC/MCC	1.7662
166	OTHER RESP SYSTEM O.R. PROCEDURES W MCC	3.7227
167	OTHER RESP SYSTEM O.R. PROCEDURES W CC	2.0068
168	OTHER RESP SYSTEM O.R. PROCEDURES W/O CC/MCC	1.3026
175	PULMONARY EMBOLISM W MCC	1.6121
176	PULMONARY EMBOLISM W/O MCC	1.0685
177	RESPIRATORY INFECTIONS & INFLAMMATIONS W MCC	2.0483
178	RESPIRATORY INFECTIONS & INFLAMMATIONS W CC	1.486
179	RESPIRATORY INFECTIONS & INFLAMMATIONS W/O CC/MCC	1.0088
180	RESPIRATORY NEOPLASMS W MCC	1.7263
181	RESPIRATORY NEOPLASMS W CC	1.2062
182	RESPIRATORY NEOPLASMS W/O CC/MCC	0.8159
183	MAJOR CHEST TRAUMA W MCC	1.4432
184	MAJOR CHEST TRAUMA W CC	0.9483
185	MAJOR CHEST TRAUMA W/O CC/MCC	0.6665
186	PLEURAL EFFUSION W MCC	1.5917
187	PLEURAL EFFUSION W CC	1.062
188	PLEURAL EFFUSION W/O CC/MCC	0.7612
189	PULMONARY EDEMA & RESPIRATORY FAILURE	1.3455
190	CHRONIC OBSTRUCTIVE PULMONARY DISEASE W MCC	1.2076
191	CHRONIC OBSTRUCTIVE PULMONARY DISEASE W CC	0.9622
192	CHRONIC OBSTRUCTIVE PULMONARY DISEASE W/O CC/MCC	0.7175
193	SIMPLE PNEUMONIA & PLEURISY W MCC	1.4378
194	SIMPLE PNEUMONIA & PLEURISY W CC	0.9976
195	SIMPLE PNEUMONIA & PLEURISY W/O CC/MCC	0.7095
196	INTERSTITIAL LUNG DISEASE W MCC	1.5396
197	INTERSTITIAL LUNG DISEASE W CC	1.0647
198	INTERSTITIAL LUNG DISEASE W/O CC/MCC	0.8137

MS-DRG	MS-DRG Title	Weights
199	PNEUMOTHORAX W MCC	1.8266
200	PNEUMOTHORAX W CC	0.9745
201	PNEUMOTHORAX W/O CC/MCC	0.7144
202	BRONCHITIS & ASTHMA W CC/MCC	0.8374
203	BRONCHITIS & ASTHMA W/O CC/MCC	0.6055
204	RESPIRATORY SIGNS & SYMPTOMS	0.6472
205	OTHER RESPIRATORY SYSTEM DIAGNOSES W MCC	1.2566
206	OTHER RESPIRATORY SYSTEM DIAGNOSES W/O MCC	0.7294
207	RESPIRATORY SYSTEM DIAGNOSIS W VENTILATOR SUPPORT 96+ HOURS	5.178
208	RESPIRATORY SYSTEM DIAGNOSIS W VENTILATOR SUPPORT <96 HOURS	2.2358
215	OTHER HEART ASSIST SYSTEM IMPLANT	12.8304
216	CARDIAC VALVE & OTH MAJ CARDIOTHORACIC PROC W CARD CATH W MCC	10.1967
217	CARDIAC VALVE & OTH MAJ CARDIOTHORACIC PROC W CARD CATH W CC	6.5932
218	CARDIAC VALVE & OTH MAJ CARDIOTHORACIC PROC W CARD CATH W/O CC/MCC	5.2809
219	CARDIAC VALVE & OTH MAJ CARDIOTHORACIC PROC W/O CARD CATH W MCC	7.9336
220	CARDIAC VALVE & OTH MAJ CARDIOTHORACIC PROC W/O CARD CATH W CC	5.1767
221	CARDIAC VALVE & OTH MAJ CARDIOTHORACIC PROC W/O CARD CATH W/O CC/MCC	4.3926
222	CARDIAC DEFIB IMPLANT W CARDIAC CATH W AMI/HF/SHOCK W MCC	8.4829
223	CARDIAC DEFIB IMPLANT W CARDIAC CATH W AMI/HF/SHOCK W/O MCC	6.2229
224	CARDIAC DEFIB IMPLANT W CARDIAC CATH W/O AMI/HF/SHOCK W MCC	7.5477
225	CARDIAC DEFIB IMPLANT W CARDIAC CATH W/O AMI/HF/SHOCK W/O MCC	5.8321
226	CARDIAC DEFIBRILLATOR IMPLANT W/O CARDIAC CATH W MCC	6.5457

MS-DRG	MS-DRG Title	Weights
227	CARDIAC DEFIBRILLATOR IMPLANT W/O CARDIAC CATH W/O MCC	5.0519
228	OTHER CARDIOTHORACIC PROCEDURES W MCC	7.5401
229	OTHER CARDIOTHORACIC PROCEDURES W CC	4.8428
230	OTHER CARDIOTHORACIC PROCEDURES W/O CC/MCC	3.7989
231	CORONARY BYPASS W PTCA W MCC	7.6784
232	CORONARY BYPASS W PTCA W/O MCC	5.5589
233	CORONARY BYPASS W CARDIAC CATH W MCC	6.924
234	CORONARY BYPASS W CARDIAC CATH W/O MCC	4.6212
235	CORONARY BYPASS W/O CARDIAC CATH W MCC	5.6898
236	CORONARY BYPASS W/O CARDIAC CATH W/O MCC	3.6128
237	MAJOR CARDIOVASC PROCEDURES W MCC OR THORACIC AORTIC ANEURYSM REPAIR	5.0355
238	MAJOR CARDIOVASC PROCEDURES W/O MCC	2.9366
239	AMPUTATION FOR CIRC SYS DISORDERS EXC UPPER LIMB & TOE W MCC	4.7275
240	AMPUTATION FOR CIRC SYS DISORDERS EXC UPPER LIMB & TOE W CC	2.5377
241	AMPUTATION FOR CIRC SYS DISORDERS EXC UPPER LIMB & TOE W/O CC/MCC	1.4922
242	PERMANENT CARDIAC PACEMAKER IMPLANT W MCC	3.5878
243	PERMANENT CARDIAC PACEMAKER IMPLANT W CC	2.5737
244	PERMANENT CARDIAC PACEMAKER IMPLANT W/O CC/MCC	1.9888
245	AICD GENERATOR PROCEDURES	4.0534
246	PERC CARDIOVASC PROC W DRUG-ELUTING STENT W MCC OR 4+ VESSELS/STENTS	3.0955
247	PERC CARDIOVASC PROC W DRUG-ELUTING STENT W/O MCC	1.9121
248	PERC CARDIOVASC PROC W NON-DRUG-ELUTING STENT W MCC OR 4+ VES/STENTS	2.8419
249	PERC CARDIOVASC PROC W NON-DRUG-ELUTING STENT W/O MCC	1.684
250	PERC CARDIOVASC PROC W/O CORONARY ARTERY STENT W MCC	2.7546
251	PERC CARDIOVASC PROC W/O CORONARY ARTERY STENT W/O MCC	1.6455
252	OTHER VASCULAR PROCEDURES W MCC	2.9443

MS-DRG	MS-DRG Title	Weights
253	OTHER VASCULAR PROCEDURES W CC	2.2817
254	OTHER VASCULAR PROCEDURES W/O CC/MCC	1.5713
255	UPPER LIMB & TOE AMPUTATION FOR CIRC SYSTEM DISORDERS W MCC	2.5388
256	UPPER LIMB & TOE AMPUTATION FOR CIRC SYSTEM DISORDERS W CC	1.5518
257	UPPER LIMB & TOE AMPUTATION FOR CIRC SYSTEM DISORDERS W/O CC/MCC	0.9529
258	CARDIAC PACEMAKER DEVICE REPLACEMENT W MCC	2.8006
259	CARDIAC PACEMAKER DEVICE REPLACEMENT W/O MCC	1.7191
260	CARDIAC PACEMAKER REVISION EXCEPT DEVICE REPLACEMENT W MCC	3.2956
261	CARDIAC PACEMAKER REVISION EXCEPT DEVICE REPLACEMENT W CC	1.4677
262	CARDIAC PACEMAKER REVISION EXCEPT DEVICE REPLACEMENT W/O CC/MCC	1.0412
263	VEIN LIGATION & STRIPPING	1.6163
264	OTHER CIRCULATORY SYSTEM O.R. PROCEDURES	2.5087
265	AICD LEAD PROCEDURES	2.2407
280	ACUTE MYOCARDIAL INFARCTION, DISCHARGED ALIVE W MCC	1.8313
281	ACUTE MYOCARDIAL INFARCTION, DISCHARGED ALIVE W CC	1.162
282	ACUTE MYOCARDIAL INFARCTION, DISCHARGED ALIVE W/O CC/MCC	0.8177
283	ACUTE MYOCARDIAL INFARCTION, EXPIRED W MCC	1.6717
284	ACUTE MYOCARDIAL INFARCTION, EXPIRED W CC	0.8024
285	ACUTE MYOCARDIAL INFARCTION, EXPIRED W/O CC/MCC	0.5602
286	CIRCULATORY DISORDERS EXCEPT AMI, W CARD CATH W MCC	1.9634
287	CIRCULATORY DISORDERS EXCEPT AMI, W CARD CATH W/O MCC	1.0321
288	ACUTE & SUBACUTE ENDOCARDITIS W MCC	3.0888
289	ACUTE & SUBACUTE ENDOCARDITIS W CC	1.8496
290	ACUTE & SUBACUTE ENDOCARDITIS W/O CC/MCC	1.2313
291	HEART FAILURE & SHOCK W MCC	1.4609

MS-DRG	MS-DRG Title	Weights
292	HEART FAILURE & SHOCK W CC	0.974
293	HEART FAILURE & SHOCK W/O CC/MCC	0.694
294	DEEP VEIN THROMBOPHLEBITIS W CC/MCC	1.0104
295	DEEP VEIN THROMBOPHLEBITIS W/O CC/MCC	0.6504
296	CARDIAC ARREST, UNEXPLAINED W MCC	1.1665
297	CARDIAC ARREST, UNEXPLAINED W CC	0.6704
298	CARDIAC ARREST, UNEXPLAINED W/O CC/MCC	0.4469
299	PERIPHERAL VASCULAR DISORDERS W MCC	1.4045
300	PERIPHERAL VASCULAR DISORDERS W CC	0.9378
301	PERIPHERAL VASCULAR DISORDERS W/O CC/MCC	0.6522
302	ATHEROSCLEROSIS W MCC	0.9999
303	ATHEROSCLEROSIS W/O MCC	0.5681
304	HYPERTENSION W MCC	1.0242
305	HYPERTENSION W/O MCC	0.5959
306	CARDIAC CONGENITAL & VALVULAR DISORDERS W MCC	1.3076
307	CARDIAC CONGENITAL & VALVULAR DISORDERS W/O MCC	0.7624
308	CARDIAC ARRHYTHMIA & CONDUCTION DISORDERS W MCC	1.2188
309	CARDIAC ARRHYTHMIA & CONDUCTION DISORDERS W CC	0.8207
310	CARDIAC ARRHYTHMIA & CONDUCTION DISORDERS W/O CC/MCC	0.571
311	ANGINA PECTORIS	0.5128
312	SYNCOPE & COLLAPSE	0.7215
313	CHEST PAIN	0.5404
314	OTHER CIRCULATORY SYSTEM DIAGNOSES W MCC	1.7589
315	OTHER CIRCULATORY SYSTEM DIAGNOSES W CC	0.9598
316	OTHER CIRCULATORY SYSTEM DIAGNOSES W/O CC/MCC	0.6211
326	STOMACH, ESOPHAGEAL & DUODENAL PROC W MCC	5.6845
327	STOMACH, ESOPHAGEAL & DUODENAL PROC W CC	2.7062
328	STOMACH, ESOPHAGEAL & DUODENAL PROC W/O CC/MCC	1.395
329	MAJOR SMALL & LARGE BOWEL PROCEDURES W MCC	5.1396
330	MAJOR SMALL & LARGE BOWEL PROCEDURES W CC	2.4981

MS-DRG	MS-DRG Title	Weights
331	MAJOR SMALL & LARGE BOWEL PROCEDURES W/O CC/MCC	1.5952
332	RECTAL RESECTION W MCC	4.7762
333	RECTAL RESECTION W CC	2.415
334	RECTAL RESECTION W/O CC/MCC	1.6208
335	PERITONEAL ADHESIOLYSIS W MCC	4.1422
336	PERITONEAL ADHESIOLYSIS W CC	2.2458
337	PERITONEAL ADHESIOLYSIS W/O CC/MCC	1.4441
338	APPENDECTOMY W COMPLICATED PRINCIPAL DIAG W MCC	3.0677
339	APPENDECTOMY W COMPLICATED PRINCIPAL DIAG W CC	1.7979
340	APPENDECTOMY W COMPLICATED PRINCIPAL DIAG W/O CC/MCC	1.2197
341	APPENDECTOMY W/O COMPLICATED PRINCIPAL DIAG W MCC	2.2109
342	APPENDECTOMY W/O COMPLICATED PRINCIPAL DIAG W CC	1.3112
343	APPENDECTOMY W/O COMPLICATED PRINCIPAL DIAG W/O CC/MCC	0.936
344	MINOR SMALL & LARGE BOWEL PROCEDURES W MCC	3.0345
345	MINOR SMALL & LARGE BOWEL PROCEDURES W CC	1.6179
346	MINOR SMALL & LARGE BOWEL PROCEDURES W/O CC/MCC	1.1755
347	ANAL & STOMAL PROCEDURES W MCC	2.2657
348	ANAL & STOMAL PROCEDURES W CC	1.3237
349	ANAL & STOMAL PROCEDURES W/O CC/MCC	0.7665
350	INGUINAL & FEMORAL HERNIA PROCEDURES W MCC	2.2798
351	INGUINAL & FEMORAL HERNIA PROCEDURES W CC	1.2628
352	INGUINAL & FEMORAL HERNIA PROCEDURES W/O CC/MCC	0.821
353	HERNIA PROCEDURES EXCEPT INGUINAL & FEMORAL W MCC	2.5349
354	HERNIA PROCEDURES EXCEPT INGUINAL & FEMORAL W CC	1.4337
355	HERNIA PROCEDURES EXCEPT INGUINAL & FEMORAL W/O CC/MCC	0.9878
356	OTHER DIGESTIVE SYSTEM O.R. PROCEDURES W MCC	3.9597
357	OTHER DIGESTIVE SYSTEM O.R. PROCEDURES W CC	2.116
358	OTHER DIGESTIVE SYSTEM O.R. PROCEDURES W/O CC/MCC	1.3008
368	MAJOR ESOPHAGEAL DISORDERS W MCC	1.6584
369	MAJOR ESOPHAGEAL DISORDERS W CC	1.048

MS-DRG	MS-DRG Title	Weights
370	MAJOR ESOPHAGEAL DISORDERS W/O CC/MCC	0.7501
371	MAJOR GASTROINTESTINAL DISORDERS & PERITONEAL INFECTIONS W MCC	1.9214
372	MAJOR GASTROINTESTINAL DISORDERS & PERITONEAL INFECTIONS W CC	1.2865
373	MAJOR GASTROINTESTINAL DISORDERS & PERITONEAL INFECTIONS W/O CC/MCC	0.8619
374	DIGESTIVE MALIGNANCY W MCC	2.0149
375	DIGESTIVE MALIGNANCY W CC	1.2631
376	DIGESTIVE MALIGNANCY W/O CC/MCC	0.8883
377	G.I. HEMORRHAGE W MCC	1.6149
378	G.I. HEMORRHAGE W CC	0.9873
379	G.I. HEMORRHAGE W/O CC/MCC	0.7179
380	COMPLICATED PEPTIC ULCER W MCC	1.7333
381	COMPLICATED PEPTIC ULCER W CC	1.0853
382	COMPLICATED PEPTIC ULCER W/O CC/MCC	0.7785
383	UNCOMPLICATED PEPTIC ULCER W MCC	1.2399
384	UNCOMPLICATED PEPTIC ULCER W/O MCC	0.8146
385	INFLAMMATORY BOWEL DISEASE W MCC	1.7089
386	INFLAMMATORY BOWEL DISEASE W CC	1.0423
387	INFLAMMATORY BOWEL DISEASE W/O CC/MCC	0.7871
388	G.I. OBSTRUCTION W MCC	1.506
389	G.I. OBSTRUCTION W CC	0.9268
390	G.I. OBSTRUCTION W/O CC/MCC	0.6341
391	ESOPHAGITIS, GASTROENT & MISC DIGEST DISORDERS W MCC	1.0958
392	ESOPHAGITIS, GASTROENT & MISC DIGEST DISORDERS W/O MCC	0.6921
393	OTHER DIGESTIVE SYSTEM DIAGNOSES W MCC	1.5632
394	OTHER DIGESTIVE SYSTEM DIAGNOSES W CC	0.9572
395	OTHER DIGESTIVE SYSTEM DIAGNOSES W/O CC/MCC	0.6666
405	PANCREAS, LIVER & SHUNT PROCEDURES W MCC	5.5911
406	PANCREAS, LIVER & SHUNT PROCEDURES W CC	2.6729

MS-DRG	MS-DRG Title	Weights
407	PANCREAS, LIVER & SHUNT PROCEDURES W/O CC/MCC	1.8068
408	BILIARY TRACT PROC EXCEPT ONLY CHOLECYST W OR W/O C.D.E. W MCC	4.0844
409	BILIARY TRACT PROC EXCEPT ONLY CHOLECYST W OR W/O C.D.E. W CC	2.3103
410	BILIARY TRACT PROC EXCEPT ONLY CHOLECYST W OR W/O C.D.E. W/O CC/MCC	1.6134
411	CHOLECYSTECTOMY W C.D.E. W MCC	3.9655
412	CHOLECYSTECTOMY W C.D.E. W CC	2.3982
413	CHOLECYSTECTOMY W C.D.E. W/O CC/MCC	1.6222
414	CHOLECYSTECTOMY EXCEPT BY LAPAROSCOPE W/O C.D.E. W MCC	3.6023
415	CHOLECYSTECTOMY EXCEPT BY LAPAROSCOPE W/O C.D.E. W CC	1.9824
416	CHOLECYSTECTOMY EXCEPT BY LAPAROSCOPE W/O C.D.E. W/O CC/MCC	1.2904
417	LAPAROSCOPIC CHOLECYSTECTOMY W/O C.D.E. W MCC	2.405
418	LAPAROSCOPIC CHOLECYSTECTOMY W/O C.D.E. W CC	1.6354
419	LAPAROSCOPIC CHOLECYSTECTOMY W/O C.D.E. W/O CC/MCC	1.1334
420	HEPATOBILIARY DIAGNOSTIC PROCEDURES W MCC	4.1182
421	HEPATOBILIARY DIAGNOSTIC PROCEDURES W CC	1.6987
422	HEPATOBILIARY DIAGNOSTIC PROCEDURES W/O CC/MCC	1.1791
423	OTHER HEPATOBILIARY OR PANCREAS O.R. PROCEDURES W MCC	4.2255
424	OTHER HEPATOBILIARY OR PANCREAS O.R. PROCEDURES W CC	2.2105
425	OTHER HEPATOBILIARY OR PANCREAS O.R. PROCEDURES W/O CC/MCC	1.4477
432	CIRRHOSIS & ALCOHOLIC HEPATITIS W MCC	1.6369
433	CIRRHOSIS & ALCOHOLIC HEPATITIS W CC	0.9076
434	CIRRHOSIS & ALCOHOLIC HEPATITIS W/O CC/MCC	0.6489
435	MALIGNANCY OF HEPATOBILIARY SYSTEM OR PANCREAS W MCC	1.7293
436	MALIGNANCY OF HEPATOBILIARY SYSTEM OR PANCREAS W CC	1.1831
437	MALIGNANCY OF HEPATOBILIARY SYSTEM OR PANCREAS W/O CC/MCC	0.878
438	DISORDERS OF PANCREAS EXCEPT MALIGNANCY W MCC	1.6993

MS-DRG	MS-DRG Title	Weights
439	DISORDERS OF PANCREAS EXCEPT MALIGNANCY W CC	0.996
440	DISORDERS OF PANCREAS EXCEPT MALIGNANCY W/O CC/MCC	0.6865
441	DISORDERS OF LIVER EXCEPT MALIG, CIRR, ALC HEPA W MCC	1.729
442	DISORDERS OF LIVER EXCEPT MALIG, CIRR, ALC HEPA W CC	0.9407
443	DISORDERS OF LIVER EXCEPT MALIG, CIRR, ALC HEPA W/O CC/MCC	0.6631
444	DISORDERS OF THE BILIARY TRACT W MCC	1.5055
445	DISORDERS OF THE BILIARY TRACT W CC	1.0386
446	DISORDERS OF THE BILIARY TRACT W/O CC/MCC	0.7239
453	COMBINED ANTERIOR/POSTERIOR SPINAL FUSION W MCC	10.0108
454	COMBINED ANTERIOR/POSTERIOR SPINAL FUSION W CC	6.9533
455	COMBINED ANTERIOR/POSTERIOR SPINAL FUSION W/O CC/MCC	5.0197
456	SPINAL FUS EXC CERV W SPINAL CURV/MALIG/INFEC OR 9+ FUS W MCC	8.7412
457	SPINAL FUS EXC CERV W SPINAL CURV/MALIG/INFEC OR 9+ FUS W CC	5.9617
458	SPINAL FUS EXC CERV W SPINAL CURV/MALIG/INFEC OR 9+ FUS W/O CC/MCC	4.8966
459	SPINAL FUSION EXCEPT CERVICAL W MCC	6.1506
460	SPINAL FUSION EXCEPT CERVICAL W/O MCC	3.7097
461	BILATERAL OR MULTIPLE MAJOR JOINT PROCS OF LOWER EXTREMITY W MCC	4.5614
462	BILATERAL OR MULTIPLE MAJOR JOINT PROCS OF LOWER EXTREMITY W/O MCC	3.2056
463	WND DEBRID & SKN GRFT EXC HAND, FOR MUSCULO-CONN TISS DIS W MCC	5.3025
464	WND DEBRID & SKN GRFT EXC HAND, FOR MUSCULO-CONN TISS DIS W CC	2.8384
465	WND DEBRID & SKN GRFT EXC HAND, FOR MUSCULO-CONN TISS DIS W/O CC/MCC	1.7896
466	REVISION OF HIP OR KNEE REPLACEMENT W MCC	4.6698
467	REVISION OF HIP OR KNEE REPLACEMENT W CC	3.1207
468	REVISION OF HIP OR KNEE REPLACEMENT W/O CC/MCC	2.5167

MS-DRG	MS-DRG Title	Weights
469	MAJOR JOINT REPLACEMENT OR REATTACHMENT OF LOWER EXTREMITY W MCC	3.3282
470	MAJOR JOINT REPLACEMENT OR REATTACHMENT OF LOWER EXTREMITY W/O MCC	2.0613
471	CERVICAL SPINAL FUSION W MCC	4.6182
472	CERVICAL SPINAL FUSION W CC	2.7547
473	CERVICAL SPINAL FUSION W/O CC/MCC	2.0033
474	AMPUTATION FOR MUSCULOSKELETAL SYS & CONN TISSUE DIS W MCC	3.504
475	AMPUTATION FOR MUSCULOSKELETAL SYS & CONN TISSUE DIS W CC	1.923
476	AMPUTATION FOR MUSCULOSKELETAL SYS & CONN TISSUE DIS W/O CC/MCC	1.065
477	BIOPSIES OF MUSCULOSKELETAL SYSTEM & CONNECTIVE TISSUE W MCC	3.1343
478	BIOPSIES OF MUSCULOSKELETAL SYSTEM & CONNECTIVE TISSUE W CC	2.1321
479	BIOPSIES OF MUSCULOSKELETAL SYSTEM & CONNECTIVE TISSUE W/O CC/MCC	1.5121
480	HIP & FEMUR PROCEDURES EXCEPT MAJOR JOINT W MCC	2.8752
481	HIP & FEMUR PROCEDURES EXCEPT MAJOR JOINT W CC	1.8373
482	HIP & FEMUR PROCEDURES EXCEPT MAJOR JOINT W/O CC/MCC	1.5071
483	MAJOR JOINT & LIMB REATTACHMENT PROC OF UPPER EXTREMITY W CC/MCC	2.3024
484	MAJOR JOINT & LIMB REATTACHMENT PROC OF UPPER EXTREMITY W/O CC/MCC	1.8358
485	KNEE PROCEDURES W PDX OF INFECTION W MCC	3.0871
486	KNEE PROCEDURES W PDX OF INFECTION W CC	2.0558
487	KNEE PROCEDURES W PDX OF INFECTION W/O CC/MCC	1.4338
488	KNEE PROCEDURES W/O PDX OF INFECTION W CC/MCC	1.6774
489	KNEE PROCEDURES W/O PDX OF INFECTION W/O CC/MCC	1.183
490	BACK & NECK PROC EXC SPINAL FUSION W CC/MCC OR DISC DEVICE/NEUROSTIM	1.7718
491	BACK & NECK PROC EXC SPINAL FUSION W/O CC/MCC	0.9522

MS-DRG	MS-DRG Title	Weights
492	LOWER EXTREM & HUMER PROC EXCEPT HIP, FOOT, FEMUR W MCC	2.85
493	LOWER EXTREM & HUMER PROC EXCEPT HIP, FOOT, FEMUR W CC	1.7806
494	LOWER EXTREM & HUMER PROC EXCEPT HIP, FOOT, FEMUR W/O CC/MCC	1.2619
495	LOCAL EXCISION & REMOVAL INT FIX DEVICES EXC HIP & FEMUR W MCC	2.8743
496	LOCAL EXCISION & REMOVAL INT FIX DEVICES EXC HIP & FEMUR W CC	1.6254
497	LOCAL EXCISION & REMOVAL INT FIX DEVICES EXC HIP & FEMUR W/O CC/MCC	1.0344
498	LOCAL EXCISION & REMOVAL INT FIX DEVICES OF HIP & FEMUR W CC/MCC	1.9228
499	LOCAL EXCISION & REMOVAL INT FIX DEVICES OF HIP & FEMUR W/O CC/MCC	0.8975
500	SOFT TISSUE PROCEDURES W MCC	3.0244
501	SOFT TISSUE PROCEDURES W CC	1.5169
502	SOFT TISSUE PROCEDURES W/O CC/MCC	0.9834
503	FOOT PROCEDURES W MCC	2.1835
504	FOOT PROCEDURES W CC	1.5082
505	FOOT PROCEDURES W/O CC/MCC	1.0282
506	MAJOR THUMB OR JOINT PROCEDURES	1.1381
507	MAJOR SHOULDER OR ELBOW JOINT PROCEDURES W CC/MCC	1.8188
508	MAJOR SHOULDER OR ELBOW JOINT PROCEDURES W/O CC/MCC	1.2568
509	ARTHROSCOPY	1.2065
510	SHOULDER, ELBOW OR FOREARM PROC, EXC MAJOR JOINT PROC W MCC	2.1482
511	SHOULDER, ELBOW OR FOREARM PROC, EXC MAJOR JOINT PROC W CC	1.3747
512	SHOULDER, ELBOW OR FOREARM PROC, EXC MAJOR JOINT PROC W/O CC/MCC	1.0033
513	HAND OR WRIST PROC, EXCEPT MAJOR THUMB OR JOINT PROC W CC/MCC	1.2327
514	HAND OR WRIST PROC, EXCEPT MAJOR THUMB OR JOINT PROC W/O CC/MCC	0.7712

MS-DRG	MS-DRG Title	Weights
515	OTHER MUSCULOSKELET SYS & CONN TISS O.R. PROC W MCC	3.0414
516	OTHER MUSCULOSKELET SYS & CONN TISS O.R. PROC W CC	1.8355
517	OTHER MUSCULOSKELET SYS & CONN TISS O.R. PROC W/O CC/MCC	1.364
533	FRACTURES OF FEMUR W MCC	1.5632
534	FRACTURES OF FEMUR W/O MCC	0.7386
535	FRACTURES OF HIP & PELVIS W MCC	1.2914
536	FRACTURES OF HIP & PELVIS W/O MCC	0.7127
537	SPRAINS, STRAINS, & DISLOCATIONS OF HIP, PELVIS & THIGH W CC/MCC	0.8831
538	SPRAINS, STRAINS, & DISLOCATIONS OF HIP, PELVIS & THIGH W/O CC/MCC	0.5863
539	OSTEOMYELITIS W MCC	2.2839
540	OSTEOMYELITIS W CC	1.3839
541	OSTEOMYELITIS W/O CC/MCC	0.9422
542	PATHOLOGICAL FRACTURES & MUSCULOSKELET & CONN TISS MALIG W MCC	1.954
543	PATHOLOGICAL FRACTURES & MUSCULOSKELET & CONN TISS MALIG W CC	1.1211
544	PATHOLOGICAL FRACTURES & MUSCULOSKELET & CONN TISS MALIG W/O CC/MCC	0.7717
545	CONNECTIVE TISSUE DISORDERS W MCC	2.2783
546	CONNECTIVE TISSUE DISORDERS W CC	1.0758
547	CONNECTIVE TISSUE DISORDERS W/O CC/MCC	0.7475
548	SEPTIC ARTHRITIS W MCC	1.9281
549	SEPTIC ARTHRITIS W CC	1.1758
550	SEPTIC ARTHRITIS W/O CC/MCC	0.7082
551	MEDICAL BACK PROBLEMS W MCC	1.5442
552	MEDICAL BACK PROBLEMS W/O MCC	0.7937
553	BONE DISEASES & ARTHROPATHIES W MCC	1.1057
554	BONE DISEASES & ARTHROPATHIES W/O MCC	0.6478
555	SIGNS & SYMPTOMS OF MUSCULOSKELETAL SYSTEM & CONN TISSUE W MCC	0.9698

MS-DRG	MS-DRG Title	Weights
556	SIGNS & SYMPTOMS OF MUSCULOSKELETAL SYSTEM & CONN TISSUE W/O MCC	0.6027
557	TENDONITIS, MYOSITIS & BURSITIS W MCC	1.4685
558	TENDONITIS, MYOSITIS & BURSITIS W/O MCC	0.8387
559	AFTERCARE, MUSCULOSKELETAL SYSTEM & CONNECTIVE TISSUE W MCC	1.7514
560	AFTERCARE, MUSCULOSKELETAL SYSTEM & CONNECTIVE TISSUE W CC	0.9852
561	AFTERCARE, MUSCULOSKELETAL SYSTEM & CONNECTIVE TISSUE W/O CC/MCC	0.5959
562	FX, SPRN, STRN & DISL EXCEPT FEMUR, HIP, PELVIS & THIGH W MCC	1.3793
563	FX, SPRN, STRN & DISL EXCEPT FEMUR, HIP, PELVIS & THIGH W/O MCC	0.6927
564	OTHER MUSCULOSKELETAL SYS & CONNECTIVE TISSUE DIAGNOSES W MCC	1.5068
565	OTHER MUSCULOSKELETAL SYS & CONNECTIVE TISSUE DIAGNOSES W CC	0.907
566	OTHER MUSCULOSKELETAL SYS & CONNECTIVE TISSUE DIAGNOSES W/O CC/MCC	0.6498
573	SKIN GRAFT &/OR DEBRID FOR SKN ULCER OR CELLULITIS W MCC	3.5286
574	SKIN GRAFT &/OR DEBRID FOR SKN ULCER OR CELLULITIS W CC	1.909
575	SKIN GRAFT &/OR DEBRID FOR SKN ULCER OR CELLULITIS W/O CC/MCC	1.126
576	SKIN GRAFT &/OR DEBRID EXC FOR SKIN ULCER OR CELLULITIS W MCC	3.3598
577	SKIN GRAFT &/OR DEBRID EXC FOR SKIN ULCER OR CELLULITIS W CC	1.7235
578	SKIN GRAFT &/OR DEBRID EXC FOR SKIN ULCER OR CELLULITIS W/O CC/MCC	0.9925
579	OTHER SKIN, SUBCUT TISS & BREAST PROC W MCC	2.8556
580	OTHER SKIN, SUBCUT TISS & BREAST PROC W CC	1.3997
581	OTHER SKIN, SUBCUT TISS & BREAST PROC W/O CC/MCC	0.8589
582	MASTECTOMY FOR MALIGNANCY W CC/MCC	1.0226
583	MASTECTOMY FOR MALIGNANCY W/O CC/MCC	0.7889

MS-DRG	MS-DRG Title	Weights
584	BREAST BIOPSY, LOCAL EXCISION & OTHER BREAST PROCEDURES W CC/MCC	1.4877
585	BREAST BIOPSY, LOCAL EXCISION & OTHER BREAST PROCEDURES W/O CC/MCC	0.8593
592	SKIN ULCERS W MCC	1.8499
593	SKIN ULCERS W CC	1.0807
594	SKIN ULCERS W/O CC/MCC	0.7523
595	MAJOR SKIN DISORDERS W MCC	1.7691
596	MAJOR SKIN DISORDERS W/O MCC	0.8285
597	MALIGNANT BREAST DISORDERS W MCC	1.6302
598	MALIGNANT BREAST DISORDERS W CC	1.065
599	MALIGNANT BREAST DISORDERS W/O CC/MCC	0.6102
600	NON-MALIGNANT BREAST DISORDERS W CC/MCC	0.9801
601	NON-MALIGNANT BREAST DISORDERS W/O CC/MCC	0.5941
602	CELLULITIS W MCC	1.43
603	CELLULITIS W/O MCC	0.8178
604	TRAUMA TO THE SKIN, SUBCUT TISS & BREAST W MCC	1.1719
605	TRAUMA TO THE SKIN, SUBCUT TISS & BREAST W/O MCC	0.6824
606	MINOR SKIN DISORDERS W MCC	1.1964
607	MINOR SKIN DISORDERS W/O MCC	0.6403
614	ADRENAL & PITUITARY PROCEDURES W CC/MCC	2.6525
615	ADRENAL & PITUITARY PROCEDURES W/O CC/MCC	1.3859
616	AMPUTAT OF LOWER LIMB FOR ENDOCRINE, NUTRIT, & METABOL DIS W MCC	4.8537
617	AMPUTAT OF LOWER LIMB FOR ENDOCRINE, NUTRIT, & METABOL DIS W CC	2.0316
618	AMPUTAT OF LOWER LIMB FOR ENDOCRINE, NUTRIT, & METABOL DIS W/O CC/MCC	1.2713
619	O.R. PROCEDURES FOR OBESITY W MCC	3.5839
620	O.R. PROCEDURES FOR OBESITY W CC	1.8258
621	O.R. PROCEDURES FOR OBESITY W/O CC/MCC	1.45

MS-DRG	MS-DRG Title	Weights
622	SKIN GRAFTS & WOUND DEBRID FOR ENDOC, NUTRIT & METAB DIS W MCC	4.2285
623	SKIN GRAFTS & WOUND DEBRID FOR ENDOC, NUTRIT & METAB DIS W CC	2.0271
624	SKIN GRAFTS & WOUND DEBRID FOR ENDOC, NUTRIT & METAB DIS W/O CC/MCC	1.1304
625	THYROID, PARATHYROID & THYROGLOSSAL PROCEDURES W MCC	2.238
626	THYROID, PARATHYROID & THYROGLOSSAL PROCEDURES W CC	1.1339
627	THYROID, PARATHYROID & THYROGLOSSAL PROCEDURES W/O CC/MCC	0.7545
628	OTHER ENDOCRINE, NUTRIT & METAB O.R. PROC W MCC	3.3978
629	OTHER ENDOCRINE, NUTRIT & METAB O.R. PROC W CC	2.3003
630	OTHER ENDOCRINE, NUTRIT & METAB O.R. PROC W/O CC/MCC	1.4359
637	DIABETES W MCC	1.3303
638	DIABETES W CC	0.8263
639	DIABETES W/O CC/MCC	0.5547
640	NUTRITIONAL & MISC METABOLIC DISORDERS W MCC	1.0896
641	NUTRITIONAL & MISC METABOLIC DISORDERS W/O MCC	0.6843
642	INBORN ERRORS OF METABOLISM	1.0463
643	ENDOCRINE DISORDERS W MCC	1.6325
644	ENDOCRINE DISORDERS W CC	1.0453
645	ENDOCRINE DISORDERS W/O CC/MCC	0.7187
652	KIDNEY TRANSPLANT	2.9736
653	MAJOR BLADDER PROCEDURES W MCC	5.8189
654	MAJOR BLADDER PROCEDURES W CC	2.8942
655	MAJOR BLADDER PROCEDURES W/O CC/MCC	1.918
656	KIDNEY & URETER PROCEDURES FOR NEOPLASM W MCC	3.2592
657	KIDNEY & URETER PROCEDURES FOR NEOPLASM W CC	1.8523
658	KIDNEY & URETER PROCEDURES FOR NEOPLASM W/O CC/MCC	1.3668
659	KIDNEY & URETER PROCEDURES FOR NON-NEOPLASM W MCC	3.2812
660	KIDNEY & URETER PROCEDURES FOR NON-NEOPLASM W CC	1.8136

MS-DRG	MS-DRG Title	Weights
661	KIDNEY & URETER PROCEDURES FOR NON-NEOPLASM W/O CC/MCC	1.2817
662	MINOR BLADDER PROCEDURES W MCC	2.7753
663	MINOR BLADDER PROCEDURES W CC	1.3713
664	MINOR BLADDER PROCEDURES W/O CC/MCC	1.0193
665	PROSTATECTOMY W MCC	2.8052
666	PROSTATECTOMY W CC	1.5506
667	PROSTATECTOMY W/O CC/MCC	0.7615
668	TRANSURETHRAL PROCEDURES W MCC	2.2481
669	TRANSURETHRAL PROCEDURES W CC	1.1938
670	TRANSURETHRAL PROCEDURES W/O CC/MCC	0.7573
671	URETHRAL PROCEDURES W CC/MCC	1.4698
672	URETHRAL PROCEDURES W/O CC/MCC	0.7699
673	OTHER KIDNEY & URINARY TRACT PROCEDURES W MCC	2.9192
674	OTHER KIDNEY & URINARY TRACT PROCEDURES W CC	2.0576
675	OTHER KIDNEY & URINARY TRACT PROCEDURES W/O CC/MCC	1.3129
682	RENAL FAILURE W MCC	1.6422
683	RENAL FAILURE W CC	1.0523
684	RENAL FAILURE W/O CC/MCC	0.6746
685	ADMIT FOR RENAL DIALYSIS	0.8994
686	KIDNEY & URINARY TRACT NEOPLASMS W MCC	1.5362
687	KIDNEY & URINARY TRACT NEOPLASMS W CC	1.026
688	KIDNEY & URINARY TRACT NEOPLASMS W/O CC/MCC	0.6852
689	KIDNEY & URINARY TRACT INFECTIONS W MCC	1.2122
690	KIDNEY & URINARY TRACT INFECTIONS W/O MCC	0.7708
691	URINARY STONES W ESW LITHOTRIPSY W CC/MCC	1.4711
692	URINARY STONES W ESW LITHOTRIPSY W/O CC/MCC	1.1044
693	URINARY STONES W/O ESW LITHOTRIPSY W MCC	1.1496
694	URINARY STONES W/O ESW LITHOTRIPSY W/O MCC	0.6539
695	KIDNEY & URINARY TRACT SIGNS & SYMPTOMS W MCC	1.2396
696	KIDNEY & URINARY TRACT SIGNS & SYMPTOMS W/O MCC	0.6453

MS-DRG	MS-DRG Title	Weights
697	URETHRAL STRICTURE	0.814
698	OTHER KIDNEY & URINARY TRACT DIAGNOSES W MCC	1.4877
699	OTHER KIDNEY & URINARY TRACT DIAGNOSES W CC	0.9518
700	OTHER KIDNEY & URINARY TRACT DIAGNOSES W/O CC/MCC	0.6533
707	MAJOR MALE PELVIC PROCEDURES W CC/MCC	1.6691
708	MAJOR MALE PELVIC PROCEDURES W/O CC/MCC	1.2024
709	PENIS PROCEDURES W CC/MCC	1.835
710	PENIS PROCEDURES W/O CC/MCC	1.3227
711	TESTES PROCEDURES W CC/MCC	1.7128
712	TESTES PROCEDURES W/O CC/MCC	0.7666
713	TRANSURETHRAL PROSTATECTOMY W CC/MCC	1.1285
714	TRANSURETHRAL PROSTATECTOMY W/O CC/MCC	0.6364
715	OTHER MALE REPRODUCTIVE SYSTEM O.R. PROC FOR MALIGNANCY W CC/MCC	1.746
716	OTHER MALE REPRODUCTIVE SYSTEM O.R. PROC FOR MALIGNANCY W/O CC/MCC	1.0053
717	OTHER MALE REPRODUCTIVE SYSTEM O.R. PROC EXC MALIGNANCY W CC/MCC	1.6782
718	OTHER MALE REPRODUCTIVE SYSTEM O.R. PROC EXC MALIGNANCY W/O CC/MCC	0.7921
722	MALIGNANCY, MALE REPRODUCTIVE SYSTEM W MCC	1.4962
723	MALIGNANCY, MALE REPRODUCTIVE SYSTEM W CC	0.9732
724	MALIGNANCY, MALE REPRODUCTIVE SYSTEM W/O CC/MCC	0.6288
725	BENIGN PROSTATIC HYPERTROPHY W MCC	1.0685
726	BENIGN PROSTATIC HYPERTROPHY W/O MCC	0.6979
727	INFLAMMATION OF THE MALE REPRODUCTIVE SYSTEM W MCC	1.3162
728	INFLAMMATION OF THE MALE REPRODUCTIVE SYSTEM W/O MCC	0.7331
729	OTHER MALE REPRODUCTIVE SYSTEM DIAGNOSES W CC/MCC	0.9642
730	OTHER MALE REPRODUCTIVE SYSTEM DIAGNOSES W/O CC/MCC	0.5786
734	PELVIC EVISCERATION, RAD HYSTERECTOMY & RAD VULVECTOMY W CC/MCC	2.5091

MS-DRG	MS-DRG Title	Weights
735	PELVIC EVISCERATION, RAD HYSTERECTOMY & RAD VULVECTOMY W/O CC/MCC	1.137
736	UTERINE & ADNEXA PROC FOR OVARIAN OR ADNEXAL MALIGNANCY W MCC	4.349
737	UTERINE & ADNEXA PROC FOR OVARIAN OR ADNEXAL MALIGNANCY W CC	1.9651
738	UTERINE & ADNEXA PROC FOR OVARIAN OR ADNEXAL MALIGNANCY W/O CC/MCC	1.1766
739	UTERINE, ADNEXA PROC FOR NON-OVARIAN/ADNEXAL MALIG W MCC	3.0553
740	UTERINE, ADNEXA PROC FOR NON-OVARIAN/ADNEXAL MALIG W CC	1.5028
741	UTERINE, ADNEXA PROC FOR NON-OVARIAN/ADNEXAL MALIG W/O CC/MCC	1.0568
742	UTERINE & ADNEXA PROC FOR NON-MALIGNANCY W CC/MCC	1.3481
743	UTERINE & ADNEXA PROC FOR NON-MALIGNANCY W/O CC/MCC	0.8787
744	D&C, CONIZATION, LAPAROSCOPY & TUBAL INTERRUPTION W CC/MCC	1.4699
745	D&C, CONIZATION, LAPAROSCOPY & TUBAL INTERRUPTION W/O CC/MCC	0.7721
746	VAGINA, CERVIX & VULVA PROCEDURES W CC/MCC	1.2251
747	VAGINA, CERVIX & VULVA PROCEDURES W/O CC/MCC	0.8471
748	FEMALE REPRODUCTIVE SYSTEM RECONSTRUCTIVE PROCEDURES	0.8784
749	OTHER FEMALE REPRODUCTIVE SYSTEM O.R. PROCEDURES W CC/MCC	2.4378
750	OTHER FEMALE REPRODUCTIVE SYSTEM O.R. PROCEDURES W/O CC/MCC	1.0159
754	MALIGNANCY, FEMALE REPRODUCTIVE SYSTEM W MCC	1.8829
755	MALIGNANCY, FEMALE REPRODUCTIVE SYSTEM W CC	1.1184
756	MALIGNANCY, FEMALE REPRODUCTIVE SYSTEM W/O CC/MCC	0.5883
757	INFECTIONS, FEMALE REPRODUCTIVE SYSTEM W MCC	1.7189
758	INFECTIONS, FEMALE REPRODUCTIVE SYSTEM W CC	1.098
759	INFECTIONS, FEMALE REPRODUCTIVE SYSTEM W/O CC/MCC	0.7719
760	MENSTRUAL & OTHER FEMALE REPRODUCTIVE SYSTEM DISORDERS W CC/MCC	0.7992

MS-DRG	MS-DRG Title	Weights
761	MENSTRUAL & OTHER FEMALE REPRODUCTIVE SYSTEM DISORDERS W/O CC/MCC	0.4952
765	CESAREAN SECTION W CC/MCC	1.1083
766	CESAREAN SECTION W/O CC/MCC	0.7526
767	VAGINAL DELIVERY W STERILIZATION &/OR D&C	0.8389
768	VAGINAL DELIVERY W O.R. PROC EXCEPT STERIL &/OR D&C	1.7754
769	POSTPARTUM & POST ABORTION DIAGNOSES W O.R. PROCEDURE	1.89
770	ABORTION W D&C, ASPIRATION CURETTAGE OR HYSTEROTOMY	0.5367
774	VAGINAL DELIVERY W COMPLICATING DIAGNOSES	0.6873
775	VAGINAL DELIVERY W/O COMPLICATING DIAGNOSES	0.4971
776	POSTPARTUM & POST ABORTION DIAGNOSES W/O O.R. PROCEDURE	0.6808
777	ECTOPIC PREGNANCY	0.7786
778	THREATENED ABORTION	0.4229
779	ABORTION W/O D&C	0.4386
780	FALSE LABOR	0.2023
781	OTHER ANTEPARTUM DIAGNOSES W MEDICAL COMPLICATIONS	0.6357
782	OTHER ANTEPARTUM DIAGNOSES W/O MEDICAL COMPLICATIONS	0.4504
789	NEONATES, DIED OR TRANSFERRED TO ANOTHER ACUTE CARE FACILITY	1.4583
790	EXTREME IMMATURITY OR RESPIRATORY DISTRESS SYNDROME, NEONATE	4.809
791	PREMATURITY W MAJOR PROBLEMS	3.2844
792	PREMATURITY W/O MAJOR PROBLEMS	1.9817
793	FULL TERM NEONATE W MAJOR PROBLEMS	3.3738
794	NEONATE W OTHER SIGNIFICANT PROBLEMS	1.1941
795	NORMAL NEWBORN	0.1617
799	SPLENECTOMY W MCC	5.1087
800	SPLENECTOMY W CC	2.5315
801	SPLENECTOMY W/O CC/MCC	1.5865
802	OTHER O.R. PROC OF THE BLOOD & BLOOD FORMING ORGANS W MCC	3.4788

MS-DRG	MS-DRG Title	Weights
803	OTHER O.R. PROC OF THE BLOOD & BLOOD FORMING ORGANS W CC	1.768
804	OTHER O.R. PROC OF THE BLOOD & BLOOD FORMING ORGANS W/O CC/MCC	1.0388
808	MAJOR HEMATOL/IMMUN DIAG EXC SICKLE CELL CRISIS & COAGUL W MCC	2.0487
809	MAJOR HEMATOL/IMMUN DIAG EXC SICKLE CELL CRISIS & COAGUL W CC	1.1725
810	MAJOR HEMATOL/IMMUN DIAG EXC SICKLE CELL CRISIS & COAGUL W/O CC/MCC	0.8689
811	RED BLOOD CELL DISORDERS W MCC	1.2431
812	RED BLOOD CELL DISORDERS W/O MCC	0.7751
813	COAGULATION DISORDERS	1.3846
814	RETICULOENDOTHELIAL & IMMUNITY DISORDERS W MCC	1.5144
815	RETICULOENDOTHELIAL & IMMUNITY DISORDERS W CC	0.9596
816	RETICULOENDOTHELIAL & IMMUNITY DISORDERS W/O CC/MCC	0.6953
820	LYMPHOMA & LEUKEMIA W MAJOR O.R. PROCEDURE W MCC	5.3673
821	LYMPHOMA & LEUKEMIA W MAJOR O.R. PROCEDURE W CC	2.2672
822	LYMPHOMA & LEUKEMIA W MAJOR O.R. PROCEDURE W/O CC/MCC	1.1632
823	LYMPHOMA & NON-ACUTE LEUKEMIA W OTHER O.R. PROC W MCC	3.901
824	LYMPHOMA & NON-ACUTE LEUKEMIA W OTHER O.R. PROC W CC	2.152
825	LYMPHOMA & NON-ACUTE LEUKEMIA W OTHER O.R. PROC W/O CC/MCC	1.2003
826	MYELOPROLIF DISORD OR POORLY DIFF NEOPL W MAJ O.R. PROC W MCC	4.5104
827	MYELOPROLIF DISORD OR POORLY DIFF NEOPL W MAJ O.R. PROC W CC	2.0111
828	MYELOPROLIF DISORD OR POORLY DIFF NEOPL W MAJ O.R. PROC W/O CC/MCC	1.2384
829	MYELOPROLIF DISORD OR POORLY DIFF NEOPL W OTHER O.R. PROC W CC/MCC	2.6088
830	MYELOPROLIF DISORD OR POORLY DIFF NEOPL W OTHER O.R. PROC W/O CC/MCC	0.9784
834	ACUTE LEUKEMIA W/O MAJOR O.R. PROCEDURE W MCC	4.3709

MS-DRG	MS-DRG Title	Weights
835	ACUTE LEUKEMIA W/O MAJOR O.R. PROCEDURE W CC	2.4817
836	ACUTE LEUKEMIA W/O MAJOR O.R. PROCEDURE W/O CC/MCC	1.2595
837	CHEMO W ACUTE LEUKEMIA AS SDX OR W HIGH DOSE CHEMO AGENT W MCC	6.3616
838	CHEMO W ACUTE LEUKEMIA AS SDX W CC OR HIGH DOSE CHEMO AGENT	3.0949
839	CHEMO W ACUTE LEUKEMIA AS SDX W/O CC/MCC	1.2496
840	LYMPHOMA & NON-ACUTE LEUKEMIA W MCC	2.7258
841	LYMPHOMA & NON-ACUTE LEUKEMIA W CC	1.5071
842	LYMPHOMA & NON-ACUTE LEUKEMIA W/O CC/MCC	0.9803
843	OTHER MYELOPROLIF DIS OR POORLY DIFF NEOPL DIAG W MCC	1.6852
844	OTHER MYELOPROLIF DIS OR POORLY DIFF NEOPL DIAG W CC	1.1997
845	OTHER MYELOPROLIF DIS OR POORLY DIFF NEOPL DIAG W/O CC/MCC	0.8043
846	CHEMOTHERAPY W/O ACUTE LEUKEMIA AS SECONDARY DIAGNOSIS W MCC	2.1717
847	CHEMOTHERAPY W/O ACUTE LEUKEMIA AS SECONDARY DIAGNOSIS W CC	0.9451
848	CHEMOTHERAPY W/O ACUTE LEUKEMIA AS SECONDARY DIAGNOSIS W/O CC/MCC	0.8235
849	RADIOTHERAPY	1.2837
853	INFECTIOUS & PARASITIC DISEASES W O.R. PROCEDURE W MCC	5.4946
854	INFECTIOUS & PARASITIC DISEASES W O.R. PROCEDURE W CC	2.729
855	INFECTIOUS & PARASITIC DISEASES W O.R. PROCEDURE W/O CC/MCC	1.704
856	POSTOPERATIVE OR POST-TRAUMATIC INFECTIONS W O.R. PROC W MCC	4.9249
857	POSTOPERATIVE OR POST-TRAUMATIC INFECTIONS W O.R. PROC W CC	2.0439
858	POSTOPERATIVE OR POST-TRAUMATIC INFECTIONS W O.R. PROC W/O CC/MCC	1.3521
862	POSTOPERATIVE & POST-TRAUMATIC INFECTIONS W MCC	1.9008
863	POSTOPERATIVE & POST-TRAUMATIC INFECTIONS W/O MCC	0.9702
864	FEVER	0.8153

MS-DRG	*MS-DRG Title*	*Weights*
865	VIRAL ILLNESS W MCC	1.3601
866	VIRAL ILLNESS W/O MCC	0.6736
867	OTHER INFECTIOUS & PARASITIC DISEASES DIAGNOSES W MCC	2.3705
868	OTHER INFECTIOUS & PARASITIC DISEASES DIAGNOSES W CC	1.068
869	OTHER INFECTIOUS & PARASITIC DISEASES DIAGNOSES W/O CC/MCC	0.7419
870	SEPTICEMIA OR SEVERE SEPSIS W MV 96+ HOURS	5.8007
871	SEPTICEMIA OR SEVERE SEPSIS W/O MV 96+ HOURS W MCC	1.8437
872	SEPTICEMIA OR SEVERE SEPSIS W/O MV 96+ HOURS W/O MCC	1.1155
876	O.R. PROCEDURE W PRINCIPAL DIAGNOSES OF MENTAL ILLNESS	2.5892
880	ACUTE ADJUSTMENT REACTION & PSYCHOSOCIAL DYSFUNCTION	0.6191
881	DEPRESSIVE NEUROSES	0.6048
882	NEUROSES EXCEPT DEPRESSIVE	0.6676
883	DISORDERS OF PERSONALITY & IMPULSE CONTROL	1.1188
884	ORGANIC DISTURBANCES & MENTAL RETARDATION	0.9452
885	PSYCHOSES	0.8899
886	BEHAVIORAL & DEVELOPMENTAL DISORDERS	0.7895
887	OTHER MENTAL DISORDER DIAGNOSES	0.8336
894	ALCOHOL/DRUG ABUSE OR DEPENDENCE, LEFT AMA	0.4021
895	ALCOHOL/DRUG ABUSE OR DEPENDENCE W REHABILITATION THERAPY	0.9742
896	ALCOHOL/DRUG ABUSE OR DEPENDENCE W/O REHABILITATION THERAPY W MCC	1.4155
897	ALCOHOL/DRUG ABUSE OR DEPENDENCE W/O REHABILITATION THERAPY W/O MCC	0.6288
901	WOUND DEBRIDEMENTS FOR INJURIES W MCC	4.0545
902	WOUND DEBRIDEMENTS FOR INJURIES W CC	1.785
903	WOUND DEBRIDEMENTS FOR INJURIES W/O CC/MCC	1.0137
904	SKIN GRAFTS FOR INJURIES W CC/MCC	2.8601
905	SKIN GRAFTS FOR INJURIES W/O CC/MCC	1.0901
906	HAND PROCEDURES FOR INJURIES	0.9991

MS-DRG	MS-DRG Title	Weights
907	OTHER O.R. PROCEDURES FOR INJURIES W MCC	3.8072
908	OTHER O.R. PROCEDURES FOR INJURIES W CC	1.8736
909	OTHER O.R. PROCEDURES FOR INJURIES W/O CC/MCC	1.1135
913	TRAUMATIC INJURY W MCC	1.3473
914	TRAUMATIC INJURY W/O MCC	0.6789
915	ALLERGIC REACTIONS W MCC	1.2545
916	ALLERGIC REACTIONS W/O MCC	0.4513
917	POISONING & TOXIC EFFECTS OF DRUGS W MCC	1.4449
918	POISONING & TOXIC EFFECTS OF DRUGS W/O MCC	0.5839
919	COMPLICATIONS OF TREATMENT W MCC	1.5883
920	COMPLICATIONS OF TREATMENT W CC	0.9405
921	COMPLICATIONS OF TREATMENT W/O CC/MCC	0.6121
922	OTHER INJURY, POISONING & TOXIC EFFECT DIAG W MCC	1.3114
923	OTHER INJURY, POISONING & TOXIC EFFECT DIAG W/O MCC	0.6556
927	EXTENSIVE BURNS OR FULL THICKNESS BURNS W MV 96+ HRS W SKIN GRAFT	13.7351
928	FULL THICKNESS BURN W SKIN GRAFT OR INHAL INJ W CC/MCC	5.3052
929	FULL THICKNESS BURN W SKIN GRAFT OR INHAL INJ W/O CC/MCC	2.0086
933	EXTENSIVE BURNS OR FULL THICKNESS BURNS W MV 96+ HRS W/O SKIN GRAFT	2.3081
934	FULL THICKNESS BURN W/O SKIN GRFT OR INHAL INJ	1.3403
935	NON-EXTENSIVE BURNS	1.2507
939	O.R. PROC W DIAGNOSES OF OTHER CONTACT W HEALTH SERVICES W MCC	2.8593
940	O.R. PROC W DIAGNOSES OF OTHER CONTACT W HEALTH SERVICES W CC	1.6821
941	O.R. PROC W DIAGNOSES OF OTHER CONTACT W HEALTH SERVICES W/O CC/MCC	1.1298
945	REHABILITATION W CC/MCC	1.2388
946	REHABILITATION W/O CC/MCC	1.1159
947	SIGNS & SYMPTOMS W MCC	1.0922
948	SIGNS & SYMPTOMS W/O MCC	0.6689

MS-DRG	MS-DRG Title	Weights
949	AFTERCARE W CC/MCC	0.9758
950	AFTERCARE W/O CC/MCC	0.5459
951	OTHER FACTORS INFLUENCING HEALTH STATUS	0.7239
955	CRANIOTOMY FOR MULTIPLE SIGNIFICANT TRAUMA	5.6781
956	LIMB REATTACHMENT, HIP & FEMUR PROC FOR MULTIPLE SIGNIFICANT TRAUMA	3.4364
957	OTHER O.R. PROCEDURES FOR MULTIPLE SIGNIFICANT TRAUMA W MCC	6.2993
958	OTHER O.R. PROCEDURES FOR MULTIPLE SIGNIFICANT TRAUMA W CC	3.6544
959	OTHER O.R. PROCEDURES FOR MULTIPLE SIGNIFICANT TRAUMA W/O CC/MCC	2.2
963	OTHER MULTIPLE SIGNIFICANT TRAUMA W MCC	2.7687
964	OTHER MULTIPLE SIGNIFICANT TRAUMA W CC	1.5026
965	OTHER MULTIPLE SIGNIFICANT TRAUMA W/O CC/MCC	0.9781
969	HIV W EXTENSIVE O.R. PROCEDURE W MCC	5.5074
970	HIV W EXTENSIVE O.R. PROCEDURE W/O MCC	2.5627
974	HIV W MAJOR RELATED CONDITION W MCC	2.481
975	HIV W MAJOR RELATED CONDITION W CC	1.3597
976	HIV W MAJOR RELATED CONDITION W/O CC/MCC	0.8967
977	HIV W OR W/O OTHER RELATED CONDITION	1.0538
981	EXTENSIVE O.R. PROCEDURE UNRELATED TO PRINCIPAL DIAGNOSIS W MCC	5.0389
982	EXTENSIVE O.R. PROCEDURE UNRELATED TO PRINCIPAL DIAGNOSIS W CC	2.8954
983	EXTENSIVE O.R. PROCEDURE UNRELATED TO PRINCIPAL DIAGNOSIS W/O CC/MCC	1.8072
984	PROSTATIC O.R. PROCEDURE UNRELATED TO PRINCIPAL DIAGNOSIS W MCC	3.3443
985	PROSTATIC O.R. PROCEDURE UNRELATED TO PRINCIPAL DIAGNOSIS W CC	1.9481
986	PROSTATIC O.R. PROCEDURE UNRELATED TO PRINCIPAL DIAGNOSIS W/O CC/MCC	1.1079

MS-DRG	MS-DRG Title	Weights
987	NON-EXTENSIVE O.R. PROC UNRELATED TO PRINCIPAL DIAGNOSIS W MCC	3.402
988	NON-EXTENSIVE O.R. PROC UNRELATED TO PRINCIPAL DIAGNOSIS W CC	1.7836
989	NON-EXTENSIVE O.R. PROC UNRELATED TO PRINCIPAL DIAGNOSIS W/O CC/MCC	1.0358
998	PRINCIPAL DIAGNOSIS INVALID AS DISCHARGE DIAGNOSIS	0
999	UNGROUPABLE	0

Index

For Product Safety Concerns and Information please contact our EU
representative GPSR@taylorandfrancis.com Taylor & Francis Verlag GmbH,
Kaufingerstraße 24, 80331 München, Germany

Printed and bound by CPI Group (UK) Ltd, Croydon, CR0 4YY

08/05/2025

01864428-0002